REFUGEES AND THE MYTH OF HUMAN RIGHTS

For those who speak but are not heard.

Refugees and the Myth of Human Rights

Life Outside the Pale of the Law

EMMA LARKING
Australian National University, Australia

Routledge
Taylor & Francis Group
LONDON AND NEW YORK

First published 2014 by Ashgate Publishing

Published 2016 by Routledge
2 Park Square, Milton Park, Abingdon, Oxon OX14 4RN
711 Third Avenue, New York, NY 10017, USA

First issued in paperback 2017

Routledge is an imprint of the Taylor & Francis Group, an informa business

British Library Cataloguing in Publication Data
A catalogue record for this book is available from the British Library

The Library of Congress has cataloged the printed edition as follows:
Larking, Emma.
Refugees and the myth of human rights : life outside the pale of the law / by Emma Larking.
pages cm
Includes bibliographical references and index.
ISBN 978-1-4724-3007-6 (hardback) -- ISBN 978-1-4724-3008-3 (ebook) -- ISBN 978-1-4724-3009-0 (epub) 1. Refugees--Legal status, laws, etc. 2. Refugees--Government policy 3. Human rights--Government policy. 4. Border security--Government policy. 5. Emigration and immigration--Government policy I. Title.
JV6346.L37 2014
325'.21--dc23

2014016248

ISBN 13: 978-1-138-05478-3 (pbk)
ISBN 13: 978-1-4724-3007-6 (hbk)

Contents

Acknowledgements

Many people at the University of Melbourne and particularly in the Centre for Applied Philosophy and Public Ethics provided me with friendship, support, encouragement and intellectual inspiration during my time studying and working there. Thank you especially to Andrew Alexandra, Lisa Ball, Irena Blonder, Tony Coady, Ned Dobos, Anna Goppal, Karen Jones, Mianna Lotz, Clare McCausland, Emma Rush, Andy Schaap, Doris Schroeder and Philippa Smales. Thank you as well to Brian Galligan and John Chesterman with whom I was fortunate to work on the 'Politics of Rights' project.

Hilary Charlesworth, Ned Dobos, Leonie Martino and Emma Rush all read parts of this book at various stages and provided helpful feedback for which I am very grateful. Andrew Alexandra and Phillip Cole read drafts of the entire manuscript and I am indebted to them for their generous support and insightful criticisms.

I am grateful to my colleagues at the Regulatory Institutions Network at ANU for providing a wonderfully hospitable, lively and supportive research community.

To all the people who have supported and cheered me on during the writing of this book, thank you. For your many kindnesses, friendship, loyalty, enriching conversation and generosity of spirit I would like to thank in particular my family, Carmen Anderson, Conrad Asmus, Rachel Chiodo, Libby Douglas, Vicki Eddey, Claire Heughan, Kate Hill, Imelda Deinla, Sam Jackson, Jo Kenny, Michael McIver, Leonie Martino, Sarah Nieuwenhuysen, Petrina O'Connor, Mark Phelan, Hannah Richardson, Rachel Scully, Ben Tootell, Jacqui Walker, and my lovely bookgroup girls.

Thank you to the publishers for their permission to reprint material that appeared in two articles in *The Australian Journal of Human Rights:* 'Human Rights and the Principle of Sovereignty: A Dangerous Conflict at the Heart of the Nation State?' *AJHR* 10 no. 1: 15–32, June 2004, and 'Human Rights, the Right to Have Rights, and Life Beyond the Pale of the Law' *AJHR* 18 no. 1: 57–88, July 2012.

Finally, my warm thanks to Rob Sorsby and all at Ashgate.

Introduction
Refugees and the Myth of Human Rights: Life Outside the Pale of the Law

In February 2014, more than 60 asylum seekers detained in a camp run by Australia on Manus Island, Papua New Guinea were badly beaten and slashed with knives and machetes. One man was shot and Reza Berati, a 23-year-old Iranian man, was killed. Media reports suggest that camp guards employed by the security contractor G4S were responsible for the attacks, supported by members of the PNG police. There are conflicting accounts of what sparked the violence, with the Australian government claiming asylum seekers at the centre were engaged in a protest that led to a riot. The asylum seekers themselves claim they were 'pulled from their rooms, beaten and told by their attackers: "You want freedom? We'll give you freedom tonight"' (Gordon and Ireland 2014).

According to the Universal Declaration of Human Rights (UDHR), 'all human beings are born free and equal in dignity and rights' (Art. 1). Wealthy liberal democracies claim to recognise the innate freedom and equality of all people and to uphold human rights but also spend billions fortifying their borders and incarcerating refugees. Written by a citizen of a wealthy liberal democracy (Australia), this book is an attempt to 'think what we are doing' (Arendt 1998, 5) and to explore the likely consequences of our actions. It examines the theoretical and institutional commitments that undergird the liberal democratic state, including its commitment to human rights, and considers to what extent contemporary border policing regimes are consistent with these commitments. The idea that humans are naturally endowed with dignity and rights and are by nature 'free and equal' is what I call 'the myth of human rights'. This myth plays an important and dangerous role in the liberal democratic state by obscuring the political effort and commitment necessary to the realisation of freedom, equality, dignity and rights. The problematic character of the myth of human rights becomes apparent when we consider the position of refugees who arrive without lawful authorisation in the state. These people cannot make rights claims based on membership of the state or their lawful right to remain; they have only their human rights to fall back on. How they are treated by the liberal state suggests that human rights are worth very little, and indeed I argue in this book that within a liberal democracy an appeal to human rights is evidence in itself that the person making the appeal is neither free nor equal. Worse than this, the appeal is likely to provoke hostility rather than evoke a sense of solidarity. These people do not stand respectfully at a distance, pleading for assistance from their home countries or camps in Africa, Asia and the Middle East and prepared to wait indefinitely for our charity and perhaps the prospects of resettlement. Instead they directly engage the law of the state, which says they must not come, pitting their bodies and their human rights against its border policing regime. Although they are often repaid for this affront with calculated brutality they are not usually deterred. The problem that they pose for the liberal democratic state and its avowed commitment to rights will not go away, no matter how high the fences it builds or how numerous the guards at its frontiers. Around the world, millions of people are prepared to suffer and to risk death in search of a better life because staying where they are seems simply untenable: '[t]his is the subtext to the plight of every [exile]: Whatever hardship he endures, he endures because it beats the hardship he escaped. Every story of exile implies the sadder story of a homeland' (Mogelson 2013).

In 2013, the number of people of concern to the Office of the United Nations High Commissioner for Refugees (UNHCR) reached an 'all-time high', coming close to 39 million (UNHCR 2013, 6). The majority were displaced within the borders of their home country; most of the rest were living in camps in neighbouring countries in the developing world – nevertheless, asylum claims in wealthy liberal states also surged (UNHCR 2013, 6; 2012b). Data compiled by UNHCR shows considerable fluctuations in asylum seeker numbers. Despite recent increases in protection applications, the total number of people seeking asylum in industrialised countries was greater in the early 1990s and at the turn of the century than it is currently. War in the former Yugoslavia contributed to an increase in protection applications in the 1990s, the invasions of Afghanistan and Iraq helped account for another increase in the early 2000s and the North African revolutions and continuing conflict in the Syrian Arab Republic largely explain current figures (see UNHCR 2012b, 7 and 12). In the future, asylum applications in wealthy liberal democracies and global refugee numbers will continue to fluctuate in response to persecution in various regions and as violent conflicts ignite or are resolved. Overall, though, internal and cross-border migrations are likely to increase as people affected by poverty as well as by natural disasters and climate change leave their homes and search for new ones.

Only a relatively small proportion of these people fall within the definition of a refugee outlined in the United Nations Convention Relating to the Status of Refugees ('the Refugee Convention'). Article 1 of the Convention provides that refugees are persons who are outside their country of nationality or, if stateless, of habitual residence and unable or unwilling to return to it because of a 'well-founded fear of persecution on grounds of race, religion, nationality, membership of a particular social group, or political opinion'. In the concluding chapter of this book I suggest that liberal democracies may be justified in drawing distinctions between some refugees, but my argument throughout employs an expansive refugee definition going well beyond that contained in the Refugee Convention.

I apply the term 'refugee' to all those who have left home because their national state is unable or unwilling to secure the conditions necessary for living what Dummett describes as 'a decent human life' 'without the threat of an unnatural death' (2001, 32), 'free from terror and allowing … a basic dignity' (2001, 34). A state's failure to secure the conditions necessary for a decent life may relate to a range of factors, including persecution of various forms, but also starvation, civil war and poverty (see Dummett 2001, 32–7). Although unable to live a decent life in their home country, if refugees have moved outside its borders their presence under the laws of the country in which they reside is either unlawful or 'legally qualified' in the sense that punitive conditions such as restrictions on freedom of movement are attached to their right to remain. This definition of what it is to be a refugee thus includes asylum seekers who wish to claim protection under the Refugee Convention but who are unlawfully present in the country in which they have applied for protection. It also includes individuals living in camps or otherwise precarious circumstances who have been assessed as 'Convention refugees' by UNHCR but who do not have stable resettlement options. For the purposes of my discussion I exclude individuals who have successfully claimed protection under the Refugee Convention and have been resettled, as long as they have permanent residency and there are no conditions attached to their residency that make it more difficult for them, by comparison with other permanent residents, to apply for and obtain citizenship. Although the definition employed here encompasses refugees wherever they are found, my discussion is concerned solely with how wealthy liberal democracies respond to refugees, and predominantly those refugees at the state's borders or living on its territory. A state's constitutive commitments are drawn into question by what happens beyond its borders, particularly given the existence of a global institutional structure – something I discuss in Chapter 9, so the position of refugees who are unable to escape their home state or are confined in camps in neighbouring regions is relevant to my argument. Existence for these refugees is precarious and they are often the target of state sanctioned discrimination and violence (see UNHCR 2006, 22–4). Nevertheless, the liberal state's commitments are most obviously and directly engaged by actions in which its agency is indisputable. In relation to refugees, these actions usually occur within the borders of the state and in the course of preventing access to its borders. There is a risk that my focus on the liberal democratic response to refugees will obscure the plight of those refugees living in other parts of the world but in my final chapter I make recommendations that apply universally.

The refugee definition outlined above is expansive but it is not arbitrary. As Dauvergne (2005, 82–3) points out, the *Oxford English Dictionary* defines refugees to include individuals 'driven from … home to seek refuge, esp. in a foreign country, from war, religious persecution, political troubles, natural disaster, etc.' (citing the fifth edition of the *Shorter Oxford English Dictionary*). Furthermore, while it is common in the Western media to characterise refugees who arrive in a state without lawful authorisation as cynical adventurers, seeking to evade legal controls and orderly migration processes in a spirit of callous defiance, it is implausible that many people take lightly the decision to leave their homes and attempt to find new ones without official assistance or protection. An expansive refugee definition reflects this. In this book, however, an expansive definition is also justified by the fact that regardless of the circumstances they left behind, people who attempt to enter a liberal democracy without lawful authorisation pose a challenge for the state and its commitment to human rights that goes to its very foundations. It is with this challenge that the book is primarily concerned.

The liberal democratic world has closed down avenues of lawful access to refugees, forcing them to rely on criminal smuggling networks known for their exploitative and abusive practices. The anodyne language of 'deterrence' that is used to justify border policing regimes masks the disturbing reality that these regimes are designed to inflict the greatest harm possible on anyone who challenges them. As a consequence, hundreds of thousands of people die en route to or while attempting to enter liberal democracies, or languish in appalling conditions in the detention camps run and financed by them. The stony logic behind the militarised protection of borders – reflected in this respect quite accurately by the language of militarisation, with border 'security' and 'protection' supplemented by border patrols,[1] 'Operational Cooperation',[2] 'Rapid Intervention' teams,[3] and 'Operation': 'Sovereign Borders',[4] 'Hold the Line' and 'Gatekeeper'[5] – is that refugees can be contained in their own countries or regions or 'deflected' to other destination countries with less aggressively punitive regimes. It is misguided to think that refugees can be deterred – as I have said, it will always be the case that for many the costs of remaining where they are outweigh the risks of leaving. It is also misguided to think that refugees are free to choose between destination countries – the realistically available options are, for most refugees, extremely limited (Spinks 2013). Nevertheless, there is some evidence to suggest that if a country's border regime is particularly harsh it can have a deterrent effect (UNHCR 2012b, 12), and there is little doubt that more open access generally would lead to a significant increase in the numbers of people moving to wealthy liberal democracies. The question is whether limiting such movement justifies current policies.

Prior to World War One territorial borders around the world were relatively porous. Border controls proliferated globally during World War One, and have

---

1 Conducted in the USA by the Border Patrol agency, a sub-agency of the Department of Homeland Security's Customs and Border Protection agency (Amnesty International, USA 2012, 7).

2 Widely known as 'Frontex', the official name for the EU's border protection agency is the European Agency for the Management of Operational Cooperation at the External Borders of the Member States of the European Union (see the Frontex website: http://frontex.europa.eu/about-frontex/origin).

3 'Rapid Intervention' teams are squads of border guards deployed by Frontex in response to 'urgent and exceptional pressure' resulting from 'large numbers of third country nationals trying to enter the territory of a [European Union] Member State illegally' (see the Frontex website: http://frontex.europa.eu/operations/rapid-intervention).

4 The Australian government has branded its current border policing regime 'Operation Sovereign Borders'. The regime is under the command of an Australian Defence Force Lieutenant General.

5 'Operation Hold the Line' and 'Operation Gatekeeper' were conducted on the USA's border with Mexico (Amnesty International, USA 2012, 20).

been tightly managed ever since. Individual states and regional groupings attempt to regulate immigration and border crossings in their own interests. In the wealthy Western world, demands for labour have often led to a relaxation in immigration policy, but Wilsher (2012, 57) argues that the 1970s marked the emergence of a 'new and diffuse climate of fear over migration', during which anyone arriving in a state without legal authorisation, 'whether seeking asylum or economic opportunity, became seen as a "security" threat'. Since the 1970s skilled and other forms of labour immigration have been encouraged when labour markets require it, but these policies co-exist alongside the vigorous policing of borders. Punitive border regimes have been defended by demonising refugees, who are now so routinely vilified that the term 'illegal' has 'broad popular and political currency' (Dauvergne 2008, 4) regardless of whether or not the person to whom it applies is seeking protection under the Refugee Convention. Although tinged by what Dauvergne (2008, 4) calls 'xenophobic paranoia' and often highly racialised, there is a calculation underlying this vilification that is at least superficially rational. Having bundled the myriad causes of refugee displacement into one, the calculation assumes that any relaxation of border controls will lead to wealthy democracies being swamped by the world's needy. Against this 'threat', liberal democratic governments, which since the 1970s have progressively dismantled social welfare safety nets and ceded power to transnational organisations and corporations, act to secure the nation through the militarised protection of borders. Refugees bear the immediate brunt of border militarisation, while global security companies and organised crime groups engaged in people-smuggling are the clearest winners from 'the worldwide panic about illegal migration' (Dauvergne 2008, 10) and corresponding border policing regimes. Politicians and nationalist political parties who gain credibility by appearing to act decisively 'in the national interest' and whose popularity rests on stoking xenophobic nationalism and inflaming distrust of refugees also gain from their promotion of border militarisation. Contrary to the arguments of the nationalists, however, most citizens of liberal democracies are not well served by the current approach.

It is true that there are significant differences between the particular refugee policies pursued by liberal democracies and their regional groupings, just as the rights traditions within these states diverge considerably, as evidenced by their varied approaches to the constitutional and legislative protection of rights. My focus here, however, is on features of the liberal democratic nation-state that are shared. A key argument pursued throughout the book is that tension between the universalism of human rights and the sovereignty of 'the people' or 'the nation' arises within all modern liberal democracies, including pluralist and multi-nation-states. Although this tension has been mediated in different ways, the issues it poses for how the state engages with refugees and for its own rights-based democratic commitments are similar. My argument that the liberal democratic state is deeply hostile to the human rights claims made by refugees at its borders or in its territory (it can simply ignore the human rights claims made by refugees on the other side of the world) holds for all such states. This hostility is explicable not only with reference to features internal to the liberal state and its political traditions, but also with reference to structural features of international law, *including* the international human rights system.

This argument can be contrasted with the now popular suggestion that human rights are gradually 'humanising' international law (see, for example, Benhabib 2005 and Sicilianos 2012). It is certainly true that international human rights treaties have proliferated since the signing of the UDHR in 1948. It is also true that international law has been increasingly concerned to ensure that human rights are secured by states and that states are held accountable for rights infringements. At the same time, however, international law affirms and upholds the sovereignty of independent nation-states, defending the principle of sovereignty as a precondition for recognising and securing the political self-determination of independent peoples. While the forces of globalisation have eroded genuine sovereign autonomy, the sovereignty of states in relation to membership, immigration and border control continues to be aggressively asserted by states and upheld by international law. The result is that the international human rights regime may assist the realisation and extension of rights to citizens and those lawfully present within states but, as I demonstrate in this book, it supports the denial of rights to refugees.

Within wealthy liberal democracies refugees live 'outside the pale of the law'. This phrase is used by Hannah Arendt in *The Origins of Totalitarianism* ('*Origins*' 1968, 277, 283, 286) to describe the plight of refugees who sought protection in the liberal democracies of Western Europe (and beyond) in the aftermath of World War One. The phrase has several layers. To be 'beyond the pale' is to be outside the bounds of the acceptable or conceivable, it is a transgression both ridiculous and unworthy of serious consideration. The experience of the post-World War One refugees was certainly one of being treated as objects of derision – the popular press referred to them as the 'scum of the earth', but the abuses inflicted on them were more grave than this, as I describe in Chapter 1. Arendt argues that the refugees were reduced to 'a condition of complete rightlessness' (1968, 296) involving their expulsion 'from humanity' (1968, 297). The word 'pale' in the expression 'beyond the pale' refers to a stake or fence paling, and historically 'the pale' fenced or demarcated an area within which a particular legal system was recognised as valid and upheld. Exclusion from the pale thus entailed exclusion from legal recognition. In Arendt's locution, to be within the pale of the law is to be recognised as a subject of law and to be protected by the physical boundary established by law. Arendt would also have been aware of darker territory delineated by the pale of the law. A 'pale of settlement' was established along the western frontier of the Russian empire in the early 1800s, establishing a vast ghetto into which millions of the empire's Jews were forced (Davitt 1903). The settlement's inhabitants had no right to roam beyond the pale, and within it they were subject to punitive laws. The pale of the law established by the liberal democratic state, on the other hand, is a privileged space within which citizens appear before each other as equals and rights bearers – as subjects and authors of the law that protects them but also sets them apart from outsiders. In an international system in which sovereign states police their borders and recognise duties to admit only their own nationals, people who have lost or been denied the protection of their own state may find themselves excluded from legal recognition and standing wherever they go. The dark side of the liberal democratic 'pale' is thus not only that those within it turn their backs on the appeals made by those outside, but that its protective boundary does not provide guaranteed assurance even to some of those within. I explore the difficulties this presents for the integrity and durability of the law itself throughout the course of this book.

Using Arendt's discussion in *Origins* as a starting point, Chapter 1 describes the experience of Europe's post-World War One refugees and their legal position in the democracies of Western Europe. Although the refugees were the objects of a complex legal regime that is virtually ignored by Arendt, she is nevertheless correct to characterise them as living outside the pale of the law, as well as to highlight the corrosive impact that this had on the rule of law and rights recognition in Western Europe. Chapter 1 concludes by introducing Arendt's curious 'right to have rights' – a right that one can have while lacking all other rights but which if denied negates all the other rights that one has.

Chapter 2 discusses Arendt's depiction in *Origins* of a distinctively modern nation-state in which rule is based on 'right' rather than 'might' and equality before the law assured. According to Arendt, sentimental nationalism undercut the revolutionary promise of the modern nation-state and helps explain its subsequent failure in Western Europe to treat refugees as the subjects of rights. As well as discussing the historical significance of nationalism, Chapter 2 introduces Arendt's critique (in *Origins* and elsewhere) of the concept of natural or human rights and the role this concept plays in legitimating the modern nation-state, as well as its reliance on the nation. Chapter 2 also considers Arendt's opposing characterisation of rights as the outcome of a certain kind of political commitment.

Chapter 3 develops the preceding chapter's account of the role of the nation in the history of human rights. It builds on that chapter's discussion of Arendt's rights critique, and introduces her distinctive understanding of politics and the public realm. It argues that Arendt's invocation of a public sphere of action provides an appropriately political basis – by contrast to sentimental conceptions of the nation – on which to establish civic solidarity in modern pluralist societies. The claim of this chapter is that an Arendtian brand of solidarity may encourage citizens of contemporary liberal democracies to uphold each other's rights and to extend legal recognition and therefore rights to outsiders.

The lineage of key concepts introduced in Part I is considered in depth in Part II. Chapter 4 focuses on the idea of the ancient 'cosmopolis' constituted by a divine law of nature. While the natural law established a universal moral community, early natural law theorists took for granted a distinction between this universal sphere of morality, governed by natural law, and the limited sphere of justice that was governed by civil law. In Parts II and III of this book, I argue that this distinction continues to have significant implications for refugees. As the subjects of human rights, refugees are relegated to a moral sphere within which they are not considered subjects of justice.

While the legitimacy of government in modern liberal democracies can be theorised in many different ways, the account of political legitimacy developed by John Locke in his *The Second Treatise of Government* encapsulates the standard conceptual apparatus for theorising the modern nation-state and exemplifies the conundrums into which the state is drawn through its dual commitment to universal rights and to the sovereignty of the people. The presuppositions that inform Locke's account of political legitimacy also structure modern international law, within which the characterisation of human rights and the importance of sovereign states as mechanisms for securing rights is distinctively Lockean. By comparison with Locke, other well-known political philosophers such as Hobbes on the one hand and Rousseau on the other have far less contemporary relevance. Chapter 5 challenges Locke's individualist and universalist credentials, demonstrating the role played by 'the public good' (as stand-in for 'the nation') in his account, and emphasising the distinctive difference that he – like his natural law predecessors – draws between the universal sphere of morality and natural rights, and the bounded sphere of justice and citizens' rights.

Immanuel Kant's political philosophy echoes Locke in many respects, but Kant goes beyond Locke in his articulation of the conditions necessary to the achievement of international peace and in his identification of 'cosmopolitan right'. It has been suggested that Kant inaugurated a new era of liberal cosmopolitanism. In Chapter 6 I argue that Kant, like Locke, in fact characterises justice, law and right as internal to the political community or the state. Chapter 6 also argues that Kant accords a privileged role, hitherto ignored by Kantian scholars, to the nation. As in the ancient global cosmopolis, cosmopolitan right and the now much discussed 'right to hospitality' establish the foundations for communicating with strangers but do not provide a basis on which political outsiders can be recognised as subjects of justice or of the rights that are secured and accorded by a rights based political community.

In the years since 1945 we have witnessed a 'rights revolution' and individuals are now accorded standing and recognition in international law to a degree unknown prior to World War Two. Chapter 7 argues that regardless of this, contemporary refugees are still consigned to live outside the pale of the law. The chapter considers how contemporary refugees are treated within liberal democracies and analyses their legal position, drawing significant parallels with the experience and position of Arendt's post-World War One refugees, and reaching similar conclusions concerning the impact of their anomalous legal status on the rule of law within the liberal state.

Chapter 8 develops the preceding chapter's explanation of how international law constructs individuals as legal persons and subjects of human rights. It also emphasises the importance of state sovereignty and considers the historical and moral foundations on which sovereignty rests. It argues that the principle of sovereignty entrenches the privileged role occupied by the nation in the history of modern nation-states, and trumps human rights in international law.

We now live in a global community. Chapter 9 considers the character of this community and supports Arendt's claim that we must assume political responsibility for all that goes on within it, while at the same time resisting the institutionalisation of a global state. The chapter discusses the conditions necessary to the adoption of global responsibility within liberal democracies, and considers the implications of recognising a universal 'right to have rights'. As a right to legal personality and political membership I argue that the right must be enforced in the form of a global Citizenship Convention. Within liberal democracies, an understanding of the significance of a right to have rights – and of what the deprivation of this right entails – should spur recognition of wide-ranging obligations to refugees, to be met in part through a multi-lateral refugee resettlement treaty between wealthy liberal states, as well as through recognition of global distributive justice obligations.

My account of the obligations owed by the liberal state to refugees will undoubtedly be considered unduly expansive by many. It may also be considered outside the realms of political possibility given how members of contemporary liberal democracies conceive of their right to police their borders, as well as the widespread – although certainly not pervasive – political inertia within these societies. A revival of political engagement is possible, however, and represents our best hope for protecting the revolutionary promise of equality on which liberal democracies are based. We take responsibility for the world we share through action in a public political sphere, and this action engenders a form of solidarity free from the taint of xenophobic nationalism. It is the only manner in which to defend political plurality while at the same time recognising and affirming our shared membership of a human community. I do not intend to downplay the hurdles to the introduction of a global Citizenship Convention along the lines I discuss in Chapter 9, nor the difficulties involved in administering and enforcing such a Convention. Similar obstacles arise in relation to forging a multi-lateral refugee resettlement treaty between liberal democracies, encouraging recognition within these democracies of global distributive justice obligations and extending legal recognition to all who come before their law. Nevertheless, the interests of the citizens of liberal democracies as much as those of all humanity lie in these achievements.

PART I

Chapter 1
Scum of the Earth I

Introduction

In 1951, in the preface to *The Origins of Totalitarianism* (*Origins*), Hannah Arendt (1968, ix) called for 'a new guarantee' for human dignity, suggesting that such a guarantee could only be supplied by 'a new law on earth'. Arendt, who was herself a refugee of Nazi Germany, argued totalitarianism might well survive the defeat of totalitarian regimes 'in the form of strong temptations which will come up whenever it seems impossible to alleviate political, social or economic misery in a manner worthy of man' (1968, 459). This possibility alone should spur the search for a new guarantee for human dignity. If we also accept Arendt's claim that the events of World War Two mean that the 'rights of man' have 'lost all validity' (1968, 447), it appears we have no choice but to seek some 'new law on earth'. There are those who would that argue totalitarianism and its attendant temptations have been comprehensively defeated, and that the great post-World War Two rights revolution – inaugurated by the establishment of the United Nations and proudly proclaimed in the Universal Declaration of Human Rights – has vindicated the rights of man. The plight of contemporary refugees, however, suggests otherwise. I consider their position in Part III of this book. In the first Part, my focus is on Europe's inter-war refugees, and the contradiction between the modern nation-state's revolutionary commitment to equality and how it treated the refugees.

In *Origins*, Arendt argues that the constitutional democracies of Western Europe were implicated in the nihilistic logic of the Nazi 'corpse factories and holes of oblivion' (1968, 459) because they responded to the continent's displaced peoples and refugees from fascism by treating these people as legal anomalies who had no rights. In doing so, she suggests they revealed their disdain for the principle of equality before the law and demonstrated that the rights of man had in fact only ever been conceived of as the rights of citizens. In this chapter I draw on a range of historical and contemporary sources to supplement Arendt's description of the situation of the refugees. Like Arendt, I focus on the fact that even countries constitutionally committed to rights recognition treated the refugees with impunity. I support Arendt's argument that the failure to accord rights to refugees had a corrosive impact within these countries, undercutting institutional rights protections and respect for the rule of law. I consider in some detail the legal position of the refugees and highlight the importance of national status for the attribution of legal personality in international law. Arendt's claim that the refugees were consigned to live outside the protective pale of the law (1968, 277 and see 283, 286, 294) is now well known, and is often taken at face value to imply that the refugees were simply ignored by the law and treated as unworthy of consideration under it.[1] In fact the refugees were the objects of a complex international legal regime, and also of punitive laws within particular states.[2] Nevertheless, I conclude that Arendt is correct to characterise them as 'outlaws' – they were a 'surplus population' whose members had no juridical personality and whose 'greatest danger' consisted in 'the abstract nakedness of being nothing but human' (1968, 300). In the final part of the chapter I discuss the distinction that Arendt draws between the specific rights that, although not 'innate' or 'inalienable', may be accorded to individuals within a legal framework based on the protection of rights, and the 'right to have rights', which in my account is a right to political membership and a legal personality. The importance of this legally constituted *persona* will be something I elaborate upon in subsequent chapters, and I will return to discuss the 'right to have rights' in greater depth in my concluding chapter.

The Inter-war Refugees

Millions of people were displaced by World War One and by the redrawing of borders, civil unrest, and revolutions that followed it.[3] Most of the refugees were for all practical purposes stateless. As Arendt (1968, 281 fn. 28) claims, it was largely immaterial whether they were *de jure* stateless, as a result of a formal denaturalisation process undertaken by their country of origin, or *de facto* stateless, because they no longer enjoyed the protection of their home country – in practise the refugees' predicament was identical (see also Holborn 1938, 680; UN 1949, 6; Weis 1979, 44). Furthermore, the majority were in this position not because of their 'political or religious convictions' (Arendt 1968, 294) or anything they had done in their country of origin, but simply because of their membership of some

1 A notable exception is Jacques Rancière, who responds to Arendt's claim that the plight of the refugees 'is not that they are not equal before the law, but that no law exists for them; not that they are oppressed, but that nobody wants even to oppress them' (1968, 295–6) by pointing out that '[a]s a matter of fact, there were people who wanted to oppress them and laws to do this' (2004, 299).

2 Arendt implicitly acknowledges as much when she refers, in a letter written in 1946 to her mentor Karl Jaspers, to her own experience of the 'infinitely complex red-tape existence of [the refugee]' (1992a, 28).

3 Up to 2 million Russians were rendered stateless after the 1917 Revolution and civil war, with Soviet Russia passing denationalisation legislation in 1921, 1924, and 1925 (Weis 1979, 119; Hathaway 1984, 350). Turkey, Greece, and Bulgaria alone produced another 2 million refugees (Skran 1995, 18), Italy at least 180,000 (UN 1949, 5), Germany at least 350,000 (see UN 1949, 5), and the Spanish civil war more than half a million refugees (Arendt 1968, 278). The rise of totalitarianism was one factor contributing to the inter-war refugee movements (Skran 1995, 16–17), but more significant numerically was the post-World War One redrawing of borders and collapse of the Russian, Austro-Hungarian, and Ottoman Empires (see Skran 1995, 18).

deprived, marginalised or stigmatised minority (Koestler 1991, 93; Arendt 1968, 294). It is these people, including after 1935 'so-called "economic migrants"' (Arendt 1968, 286), who provide Arendt's paradigm case study – individuals persecuted not because of their commitments or activism, but simply because of who they were (1968, 294–5). Designated by their persecutors as 'the scum of the earth', they would be recognised and treated as such wherever they went (Arendt 1968, 269, 287).[4]

As economic conditions worsened throughout the 1930s, hostility towards refugees in the countries of Western Europe increased, and xenophobia and anti-Semitism were rife (Koestler 1991, 46; Skran 1995, 27; Zucotti 1993, 24–7). Western Europe's constitutional democracies constructed barriers to refugee entry, denied permission to reside or remain, and expelled refugees (Holborn 1938, 698; Jennings 1939, 105, 108; Marrus 1982, 84; Skran 1995, 123, 130–31, 133). The refugees were excluded from ordinary engagement in society with what Marrus (1982, 84) describes as a 'punctilious, almost Kafkaesque formality'. The minority of refugees who had passports, and thus evidence of their identity and former national status, might have them confiscated at any moment for the smallest infraction – such as being unable to provide the police with evidence of a fixed address (Skran 1995, 133; Marrus 1982, 84; Zucotti 1993, 26). Valid passports and travel or residency visas were necessary not only in order to establish one's identity and travel legally across the borders of countries, but also 'for normal existence within countries' (Holborn 1938, 683). Without a passport, one could not stay in a hotel or enter a hospital (Marrus 1982, 84). One could not work legally, qualify for social or welfare benefits, or even apply for a visa or temporary residence permit (Holborn 1938, 683; UN 1949, 8–9). In fact, one could not 'marry, be born, or die without creating legal problems, to which there [was] no solution' (Skran 1995, 103 and see UN 1949, 17–18). Without work or other rights, the refugees were constantly forced into law-breaking acts (Arendt 1968, 286; Marrus 1982, 84). Many obtained false identity documents or crossed secretly into states where the prospects for survival appeared more promising (Holborn 1938, 689; UN 1949, 14). The refugees thus adopted 'that very posture of illicit activity and secretive behaviour which was so much a part of anti-foreign and anti-Semitic propaganda' (Marrus 1982, 84 and see UN 1949, 24).

The practice of imprisoning refugees in specially established internment camps became increasingly common in the lead up to World War Two (Arendt 1968, 288; Holborn 1938, 689 and 693; Skran 1995, 216–18; Wilsher 2012, 108; Zucotti 1993,

4 Arendt (1968, 269) takes the phrase 'scum of the earth' from a boast made in 1938 in the official SS newspaper, the Schwarze Korps, that 'if the world was not yet convinced that the Jews were the scum of the earth, it soon would be when unidentifiable beggars, without nationality, without money, and without passports crossed their frontiers'. The phrase was also used more widely in the popular press to refer to refugees, and Arthur Koestler (1991) takes it as the title of his book describing his detention in 1939–1940 in a French internment camp for political suspects.

26). Refugees without valid visas lived under the constant threat of imprisonment. Expelled from one country, they were liable to imprisonment either for failing to comply with the expulsion order or for illegally entering another country. There was no avenue of legal recourse against imprisonment in these circumstances. The refugees were caught in 'a conflict between two sovereign wills, the one expelling them, the other forbidding their entry. There was no place left to go, and in many cases vagrancy or suicide were the only alternatives of the refugee' (Holborn 1938, 689). France alone spent 3 million francs a year imprisoning undocumented or 'undesirable' aliens (Holborn 1938, 689 fn. 41). Thus, as Arendt (1968, 288) points out, 'even though there were considerable differences in the treatment of their inmates', 'concentration camps were … provided for the same groups in all countries … if the Nazis put a person in a concentration camp and if he made a successful escape, say, to Holland, the Dutch would put him in an internment camp'.

The Refugees' Legal Status

In Arendt's account (1968, 277, 286), the intolerable position in which the inter-war refugees found themselves was a function of the fact that they were forced to live – or to die – 'outside the pale of the law'. In 1949, the United Nations' Ad Hoc Committee on Refugees and Stateless Persons ('UN Committee on Refugees', 6–8) used similar language to describe the stateless. A person who is stateless – whether *de jure* or *de facto* – is, it said, 'an anomaly', 'having no definite legal status' and 'obliged to live outside the law'. Initially, political asylum offered the only possible escape from this impasse, and although Arendt (1968, 280 and see 284–5) is disparaging of states' failure to accord asylum to refugees *en masse*, it was used on a significant scale to grant sanctuary or even permanent protection to particular individuals (Holborn 1938, 681). Those most likely to be awarded asylum were not, however, Arendt's paradigm refugees – persecuted simply on the basis of their class or race or minority status, but predominantly members of Europe's progressive elites who were outcasts because of their anti-fascist political convictions. Furthermore, the principle of asylum did not provide even these refugees with an enforceable claim to protection, and many were simply absorbed into the faceless ranks of Europe's shifting population of '*indésirables*' (Arendt 1968, 259). In his account of his 1939–1940 detention in a French internment camp for political suspects, the Hungarian Jewish journalist Arthur Koestler (1991, 71) notes that those who had once been considered 'the martyrs of Fascist barbarism', had – like their fellow displaced peoples – very quickly 'become the scum of the earth': 'having been labelled "refugees" and beaten out of three or four countries, [we] went about as if carrying an invisible leper's bell'.

The fact that all the refugees had lost the protection of their national governments in the context of an international system within which the primary actors are states rather than individuals was very significant. The system takes for granted that '[t]he normal individual is a national of some state enjoying the protection of the government of that state' (Jennings 1939, 99). Nationality is the mechanism through which individuals' legal identity, and therefore their rights, are recognised and protected outside their home state (see Weis 1979, 162). People without national status are deprived of legal standing not only in their home state but also of protection and standing in other states and in the international sphere. A person's 'nationality' in this sense refers to a 'politico-legal' concept of international law, denoting membership of a sovereign nation-state (Weis 1979, 3).[5] In the international sphere, to be a national of a state means to be a member of an entity that has its own standing and personality; that is a subject of international law (Weis 1979, 13). Individuals are 'connected with international law' through their state membership (Weis 1979, 13) and historically they were objects rather than subjects of international law (McCorquodale 2006, 307–8; Weis 1979, 32).

In the domestic sphere, bonds of nationality are 'the juridical and political link' ('Messih v. Minister of the Interior', in Weis 1979, 31) uniting individuals with their state and constituting each individual's legal personality, as well as the legal community of the state itself (Brownlie 2003, 497). Through the exercise of 'national' or 'personal' jurisdiction, states establish the particular attributes of a person's legal personality, imposing 'legal characterisations upon persons' (Lowe 2006, 340) under marriage laws, for example, or laws relating to the age of majority. Nationality establishes a reciprocal relationship between the individual and the state; it is often described as a tie or a contract under which protection is owed by a state to its subjects and allegiance owed by the subjects to their state (Weis 1979, 29–32). Nationality provides the basis upon which individuals appear before and are recognised within domestic law; it is the foundation on which they assert their rights against the state (see Weis 1979, 29–30). The content of these rights, as well as the duties associated with nationality, are determined by the state's own laws.

All individuals are 'aliens' in respect of states of which they are not, within the terms of the state's own legislation, nationals (Tiburcio 2001, 1). But in addition to states' national or personal jurisdiction, states exercise territorial jurisdiction. According to the doctrine of the sovereign equality of states, each state has legal competence in respect of its territory and the population in that territory and within its territorial jurisdiction is entitled to develop policy free from external interference.[6] An alien on the territory of another state is subject

5 Nationality in the politico-legal sense is closely related to citizenship – both are grounded in state membership and the terms are often used interchangeably, but the language of citizenship is more common in association with the domestic aspects of membership, while that of nationality is generally used to refer to those aspects of membership relevant in international law (Tiburcio 2001, 17; Weis 1979, 4–5).

6 Given the national principle allows states to extend the application of their laws to nationals living outside their territorial borders (Lowe 2006, 345), conflicts may arise in which more than one state legislates in respect of the same conduct. In practise, however,

to the territorial jurisdiction of that state and thus bound by its laws. Aliens may also receive legal recognition and be attributed certain rights under the laws of their host state (Brownlie 2003, 500; Lowe 2006, 342) but this is within the state's sovereign discretion. Historically, the host state's responsibility in international law to the alien and the alien's rights in respect of the state were founded solely on inter-state duties, with aliens traveling and living abroad under the protection of their national state. The national state provided, as it still does, all those services, including the provision of identity documents, necessary to allow its nationals 'to carry out the normal formalities of civilian life' while living in another country (UN 1949, 24). Meanwhile, the legal standing and identity of individuals in their national state was recognised within another state's borders in accordance with principles of inter-state reciprocity, usually enshrined in a treaty between the particular states (Brownlie 2003, 498; Holborn 1938, 690 fn. 45; Tiburcio 2001, 12; UN 1949, 11–12).

As the UN Committee on Refugees (1949, 23) points out:

> Every state protects its nationals. Its protective influence extends beyond its frontiers. The mere fact that a person possesses a nationality, i.e. that he is linked to a state by a bond of allegiance, brings him within the orbit of the law, and determines his legal status; in short it secures for him a standing which the stateless person, not being a member of any national community, does not enjoy.

The right to exercise diplomatic protection in accordance with the law of state responsibility for injuries to aliens provides that a wrong under international law inflicted by the organs of one state upon a national of another is an injury against the latter state that it is entitled to prosecute.[7] The Permanent Court of Justice (in Steiner and Alston 2000, 82) made it clear in 1924 that the law is concerned with states' rather than individuals' rights: '[b]y taking up the case of one of its subjects and by resorting to diplomatic action or international judicial proceedings on his behalf, the state is in reality asserting its own rights – its rights to ensure, in the person of its subjects, respect for the rules of international law'. Without the protection of their home state, and unable to establish a claim to political membership or legal standing in any other state, the inter-war stateless could be treated with impunity. Regardless of how they were treated, they had no recourse to legal remedies (UN 1949, 44).

---

this occurs infrequently, with states recognising other states' national jurisdiction for the purposes of establishing individuals' legal status and – on the other hand – generally refraining from exercising their extra-territorial jurisdiction in a manner at odds with other states' territorial jurisdiction (Lowe 2006, 347).

7 Before a state can extend diplomatic protection to its national, however, the national is expected to have exhausted any remedies available within the state accused of inflicting the wrong (Brownlie 2003, 374 and 501; Steiner and Alston 2000, 82).

Europe in the inter-war years was thus confronted with the problem of hundreds of thousands of refugees living in a legal vacuum. The international response to this crisis was piecemeal. The League of Nations was initially spurred into action in 1921 by calls for a collaborative response from those states most immediately affected by the refugee influx (Holborn 1938, 682), combined with the advocacy of international relief organisations on behalf of those Russian refugees rendered stateless after the 1917 Revolution (Skran 1995, 85). The League Council established a High Commissioner for Russian Refugees and in 1922 the Nansen passport system – named after Fridtjof Nansen, the first High Commissioner for Refugees – was devised specifically for the Russian refugees (UN 1949, 59–60). Over the years the system was gradually extended to include a range of other refugee groups, including Armenian refugees (Holborn 1938, 684 fn. 15), 'Assyrians and other Christian minorities from the former Ottoman Empire' (Skran 1995, 113; Holborn 1938, 686), refugees from the Saar region (Jennings 1939, 100 fn. 4), and Czechoslovakian refugees from the Sudentenland (UN 1949, 27). At the outset, it created a special internationally valid certificate of identity for Russian refugees to substitute for a national passport (Holborn 1938, 684). Insofar as the certificate attested to a person's identity and the fact that he or she was formerly a Russian national, it facilitated travel across international borders and provided what Skran (1995, 104–5) describes as 'a modicum of legal status'.

But Nansen certificates were vastly inferior substitutes for national passports and the national status of which valid passports are evidence. While the 1922 Arrangement that established the system recommended states parties grant transit visas upon request to certificate holders, this was dependent on the refugees already having a visa in respect of the country to which they wished to travel. The Arrangement provided no guarantee in respect of the grant of such visas. Furthermore, it specified that 'the grant of the certificate does not in any way imply the right of the refugee to return to the state in which he obtained it'. This provision dramatically reduced the likelihood of refugees being granted entry visas to other countries. Speaking about arrangements to improve the status of stateless people after World War Two, the UN Committee on Refugees (1949, 43) noted that a 'right to return' clause 'alone makes it possible to obtain an entry visa for other countries'.

In 1933, the Convention Relating to the International Status of Refugees codified the Nansen certificate Arrangements, making them legally binding for signatory states (UN 1949, 71). Parties to the Convention undertook to issue Nansen certificates, 'valid for not less than one year' to those Russian and Armenian refugees 'residing regularly in [their] territory' (Art. 2). Certificates issued under the Convention automatically included a right to leave and to return to the territory of the issuing state (Art. 2). Skran (1995, 136) points out that the Convention broke new ground in treaty law by containing the first ever prohibition against expulsion and refoulement, or return to the borders of a state in which a person faces persecution. The prohibition was, however, extraordinarily weak. It was open to qualification on the basis of concerns relating to 'national security or public order' and was widely interpreted as applying only to refugees to whom asylum had already been granted (Skran 1995, 136). Skran (1995, 72) notes that the 'national security or public order' qualification could be broadly interpreted, allowing for the expulsion of refugees in periods of recession or times of war. Furthermore, where such expulsion was prevented by border controls imposed by other countries, the parties reserved 'the right to apply such internal measures as [they deemed] necessary' (Art. 3). This clause provided a basis on which the detention of refugees could be legitimated within the terms of the Convention.

The Convention also dealt with refugees' juridical condition, specifying their personal status should be governed by the law of their country of domicile, or in the absence of domicile, the law of their country of residence (Art. 4). It specified that rights acquired under the refugees' former national law, particularly those associated with marriage, should be respected (Art. 4); and that refugees should have 'free and ready access to the courts of law' (Art. 6). In addition, the Convention stated that restrictions on refugees' entry to the labour market should be relaxed (Art. 7); and that 'the most favourable treatment' accorded by parties to foreign nationals should be extended to refugees residing in their territory in relation to industrial accidents (Art. 8) and to welfare and relief (Arts 9, 10 and 11). In relation to education, the Convention specified that refugees should be accorded 'treatment as favourable as other foreigners in general' (Art. 12). Parties undertook not to impose special duties or taxes on refugees, except those costs associated with the administration of the Nansen regime (Art. 13). Parties also agreed not to refuse those rights to refugees that were generally extended to foreigners subject to reciprocity (Art. 14). Notably, however, certificates were issued by signatory governments rather than League of Nations delegates, so accession to the system was no guarantee of compliance (Skran 1995, 120). In practise, Nansen certificates were expensive and difficult – if not impossible – to obtain (Skran 1995, 108, 120 table 12, 121; Holborn 1938, 684).

German government opposition initially prevented the extension of the Nansen passport system to refugees from the Third Reich (UN 1949, 26). A separate High Commissioner's Office for German Refugees was established in October 1933, although the League of Nations eventually took over administration of the Office and in 1938 amalgamated the refugee work being conducted on its behalf (UN 1949, 26–7). A provisional agreement in 1936 and a Convention in 1938 provided for the issue of travel documents to German refugees,[8] and contained protections similar to those provided to Nansen refugees. The position of Austrian refugees was ostensibly assimilated with that of German refugees in September 1939, although only three countries signed the Additional Protocol extending the 1938

8 In addition to 'persons possessing or having possessed German nationality', the Convention covered 'stateless persons not covered by previous Conventions or Agreements who have left German territory after being established therein and who are proved not to enjoy, in law or in fact, the protection of the German Government' (UN 1949, 39). The 1936 provisional agreement had excluded stateless people from its refugee definition.

Convention to refugees from Austria (UN 1949, 27, 33 and 39). The support and resources provided by the League to the High Commissioner were paltry, and the powers exercised by his Office 'rigidly limited' (Lafitte 1940, 61). In 1938, in recognition, Skran (1995, 78) says, of 'the declining prestige of the League of Nations', the Evian Conference agreed to establish an additional organisation to deal with refugees from the Third Reich, the Intergovernmental Committee on Refugees (IGCR). The IGCR functioned from 1938 until 1 July 1947.

The various organisations created to deal with refugee issues during the inter-war years received funding from the League of Nations Council and Assembly, and drew on the League Secretariat for expert advice (Skran 1995, 76). Skran (1995, 76) points out that the League Assembly was a representative body in which decisions were made by consensus, so any significant measures taken on behalf of refugees required the support of all members of the League. This was particularly significant given membership of the League included Germany and other refugee producing countries such as Romania – which passed nationality laws in 1924 that made around 100,000 Jewish citizens stateless (Skran 1995, 94). No funding was provided directly for refugee relief; instead the High Commissioner's Office and its successors were expected to coordinate the efforts of individual governments and charitable institutions (Holborn 1938, 687; Hathaway 1990, 138).

Writing in 1940, Lafitte (1940, 62) argued that '[t]he urgent need of the refugees is precisely for an independent Protecting Power which can ensure to them some of the rights and backing which the ordinary citizen enjoys when in a foreign country, by virtue of having a Government of his own to protect him'. This protection was never provided to the inter-war refugees, even to the Russian refugees for whom the Nansen regime was initially created and thus who could be regarded as 'the aristocracy of the stateless people' (Arendt 1968, 281 fn. 30). The Nansen certificates and their equivalents only ever provided temporary legal recognition and were never considered a pathway to resettlement or naturalisation (Goodwin-Gill and McAdam 2007, 358). Furthermore, it remained virtually impossible for refugees to obtain visas, including transit visas, unless they were sponsored by an individual or organisation prepared to take financial responsibility for them.[9] In addition, widespread failure by signatories to incorporate the Nansen Arrangements into domestic law meant the refugees' legal status remained anomalous, and the many reservations attached to the Arrangements ensured that when honouring their obligations became politically contentious within the signatory state, they could be easily evaded (see Holborn 1938, 684; Jennings 1939, 98; Skran 1995, 108 and 120; and in relation to the UK experience, Lafitte 1940). Despite the scale of the refugee problem and the clear and urgent need for a co-ordinated response, democratic governments in Europe and around the world 'consistently refused to create a world-wide migration service' (Skran 1995, 99) or to institute a comprehensive strategy to provide the legal recognition and permanent protection that the refugees so desperately needed. Holborn (1938, 688)

9 See Lafitte 1940, 22, 24 and 37 in respect of the refugees from Germany.

suggests that all schemes aimed at longer term solutions, such as those providing for the mass resettlement of refugees, 'failed through inability to secure necessary funds'. The failure was also, and more fundamentally, a result of the unwillingness of states to accept obligations that would limit their sovereign freedom in relation to naturalisation and immigration.

Erosion of the Rule of Law

While at a diplomatic level and among international aid organisations efforts were certainly made to provide coordinated assistance to the refugees, Arendt (1968, 284) is critical of the fact that the overwhelming response to them within host countries was preoccupation with the question of removal – how could the refugees 'be made deportable again?' Naturalisation *en masse*, which would have gone a long way to dissolving the problem, was never seriously entertained (Arendt 1968, 284–5; Holborn 1938, 682; Skran 1995, 103).[10] Not only did host countries refuse to address the predicament of the refugees through naturalisation, but the democracies of Western Europe actually succumbed to the 'totalitarian infection' (Arendt 1968, 278) sweeping Europe by revoking previous naturalisations and legislating to allow for the future denaturalisation of large groups of permanent residents. As Arendt points out,

> there was hardly a country left on the Continent that did not pass between the two wars some new legislation which, even if it did not use [the sovereign right of denationalisation] extensively, was always phrased to allow for getting rid of a great number of its inhabitants at any opportune moment. (1968, 278–9 and 284–5; and see Marrus 1982, 83)

In this way, denationalisation became a 'powerful weapon of totalitarian politics' (Arendt 1968, 269), practically ensuring that groups persecuted by their own governments would become targets of hostility and persecution everywhere.

The precarious position of the refugees was exacerbated by the fact that many democracies simply devolved responsibility for the refugees to the police (Arendt 1968, 287). In the early 1930s regulations were introduced in France to enhance the Ministry of the Interior's enforcement powers in respect of expulsions (Skran 1995, 131; and see Arendt 1968, 287 fn. 44). The Ministry acted through the police, and while '[i]n theory, the expulsion order came from the Minister … in practice, orders could be issued by local policemen' (Skran 1995, 132). In many states, expulsions were undertaken secretly (Jennings 1939, 105; Skran 1995, 135) and no appeal mechanisms were provided to the refugees (Jennings 1939,

10 While it was considered as a response to the Russian refugees (Arendt 1968, 281), many of the Russians considered naturalisation a mark of disloyalty to their home country and so refused it (Holborn 1938, 682).

106). It is not surprising, then, that in their dealings with the refugees, the police themselves began to commit illegal acts, smuggling people across borders in order to be rid of them, with the result that police in neighbouring countries routinely did the same (Arendt 1968, 283–4; Marrus 1982, 84; Holborn 1938, 693 fn. 61). Arendt (1968, 287) concludes that in the exercise of their authority over the refugees, the police could no longer be characterised as 'an instrument to carry out and enforce the law', but instead functioned as 'a ruling authority independent of government and ministries' (see also Skran 1995, 132). The police in a number of Western European countries went so far as to establish strong links with the Gestapo (Arendt 1968, 289),[11] so that when war broke out and the Nazis occupied countries such as France, the local police not only did little to oppose them, but often actively co-operated in their oppression of the domestic population. The story of this collaboration is now widely known (Koestler 1991, 71 and 74–5; Deak 2000, 6; Marrus and Paxton 1982, 703 and 706; Jenkins 1988, 142–3).[12]

In the lead up to and after the outbreak of war, Britain, Canada, Australia, the US and Peru also succumbed to Europe's totalitarian infection. They refused asylum to many of Europe's refugees and restricted the movement of those refugees whom they did accept, often through mass imprisonment. They also imprisoned citizens and long-term residents with links such as ancestral ties to the axis countries. All were branded 'enemy aliens' regardless of their attitude – and often their opposition – to fascism. The indiscriminate nature of these internments, as well as the punitive conditions in the camps, provoked criticism from civil libertarians, but the incarceration regimes were also a populist measure that received broad community support (see Bashford and Strange 2002).[13] Eventually the critics succeeded in forcing reviews of some aspects of the detention regimes in some countries, but it was not until years after the war that the full scope of the internment regimes was recognised and their legacy of injustice gradually acknowledged.[14] Dyzenhaus and Thwaites (2007, 9) claim the majority's endorsement of detention in cases such as Liversidge, in the UK and Korematsu in the USA, came afterwards to be 'regarded as badges of shame'. A precedent for these internments had, however, been set in Australia, Britain and the USA during

11 As well as the GPU, the USSR's foreign intelligence service.

12 Koestler (1991, 46) also points out that after war broke out but prior to the Nazi occupation of France, '[t]he country was living under the loi des suspects, which gave police practically uncontrolled power over the individual'.

13 Bashford and Strange (2002, 523) note that while the internment of refugees and other 'enemy aliens' in Australia was governed by the Hague Convention on prisoners of war, the reality of conditions in detention was often at odds with the principles propounded by the Convention. For further details of the wartime internment regimes see Lafitte, 1940; Bashford and Strange 2002; Larkin 1996.

14 For conflicting views on the precedent set by wartime internment in Australia see McHugh and Kirby JJ's reasons in 'Al-Kateb v. Godwin', at [55]-[61] (McHugh) and [162]-[166] (Kirby, in dissent).

World War One (see Bashford and Strange 2002, 517–19; and in relation to the USA and UK, Wilsher 2012, 29–34 and 45–53).

The Right to have Rights

According to the eighteenth century's pronouncement of the rights of man, the inter-war refugees should have been able to fall back on their fundamental human rights (Arendt 1968, 300). The American Declaration of Independence and the French Declaration of the Rights of Man and of the Citizen state that all men are born with rights, and that civil law is founded upon and 'secures' or 'preserves' these pre-existing 'inalienable' rights:

> We hold these truths to be self-evident: That all men are created equal; that they are endowed by their Creator with certain unalienable rights; ... that, to secure these rights, governments are instituted among men. (Declaration of Independence, US General Congress, 4 July 1776)

> [T]he National Assembly recognizes and proclaims, in the presence and under the auspices of the Supreme Being, the following rights of man and of the citizen: Men are born and remain free and equal in rights ... The aim of all political association is the preservation of the natural and imprescriptible rights of man. (Declaration of the Rights of Man and of the Citizen, National Assembly of France, 26 August 1789)

Having severed or been cut off from all ties with their national governments, however, the refugees could not appear before the law in their host countries – even in those countries in which the law was based on rights. They could neither claim rights nor appear in a court of law to argue that their rights had been abused.[15] This was the case even though refugees were the objects of punitive laws and regulations. Occasionally they received a provisional or qualified form of legal status under the Nansen Arrangements, but they lacked legal personas on the basis of which they could appear before the law as the subjects of rights. They were neither equal subjects of law nor the subjects of rights under it. The resulting reality for the refugees was vagrancy, incarceration, and subjection to arbitrary rule by the police.

---

15 While broadly adopting Arendt's diagnosis of the dilemmas the inter-war refugees confronted, Benhabib (2004, 68–9) implies that the League of Nations afforded effective protection to many refugees, and she says that those 'without passports were recognized as entitled to legal protection'. I argued in the previous section against this conclusion, and following Arendt, argue here that the failure to accord the refugees legal status was the key to their predicament.

Ironically, the commission of an act in breach of the criminal law actually improved a refugee's legal position. Arendt (1968, 286) points out that the refugee accused of a crime became an 'exception provided for by law' as opposed to an exception 'outside the pale of the law' altogether. Ordinarily speaking, the law acknowledges only 'one difference between human beings, the difference between the normal noncriminal and the anomalous criminal', but even the anomalous criminal is recognised by and has rights under the law (Arendt 1968, 287). Thus,

> [t]he same man who was in jail yesterday because of his mere presence in this world, who had no rights whatever and lived under threat of deportation, or who was dispatched without sentence and trial to some kind of internment because he had tried to work and make a living, [could] become almost a full-fledged citizen because of a little theft. (Arendt 1968, 286)

By virtue of the theft he became visible in the eyes of the law and entitled to its protections – he was granted again 'some kind of human equality' (1968, 286). Accorded a legal personality, he could be judged not simply for who he was, but on the basis of what he had done and his actions could again influence his destiny in the world. The importance of this for Arendt cannot be overstated. It helps explain the significance of her 'right to have rights' and her claim that to have such a right 'means to live in a framework where one is judged by one's actions and opinion' (1968, 296–7; and see 295; and 1978, 230). The non-criminal refugee, whose existence was anomalous in the eyes of the law, was by contrast merely an object to be disposed of as expeditiously as possible by the police. It is in this sense that Arendt distinguishes between those rights that – although proclaimed as 'human' rights are actually 'the varying rights of citizens in different countries' (1949, 24), and the right to political membership and a legal personality, or the 'right to have rights'.

According to Arendt, citizens may be deprived of particular rights ordinarily described under the rubric of human rights without thereby being reduced to a condition of 'absolute rightlessness':

> The solider during the war is deprived of his right to life, the criminal of his right to freedom, all citizens during an emergency of their right to the pursuit of happiness, but nobody would ever claim that in any of these instances a loss of human rights has taken place. (1968, 295)

The curtailment of rights in accordance with law is not an affront to a person's legal personality on the basis of which he or she is recognised as an equal subject of law and a bearer of rights. On the other hand, certain rights may be accorded – although Arendt admits, 'hardly enjoyed' – to refugees living 'under conditions of fundamental rightlessness' (1968, 295). Thus the movements of people living outside the pale of the law may be less restricted than those of prisoners incarcerated under the criminal law; and if they are locked up in a democratic country they may have greater freedom of opinion than they would while living 'in an ordinary despotism', but none of this, Arendt says, 'changes in the least their fundamental situation of rightlessness' (1968, 296). Within the internment camp, the stateless thought what they liked and received regular meals, but 'the prolongation of their lives [was] due to charity and not to right, for no law [existed] which could force the nations to feed them … and their freedom of opinion [was] a fool's freedom, for nothing they [thought mattered] anyhow' (1968, 296). Even the rightlessness suffered by those who died in Germany's concentration camps was not, Arendt (1968, 296) claims, primarily a result of the fact that the victims were deprived of their right to life, but rather that before they were actually killed they were rendered superfluous. Thus the Nazis:

> started their extermination of Jews by first depriving them of all legal status … and cutting them off from the world of the living by herding them into ghettos and concentration camps; and before they set the gas chambers into motion they … carefully tested the ground and found to their satisfaction that no country would claim these people. The point is that a condition of complete rightlessness was created before the right to live was challenged. (1968, 296)

The apparent contradiction in Arendt's claim that the Jews were made completely 'rightless' *before* being deprived of the right to life is explained by her identification of the 'right to have rights' as a precondition for having any of those fundamental rights usually described as human rights but which she argues are actually the rights of citizens. Without a 'right to have rights' even those Jews who managed to escape the gas chambers did not have a genuine right to life because their lives did not warrant the protection of any law – except the occasional law of exception such as that set up by the Nansen passport regime. Whether they lived or died had become a question of charity rather than of justice and of right.

Skran (1995, 9) argues that the League of Nations' notorious failure to assist Jewish refugees from the Third Reich in 1938–39 – 'a period when the entire organisation was disintegrating' – should not be seen as symptomatic. She points out that prior to this the League successfully assisted huge numbers of inter-war refugees. Furthermore, she claims that these efforts produced a 'lasting legacy of refugee assistance' (1995, 9). In her view,

> these first twenty years of international refugee assistance should be recognized as a time of great creativity and innovation, a time when much was accomplished with minimal resources, and a time when millions of refugees were helped to begin new lives. (1995, 9)

She concludes that '[t]his work is, in fact, a tribute to the "idealists", a generation of leaders who created and supported the League of Nations in those tumultuous years'. In *Origins*, Arendt could hardly be more scathing of the efforts made on the refugees' behalf by such 'idealists'. She notes that as the institution of asylum crumbled in the face of the huge numbers of refugees, '[t]he only guardians of the right of asylum were the few societies whose special aim was the protection of human rights' (1968, 280 and 281 fn. 27). Yet these societies were politically incompetent, and could not possibly be taken seriously (1968, 292). 'In language and composition', she says, they 'showed an uncanny similarity ... to that of societies for the prevention of cruelty to animals' (1968, 292). From her perspective,

> No paradox of contemporary politics is filled with a more poignant irony than the discrepancy between the efforts of well-meaning idealists who stubbornly insist on regarding as 'inalienable' those human rights ... enjoyed only by citizens of the most prosperous countries, and the situation of the rightless themselves. (1968, 279)

From Arendt's point of view, the horrors of the gas chambers present an unavoidable obligation. We must view history through their lens. That thousands were saved from them does not alter the reality that millions died in them – and not before it was clear to the Nazis that the rest of the world had turned its back on these people. Skran (1995, 53) herself makes clear that with war looming, avenues of escape for refugees from Europe were barred in order 'to prevent a mass influx'. Ships such as the now notorious St Louis 'travelled from port to port seeking a country willing to accept their human cargo' (Skran 1995, 53). Few countries were willing, and as a result the majority of the 937 passengers on board the St Louis were, like so many others, forced back to Europe where they would become fodder for the gas chambers (see Lafitte 1940, 22–3). The fact that refugees in the inter-war years were seen as objects of charity or 'humanitarian assistance' rather than as subjects of justice, law and rights is the crucial distinction that Skran's perspective does nothing to undercut. As humanitarian sentiments evaporated in the lead up to World War Two, the refugees were left without recourse.

Chapter 2
Rights and the Nation-state

Introduction

How can states in which the legitimacy of government depends on its claim to secure rights with which all are born nevertheless deny legal standing and the capacity to make rights claims to refugees? In this chapter I begin to address this question by discussing Arendt's account in *Origins* of the birth and subsequent decline of a distinctively modern nation-state in Western Europe. Arendt characterises the modern state as a legal institution founded on the 'new revolutionary concept of equality' (1968, 11). As such, the state should secure an 'open society' based on the equality of all who come into contact with it – its legal order should be 'open to all who happen to live on its territory' (1994, 208). Notably, however, the state was also founded on the consent of its citizens, who in Arendt's account constitute a nation, or 'a closed society to which one belongs by right of birth' (1994, 208). Arendt considers the combination of state and nation to have tremendous potential as the locus for an emancipatory and republican politics, particularly in the context of an international sphere based on the concept of a 'comity of nations'. But in her account this potential was never fully realised. Instead, the nation-state's commitment to equality was fatally undercut by 'sentimental nationalism', involving 'the conquest' of the state by the nation (1994, 208). In the international sphere, this translated into the aggressive assertion of national sovereignty and undercut any prospect of creating a genuine community of nations.

Arendt's characterisation in *Origins* of a modern revolutionary nation-state, while ostensibly historical, is implicitly framed by her conception of the nation as an idealised site of political emancipation. The nation as the locus of revolutionary politics – thus the *political* nation – certainly played a crucial role in the evolution of the nation-state, but the exact nature and extent of this role is the subject of debate, as is the history of Western European nations more generally.[1] These controversies

1 Arendt's history of the modern nation-state has been criticised on a number of grounds. For example, Brunkhorst (1996, 193) suggests that Arendt incorrectly characterises the French nation as ethnically homogenous and, moreover, that she is wrong to suggest that the nation 'conquered' the French State and its legal institutions. But while the principle of the self-determination of nations may not have explicitly 'play[ed] a significant role in … the French Revolution' – as Arendt herself would agree, focusing as she does on the role of the political nation in the Revolution – nor 'in the way later republics saw themselves' as Brunkhorst suggests, Arendt is correct to highlight the importance of appeals to ethnic and cultural homogeneity in French society in the late nineteenth and early twentieth centuries.

are not insignificant, but nor do they undercut the power of Arendt's invocation of political nationhood and her contemporaneous insistence of the dangers posed by nationalism. Throughout her life, Arendt would continue to warn of the threat posed by nationalism and to emphasise its influence in the context of a world based on the sovereignty of nation-states.[2] While our contemporary political landscape is defined by national, multinational and pluralist states, almost all are in some sense the progeny of Western Europe's original nation-states and we continue to rely on the rubric of the 'nation-state' at the same time as we are bedevilled by its dual commitment to impartial rights recognition and national sovereignty.

A version of this dual commitment is theorised by Jürgen Habermas (2001, 58–129; 2001a) through his analysis of democratic legitimacy in terms of the 'co-originality' of popular sovereignty and human rights.[3] Habermas' (2001, 60) account of 'the revolutionary birth of modern nation-states', although oriented from the standpoint of a globalising world, also bears many similarities to Arendt's account and like Arendt, Habermas points out that '[t]he form of national organization that emerged from the American and French revolutions has successfully spread over the entire world' (2001, 62). In Habermas' analysis, the achievement of the modern nation-state was to establish a form of 'civil solidarity' among strangers (2001, 64). The boundaries of the state extend well beyond any ties established by family, village, city or province, but nevertheless it successfully unites its members, forging an enduring political association ostensibly based on the commitment to individual rights. In Arendt's critique, the enduring quality of this commitment has relied dangerously on a form of solidarity achieved through members' sentimental identification with the nation. From Habermas' more optimistic perspective, the commitment to rights within the modern nation-state operates in tandem with the exercise of popular sovereignty, encouraging democratic inclusivity and militating

---

Also contentious is Arendt's claim that an appreciation of national homogeneity grew out of the developing political consciousness of the lower classes. Smith (2004, 19) recognises the presence of a range of ethnic groups within Western European nations, but like Arendt he characterises these nations as traditionally based on one dominant and relatively homogeneous ethnie that shared 'a myth of common origins and ancestry'. Notably, however, Smith (2004, 21) sees the national solidarity that arose in Western Europe as initially restricted to the elites rather than as a product of the emancipation of the peasant classes. He suggests that nations in countries such as France and England were partly the outcome of the state's 'bureaucratic incorporation' – via the imposition of the dominant ethnie's language, culture and religion – 'of the middle (and much later the lower) classes of the state's population' (2004, 21). This picture conveys a top down impression of the formation of national consciousness, as opposed to Arendt's bottom up account. The difference is not merely one of emphasis, but Arendt's account is defensible in the light of her focus on the French Revolution, which at least initially tied the idea of national sovereignty to that of the 'freedom of the people' (see Arendt 1968, 231).

2 See, for example, 'The Nation' (1994, 207; published in 1946); and *Men In Dark Times* (1995, 82; written in 1958).

3 See as well Benhabib 2004, 43–6 and Brunkhorst 2000.

against exclusionary populism.[4] It is no negative, in Habermas' view, that the state's rights-based law is legitimated not solely by reference to traditional liberal rights but also democratically, on the basis that it is authored by the members of the body politic (2001, 65). Habermas (2001, 118) recognises the tension between the universal, individualistic character of human rights and the sovereign autonomy of the people who are the subjects of rights only because they are co-authors of the law under which rights are accorded, but he does not think that this tension is fatal either for the impartial promise of a rights-based law or for the concept of democratic legitimacy. I consider how he thinks the two can be reconciled in Chapter 8. Arendt's account of the anti-political implications of the eighteenth-century's pronouncement of the rights of man, including its resort to the nation as the bedrock of rights, is my focus in Chapter 3, but I introduce that account in the last section of this chapter, drawing on Arendt's alternative understanding of equality as a political commitment secured by law. This understanding is implicit in *Origins* and is developed, although in piecemeal fashion, throughout the entire body of Arendt's work. I also briefly discuss Habermas' co-originality thesis again in this section. I begin, however, with Arendt's story of the birth and decline of the modern nation-state – a story that usefully backgrounds and serves to clarify these concerns with the source of political authority, law and rights.

The Birth and Decline of the Modern Nation-state

Arendt describes the plight of the inter-war refugees in Chapter 9 of *Origins*, titled 'The Decline of the Nation-state and the End of the Rights of Man'. Arendt's story here of the nation-state's demise needs to be read in the light of her account, earlier in *Origins*, of the rise of the nation-state in Western Europe.[5] Arendt (1968, 230) argues that the French Revolution marked the birth of a distinctively modern nation-state that would reach 'the height of its development' in the 1800s (1968, 11), but that by the end of the century was already in fatal decline. France is Arendt's '*nation par excellence*' (1968, 276), and her analysis focuses on France as an exemplar of the revolutionary nation-state, demonstrating both its republican potential and its tragic failure, and in doing so revealing a pattern that was to some extent followed in all of Europe's nation-states (1968, 79). The original nation-states combined single nations – in Western Europe the 'comparatively recent' product of the late eighteenth- and early nineteenth-centuries (1968, 230), with the institutional apparatus of states that had evolved gradually in the seventeenth- and eighteenth-centuries out of absolute monarchies (1968, 14).

4 In his later work, Habermas (2008, 237) recognises more explicitly the part played by nationalism in providing 'a basis for civic solidarity' within nation-states and he characterises nationalism as 'a stubborn mindset that [has been] historically closely interconnected with the formation of the nation-state'.

5 In discussing this account I also draw on Arendt's comments in 'The Nation' (1994).

In Arendt's analysis (1968, 125), Western Europe's nations represented an 'homogenous population's active consent to its government' and its will to preserve a cultural and political heritage grounded in a particular territory. They were founded on the emancipation of the 'firmly rooted' peasant classes (1968, 229–30) and came into being around the time of the French Revolution:

> When peoples … acquired a consciousness of themselves as cultural and historical entities, and of their territory as a permanent home, where history had left its visible traces, whose cultivation was the product of the common labor of their ancestors and whose future would depend upon the course of a common civilization. (1968, 229; and see 1994, 208)

As a result of the association between territory and recognition of a common history and a shared political future, Arendt (1968, 232) argues that Western Europe's nations were not by inclination expansionary but instead that their members had a sense 'of responsibility for a common, limited community'.

Arendt (1994, 208) depicts states, on the other hand, as power institutions that are inclined externally towards aggression and the accumulation of additional territory. Insofar as the modern state was transformed through the emancipation of the nation, however, it was linked to 'the identification of nationals with their territory' and 'limited by definite boundaries' (1968, 231). Thus Arendt describes those nineteenth-century statesmen who opposed imperialism as being guided by the 'national principle' on the basis of which they tended naturally to think 'in terms of the established national territory' (1968, 124–5 and 127; and see 1994, 208). Historically, the declining power of the monarchy and the old ruling classes enabled the forging of body politics based on the 'new revolutionary concept of equality' and the principle of consent to government (1968, 11). Equality within the national body would henceforth be realised through popular representation (1968, 229) and mutual rights recognition. This is what Habermas (2001, 113–29; 2001a) would later theorise as the co-originality of rights and popular sovereignty, and which Arendt calls 'the stern Jacobin concept of the nation based on human rights [and a …] republican view of communal life which asserts that (in the words of Clemenceau) by infringing on the rights of one you infringe on the rights of all' (1968, 106).[6]

Although based on the idea of human rights, Arendt argues nations continue to represent the bounded social, cultural and historical milieu into which a person is born; a nation is 'a closed society to which one belongs by right of birth' (1994, 208). Thus the political, rights-based nation is founded on and remains grounded in a cultural and historical nation. Nevertheless, through the development of an independent machinery of government in the form of the modern state (1968, 11), the nation-state should have been able to extend the principle of equality

6 The 'stern Jacobin concept of the nation' was in fact abandoned by the Jacobins themselves when they came to power in 1793. See Arendt 2006, 232–40.

to all who came before it. Because historically the structure of the state was 'derived from centuries of monarchy and enlightened despotism', it 'inherited as its supreme function the protection of all inhabitants in a territory no matter what their nationality' (1968, 230). This function should have been entrenched by the establishment of the state as the foundational legal institution of the body politic (1968, 230–31). Ideally, the state secures 'an open society, ruling over a territory where its power protects and makes the law. As a legal institution, the state knows only citizens no matter of what nationality; its legal order is open to all who happen to live on its territory' (1994, 208). Arendt (1968, 91) describes the nineteenth century's 'greatest achievement' as 'the complete impartiality of the law' and she claims that at the turn of the century, despite the rot that had set into the institutions of the state, 'the doctrine of equality before the law was still … firmly planted in the conscience of the civilized world' (1968, 91).

In theory, the modern state should have operated above the interests of classes or particular parties and 'in splendid isolation' represented the national interest (1968, 11; and see 38). In fact, government was invariably formed by parties who represented the interests of their particular constituents and engaged in open contests for power. Nevertheless, Arendt (1968, 38) argues that during the brief ascendancy of the original nation-states, the role of the state was premised on the assumption that national government was obliged to transcend partisan interests and to act on behalf of the entire nation. The rise of bourgeois society, however, with its centrifugal tendencies, also meant that the state in the exercise of this role was forced to claim and to wield strong centralising powers.

Based internally on the emancipation of its body politic, externally the nation-state should have functioned in a spirit of solidarity. Arendt (1968) describes this conception of the 'equality and solidarity of all peoples' (1968, 161) as 'the great principle upon which national organizations of peoples are built' and 'the central pillar of genuine nationhood' (1968, 166). Her invocation of a 'comity of nations' (1968, 161, 287) in this context can be contrasted with a conception of international law based on the sovereign autonomy of states interested primarily in their own preservation and power vis-à-vis other states – a conception that appears in the theories of Locke and Kant, whom I discuss in Part II, and that accurately characterises the contemporary international sphere, as I demonstrate in Part III. The notion of a comity of nations relies, Arendt claims, on an older ideal of international law according to which 'the idea of humanity' regulates and qualifies the interests of independent polities (1968, 157). Rather than clearly identifying with this concept of a fellowship of nations, however, Western Europe's nations asserted their sovereign independence, identifying themselves with the state as a power institution and claiming 'expansion as a national right' (1994, 208). The result was that imperialism and the 'race thinking' used to justify it became an 'ever-present shadow accompanying the development of the comity of European nations' (1968, 161). This comity was never securely established, though it functioned for some time in an ad hoc manner. Furthermore, the practise of power politics made even the principle of sovereign state equality 'a mockery except for giant states' (1968, 269).

Internally, none of Western Europe's nation-states ever developed into genuine republics capable of fully realising the political equality of their members (1968, 12). Instead, while the functional independence of the state grew out of the inability of any one social group to assert absolute political dominance, ensuring that 'political rule no longer depended upon social and economic factors' (1968, 38), these factors continued to ensure the division of society along class lines (1968, 12). The strain placed on the nation-state by what Arendt (1968, 12) describes as a 'fundamental contradiction' between the 'inequality of the class system' and the concept of political equality was also fatally exacerbated by the 'victory of bourgeois values over the citizen's sense of responsibility' (1968, 80). Thus class divisions ensured that the interests of citizens were at odds, and the triumph of bourgeois values – which allowed competitive commercial relations to dominate in the public sphere – destroyed the possibility of achieving cohesion through the collaborative engagement of all citizens in the project of self-government.

Arendt charts the path to this 'victory of bourgeois values' in some detail, discussing its appearance both within the machinery of the state and in society more generally. In the late 1880s, for example, the Panama scandal, in which hundreds of French politicians were exposed as having received bribes from the Panama Company executive in return for their support of public loans backed by parliament, revealed the perverse fact that 'members of Parliament and civil servants had become businessmen' (1968, 96) and government degraded into factions acting either in their own interests or in the interests of their particular constituents. Arendt also analyses the growth of the bourgeoisie as a political class whose members began to exert pressure on government when their wildly speculative international investments (in which small 'absentee shareholders' were involved along with the owners of capital) began to look precarious (1968, 136). In order to protect its citizens' investments in the New World, Arendt (1968, 137) says that the nation-state was led down the path of imperialism and into the perfidious position of denying abroad the applicability of the rule of law that was supposed to govern at home. Arendt concludes that imperialism's 'surprising originality' stemmed from the fact that it was not actually a political principle at all, 'but had its origin in the realm of business speculation, where expansion meant the permanent broadening of industrial production and economic transactions characteristic of the nineteenth century' (1968, 125). Canovan (1999, 105) emphasises the disturbing implications, as Arendt saw them, of this take-over by business of the public realm: '[c]apitalism had already undermined the stable human world and uprooted people by turning stable property into fluid wealth. Once this economic dynamism was imported into politics it generated a drive for expansion that was limitless, global and quite detached from national interests'. Racism flourished as a means of psychologically reconciling the conflict between the principle of government by consent within the nation-state and its negation abroad, and it provided fertile ground for the growth of sentimental nationalism (Arendt 1968, 160; and see Benhabib 1996, 75–86; 2004, 51–2).

Political Nationhood and Constitutional States

While Arendt argues in *Origins* that the formation of Western Europe's nations depended on cultural homogeneity and strong links to a fixed territory, her later work makes clear that these conditions are neither necessary nor sufficient for the creation of *political* nations or nations based on rights and consent. Her later work also demonstrates that a body politic founded on equality may be forged by 'a people' that does not share national traditions. Through mutual promises such a people can found a political nation that only subsequently forges a more developed national identity. Arendt also emphasises, in *Origins* as well as in her later work, that 'the people' who found the nation and establish the constitutional state are not an organic unity moved by one general will. Although usually bonded by culture and history as well as political commitment, the people who comprise a political nation are a 'factual plurality' (2006, 50). And while one is born into a nation (1994, 208), political forms of national consciousness have nothing to do with 'personal' or 'inherent' qualities supposedly found in a person's 'Slavic, or Germanic, or God-knows-what soul' (1968, 231–2). Nor have they anything to do with a collective sense of innate superiority, although they do involve a justified sense of 'national pride' (1968, 232) because they are conscious of historical achievements, and not least the creation of a political body founded on equality. This justified patriotism is a specifically public virtue, however, and it goes along with a sense of civic responsibility: '[i]t is a matter of public concern and civilization' (1968, 231). Furthermore, the political nation is outward looking rather than xenophobic and, consistent with the idea of a 'comity of nations', sees itself in solidarity with other nations based on equality and with peoples struggling for the achievement of political equality. Thus for Arendt the nation has two great tasks: to 'guarantee true sovereignty of the people within [and] to establish a just relationship among different peoples beyond the national borders' (in Beiner 2000, 45).

This explains Arendt's sharply critical attitude during and after World War Two towards those Zionist elites who ignored any 'genuinely national revolutionary movement which sprang from the Jewish masses' and that might have been fostered on the basis of 'an alliance with all progressive forces in Europe' (in Beiner 2000, 46). In her view, these elites subverted the true principles of Jewish nationhood because they 'felt no solidarity with other oppressed peoples whose cause, though historically otherwise conditioned, was essentially the same [as their own]' (in Beiner 2000, 47). Similarly, in *Origins* Arendt commends Europe's socialist parties for their fidelity to the idea, bequeathed by the French Revolution, of 'a "nation among nations", all of which belong to the family of mankind', but she is critical of the fact that they failed, in the context of a world of sovereign power states, to translate this idea into 'an articulate political theory' (1968, 40–41).

Her argument here seems to implicitly support that which she says remained an 'inarticulate hope' for the socialist parties: a form of global federalism embracing 'all nations on equal terms' and based upon the 'national liberty and independence of all oppressed peoples' (1968, 41).[7]

As Arendt's account of Jewish nationalism demonstrates, the most important ingredient of political nationhood is that it represents an emancipatory political movement, expressing its members' shared commitment to securing a stable, ongoing and egalitarian political association. While Arendt thinks that the future of such an association requires a territorial base, she does not think all members of the nation must reside in the one territory,[8] and she definitely does not believe that the nation requires or is entitled to a state of its own. Her remarks in the essay, 'The Nation', and her analysis in *Origins* are part of a sustained attack on 'the nineteenth-century identification of [the] nation [with the] state' (1994, 208). Arendt was also withering in her criticism of the proponents of a uni-national Jewish state in Palestine, and in the early 1940s she argued instead in favour of a form of Jewish–Arab federalism within which the nations would co-exist as equals, with neither being relegated to minority status in (Beiner 2000, 47).[9]

Arendt does, however, clearly relate the revolutionary potential of the nation to the fact that it is a society into which one is born rather than an association that one may seek to join. This reflects her belief that politics will not flourish unless it has roots in a fertile culture that unites individuals and encourages their commitment to a common future. Such a culture is usually distinguished by language and traditions that inform its members' individual development. This is one's communal 'home'; its distinctive character may sustain one, just as its landscape may come to seem one's 'natural shelter'.[10] Its vitality enriches its individual members and sustains

7 In Chapter 9, I suggest that Arendt's thought ultimately supports only a very circumscribed form of global governance.

8 According to Young-Bruehl (2004, 174), Arendt 'warned Zionists against centering their attention exclusively on Palestine, to the neglect of the Diaspora Jews who would never be Palestinians'.

9 See also many of Arendt's essays in *The Jewish Writings* (2007), including 'Zionism Reconsidered' (343–74); and also Kohn 2007, xix–xx; Young-Bruehl 2004, 173–84; and Arendt 1994, 210, in which she quotes Delos: 'The real function of the state is the establishment of a legal order which protects all rights', and adds: 'and this function is not at all affected through the number of nationalities which are protected within the framework of its legal institutions'.

10 In 1943, Thomas Mann (1998, 263) described the tragedy for a German writer in exile in terms that resonate with Arendt's account: 'it is our destiny to carry on this battle … against the land whose speech is the spiritual material in which we work, against the land in whose culture we are rooted, whose tradition we administer, and whose landscape and atmosphere should be our natural shelter'. See also Arendt's account in Origins of the significance for the stateless people of the loss of their home – which she says 'meant the loss of the entire social texture into which they were born and in which they [had] established for themselves a distinct place in the world' (1968, 293).

humanity through its contribution to diversity. While this seems to imply that the principle of nationality is 'a portable private matter, inherent in [one's] very personality', Arendt's insight is that one is born into a nation by virtue of being born into a particular cultural milieu, but this milieu must also have a political character if it is to provide a foundation for human freedom. Internally it must be based on mutual rights recognition and externally on the concept of a comity of nations. If the members of the nation fail to take political responsibility also as citizens of a law based state, and instead think of the nation merely as their natural inheritance, they depoliticise and mystify it, transforming it into a sentimental phenomenon. Furthermore, while 'the authentic origins of all human existence' are to be found in 'national traditions' (1995, 87), these traditions may also stifle politics. In a 1946 letter to Karl Jaspers, Arendt connects a sense of freedom in America, and the apparent flourishing of politics, with the absence of any 'truly national tradition' (in Beiner 2000, 44).[11]

Although deeply critical of the mass culture which she thought dominated social life in the United States, Arendt was a great admirer of American political culture.[12] She considered American constitutionalism an excellent defence against tyranny and a solid basis for the establishment of an engaged polity. The American example also demonstrates that the nation is not the sole crucible for an emancipatory politics. Constitutionalism is a 'form of government in which people are bound together not through historical memories or ethnic homogeneity, as in the nation-state ... but through the strength of mutual promises' (Arendt 1972, 87). Thus a rights based constitution may be achieved not only through the '"progressive history" of a nation', but also through 'the deliberate attempt by a whole people at founding a new body politic' (Arendt 1994, 136). As Arendt's analysis of Eastern and Southern European nationalism (which I discuss in the next section) demonstrates, however, the development of sovereign aspirations among peoples that do not yet share a progressive politics is fraught. Here aspirations to political autonomy are not matched by a thriving or emancipatory political culture. The American experience can be distinguished from the Eastern and Southern European debacle in Arendt's account because the American Revolution witnessed a genuine explosion of political engagement and built upon the constitutional commitments of the separate states that were already 'organized in self-governing

11 Arendt was writing from the vantage point of the recent Jewish émigré. Staying with an American family in the months just after her arrival in America, she was impressed by their personal political engagement although alienated by many of their opinions and the social milieu within which they moved (see Young-Bruehl 2004, 164–6).

12 Arendt's attitude to the health of the political sphere in her adopted home would change considerably over the years. While she continued to admire the republican principles of eighteenth-century America and to defend American constitutionalism, she was increasingly concerned about social forces such as mass conformism that threatened the political sphere in the nineteenth- and twentieth-centuries (see Young-Bruehl 2004, 210).

bodies' (1994, 156). Instead of seeking recourse to the language of ethnic or racial superiority, Arendt portrays the American revolutionary experience as consistently oriented towards the establishment of political institutions.[13]

What Arendt means to invoke when she speaks most glowingly of the nation then, are cultural and political traditions that are rich and vibrant and thus capable of nourishing both the individuals who participate in and contribute to them, and the distinctive political communities sustained by them. While she is extremely wary of romanticising such traditions (see Canovan 1996, 13), Arendt also thinks that their annihilation by the globalisation of culture and politics would result in 'a shallowness that would transform man, as we have known him in five thousand years of recorded history, beyond recognition' (1995, 87).

Nationalism

Although not entirely consistent in her use of the term, generally speaking 'nationalism' is used as a pejorative by Arendt to signify 'the conquest of the state through the nation' (1994, 208). In light of her account of the state as a 'supreme legal institution' (1968, 230), this conquest involves the subversion of the rule of law to the will of the nation, and historically it coincided with the nation's identification with the state as a power institution and thus with its expansionary tendencies. The subversion of the law of the state to the will of the nation is dangerous in itself. It becomes particularly problematic when the 'nation' no longer refers either to the historical and sociological phenomenon that Arendt says arose in Western Europe and which was based – if only fleetingly – on the emancipation of the 'firmly rooted' peasant classes; nor more generally to the political nation – in other words, to a normative ideal of emancipatory politics. Instead, the 'nation' that conquers the legal institution of the state in Arendt's critique of nationalism refers to a group of people bonded by 'sentimental', or worse, 'ethnic' or 'tribal' forms of national consciousness (1994, 209).[14]

The subversion of the state as legal institution to a sentimentalised perversion of the nation represented a response to the class conflict that divided citizens in Western Europe's nation-states, and the political alienation that was a consequence

13 Here Arendt's analysis is too sanguine. The political consciousness of the American states was forged not only in opposition to British domination but also through oppression of the country's indigenous inhabitants. For a convincing critique see Breen (2012, 29).

14 My analysis here differs somewhat from the taxonomy of Canovan's account in the essay, 'Is there an Arendtian case for the nation-state?' although the substance is very similar. Canovan says Arendt distinguishes in Origins between the 'worldly' nationalism of the established nation-states (a positive political force) and the 'worldless' or 'tribal' nationalism of Europe's proto-totalitarian forces (1999, 104). In my account, what Canovan calls the worldly 'nationalism' of Western Europe's nation-states was the justified pride in 'political nationhood' that I discussed in the preceding section, which was ultimately perverted into sentimental nationalism.

of the spread of bourgeois values. In such an environment, ideological recourse to a common origin seemed to provide the only secure basis on which to justify a continuing political association. As Arendt (1968, 230) puts it, 'the interest of the nation as a whole was supposedly guaranteed in a common origin, which sentimentally expressed itself in nationalism', and nationalism 'became the precious cement for binding together a centralized state and an atomized society, and it actually proved to be the only working, live connection between the individuals of the nation-state' (1968, 231; 1994, 209).

Although not in itself necessarily racist or race-based, sentimental nationalism is readily transformed into a race-based ideology that equates a common national origin with pseudo-scientific conceptions of separate races, some of which are superior to others. Even where this is not clearly articulated, Arendt points out that the 'transformation of nations into races' occurs readily 'under the conditions of an accumulating society [in which there is] no other unifying bond available between individuals who in the very process of power accumulation and expansion are losing all natural connections with their fellow-men' (1968, 157). These were the conditions that eventually prevailed in the nation-states of Western Europe. Nevertheless, older national institutions continued to some degree to buffer 'the megalomania of imperialist aspirations' and to ensure some degree of fidelity to the rule of law (1968, 124).

The situation was even more serious in other parts of Europe, where nations did not grow out of territorially rooted populations but where nationalism was nevertheless fostered by the spirit of a century that simply took for granted that 'peoples' constituted 'nations' (Arendt 1968, 232). The disenfranchised populations of Austria-Hungary, Czarist Russia and the Balkans sought, Arendt says, to dignify their status through claims to nationhood, but they were territorially intermingled peoples 'for whom nationality had not yet developed beyond the inarticulateness of ethnic consciousness' (1968, 231). Lacking 'the Western national trinity of people-territory-state', they resorted to tribal nationalism and pride in membership of an inter-European folk community (1968, 232). In the case of Germany and Russia, which combined 'some kind of national home country … with a large, dispersed irredenta', Arendt describes the evolution of tribal nationalism into a new form of organisation: the 'pan-movements' (1968, 232). The pan-German and pan-Slav movements were based on tribalism, inflamed by race-thinking, and virulently anti-Semitic (see 1968, 238 and ff.). Within the movements, nationalist ideologies substituted for 'political nationhood' (1968, 166). While their spirit pre-dated imperialism, Arendt argues that the movements 'crystallised' in Central and Eastern Europe in response to the West's dramatic imperialist expansion in the 1880s (1968, 222). With little prospect of acquiring overseas colonial possessions of their own, the nascent and territorially intermingled nations of Central and Eastern Europe developed a continental imperialist mentality, which along with overseas imperialism exhibited a basic 'contempt for the narrowness of the nation-state' (1968, 223). In Arendt's account, tribal nationalism influenced both Nazism and Bolshevism, which she argues 'owe more to Pan-Germanism and Pan-Slavism (respectively) than to any other ideology or political movement' (1968, 222).

The Minority Treaties and the Refugees

The rise of nationalism was given new impetus after World War One when national self-determination was adopted as the key organisational principle for the redrawing of Europe's borders. For Arendt (1968, 275), recognition of a right to national self-determination represented nationalism's victory in Europe and implicit acknowledgment of 'the supremacy of the will of the nation over all legal and "abstract" institutions'. The victorious powers at the conclusion of World War One were seduced into supporting the right because it represented the status quo for Western Europe, and in their efforts to preserve a decaying system they sought to extend it (1968, 271). They were faced, however, with the problem of a 'power vacuum' left by the dissolution of the Austro-Hungarian, Czarist and Ottoman empires,[15] combined with the difficulty posed by the 'belt of mixed populations' (1968, 268) in Southern and Eastern Europe – namely a muddle of different national groupings that were territorially intermingled but that had all acquired aspirations to national self-determination.

The solution forged by the Peace Treaties was to create different classes of citizens within the newly demarcated succession states:

> The Treaties lumped together many people in single states, called some of them 'state people' and entrusted them with government, silently assumed that others (such as the Slovaks in Czechoslovakia, or the Croats and Slovenes in Yugoslavia) were equal partners in the government, which of course they were not, and with equal arbitrariness created out of the remnant a third group of nationalities called 'minorities'. (1968, 270)

The minorities were assumed to require additional protection for their cultural and social rights, and thus the newly created states were bound in accordance with the Minority Treaties to observe special regulations in respect of their minority populations, and the League of Nations was given the responsibility of ensuring these regulations were observed (1968, 272; and see Steiner and Alston 2000, 93–6). These precautions failed to satisfy the minorities, however, who 'considered the Treaties an arbitrary game which handed out rule to some and servitude to others' (Arendt 1968, 270). Nor did they satisfy the succession states themselves, because they were thereby denied genuine sovereign autonomy and equal standing in the community of nation-states (1968, 270–71). The result was widespread disloyalty

15 While Arendt does not mention the Ottoman empire, its break up also contributed to the problem.

among the minorities to the governments inflicted upon them and oppressive treatment of the minorities by those governments (1968, 272).

Although responsible for ensuring observance of the Minority Treaties, the League of Nations subsequently demonstrated its sympathy for the predicament of the new governments, and Arendt (1968, 272–3, 275) argues its representatives took for granted that the Treaties were really a staging post on the road to the 'assimilation or liquidation' of the minorities. While this proved hopelessly misguided given the sheer numbers of the minorities and 'the numerical and cultural weakness of the so-called state peoples', it points to what Arendt describes as the true significance of the Treaties (1968, 273). She argues that by creating an international body to act as security for the Treaties and their subjects, the peacekeepers created a 'law of exception' whose existence simply served to underline the reality that within the decaying system of European nation-states, 'only nationals could be citizens, only people of the same national origin could enjoy the full protection of legal institutions' (1968, 275).

It was tempting for observers at this time to treat the nationalist conflicts that divided the succession states of Eastern and Southern Europe as a localised problem that could have little influence on the political future of the older established democracies of Western Europe (Arendt 1968, 268). But the minorities in the succession states and the refugees of World War One and the political upheavals that followed it became 'two victim groups' that would have a profoundly destabilising influence on the whole of Europe (Arendt 1968, 268). The refugees were in an even worse predicament than the minority peoples, who at least '*de jure* ... belonged to some political body even though they needed additional protection' for some rights (Arendt 1968, 276). The refugees had lost along with the protection of their own polity the right to recognition and protection anywhere at all.

At the time the Minority Treaties were drafted, it was argued that the older European nations did not require similar provisions in respect of minorities because they had 'constitutions which implicitly or explicitly ... were founded upon the Rights of Man, [so] that even if there were other nationalities within their borders they needed no additional law for them' (Arendt 1968, 276). The conceit of this claim was unmasked by the arrival of the refugees, whose appearance in Western Europe exposed the damage already wrought by sentimental nationalism and the degree to which the modern state had been transformed 'from an instrument of the law into an instrument of the nation' (Arendt 1968, 275). As discussed in Chapter 1, the liberal democracies of Western Europe proved incapable of integrating the refugees or of arriving at an internationally recognised solution to their predicament. The result was that literally millions of people found themselves with nowhere to go and no one to turn to for protection.

The refugee problem revealed 'what had been hidden throughout the history of national sovereignty, that sovereignties of neighboring countries could come into deadly conflict not only in the extreme case of war but in peace' (Arendt 1968, 278). Although control over naturalisation and the power to expel people from the territory of the state were core principles of sovereignty in international law, the stability of the nation-state system had in fact depended on the old concept of a comity of nations. This had been realised, although only in partial fashion, through 'a spirit of unorganized solidarity' among states that prevented them from exercising their sovereign powers without regard for their fellow states (Arendt 1968, 278). Confronted by mass people movements, however, this solidarity crumbled.

Politics and the Myth of Human Rights

In *Origins*, Arendt argues that the eighteenth century's rights declarations, which signalled the coming of age of the modern nation-state, at the same time undercut its revolutionary potential by assuming that the sole aim and end of government is to secure the natural rights of man. Whereas previously the exercise of political power had been justified on the basis of divine right, or the customs and privileges of history, the declarations pronounce man and his 'newly discovered dignity' as the source of law (1968, 298). In doing so they have had what can be described as *anti-political* implications for Arendt. The subject of the declarations is an abstraction: 'man' (now 'the human') is a depoliticised figure within whom rights apparently arise quite naturally, even in the event he finds himself living in complete isolation. The folly of characterising man as the natural subject of rights was demonstrated by the appearance *en masse* after World War One of individuals whose ties with their political communities had been severed and who therefore appeared to embody the subject of the declarations. Rather than treating these people as the bearers of 'natural, unalienable, and sacred rights' (French Declaration 1789, preamble), as we saw in Chapter 1 even countries whose constitutions were based on rights-recognition treated them as the scum of the earth. In short, the 'world found nothing sacred in the abstract nakedness of being human' (Arend 1968, 299).

It is unlikely to do so, no matter what conception of 'human nature' we attribute to the individual subject of rights. Contrary to what I am calling the myth of human rights, rights do not arise automatically as a consequence of innate qualities shared by all human beings and 'subject to the same laws of growth as that of the individual' (Arendt 1968, 298). Nor, however, can they any longer be attached to 'the privileges which history ha[s] accorded certain strata of society' (Arendt 1968, 298) – this was the revolutionary import of the new nation-state. In this revolutionary incarnation, rights are attributed and upheld in the context of a political community within which individuals who are naturally differentiated by character, physical strength, intellect and other capacities nevertheless bind themselves to act in accordance with a law that constitutes each as equal. On the basis of this constitutive law[16] – which functions at both the metaphorical and the

16 The 'basic law' in Kant's terminology.

institutional level, each has equal standing to claim those rights recognised – if at all – either in the constitution or through the passage of constitutionally valid laws. As Arendt puts it: 'We are not born equal; we become equal as members of a group on the strength of our decision to guarantee ourselves mutually equal rights' (1968, 301). Equality is 'simply … a working principle of a political organization in which otherwise unequal people have equal rights' (1968, 54).

For Arendt, then, the equality that individuals may share 'in the eyes of God' or in the face of their common mortality is specifically apolitical (see 2007a, 725; 2007b, 949). It is a matter of individual recognition – through one's dialogue with self, or in the exercise of one's conscience – and as such, while it may motivate action in the sphere of politics, it cannot *of itself* (in the course of natural events, as it were) determine what occurs in this sphere. In the Greek polis, in which equality as a principle of political organisation was first realised, there was little danger of mistaking its political character because membership of the community of equals was confined to the select few (see 2007b, 949). While it is true that there were classical thinkers who posited a 'cosmic law … universal in every respect, applicable to all things and to every man' (2007a, 718), this conception of a transcendent and universal law was, Arendt argues in 'The Great Tradition', at odds with the 'pre-philosophical Greek political experience' (2007a, 716). In this experience, which I consider further in Chapters 3 and 4, law is an artefact and a mechanism for securing the boundaries of the public sphere. It both constitutes a shared public space and within that space allocates each individual equal space within which to act and to exercise power.

Thought of in this manner as the outcome of political engagement rather than the realisation of a natural or preordained distribution of power, equality requires more than the attribution of specific rights, it requires the protection of each person's status both as a political participant and a subject of rights. This protection is achieved through the mutual recognition of legal personality, which not only allows individuals equal recourse to the law but is also a precondition of action in a political sphere that is regulated and structured by the law. Here Arendt is also drawing on a Roman understanding of law as establishing relationships (see Breen 2012). Equality is achieved 'in the sense that everybody [is] equally entitled to his legal personality, to be protected by it and, at the same time, to act almost literally "through" it' (Arendt 2006, 98).

Wearing their legal personas like masks (although masks through which their own voices are heard (Arendt 2006, 97)), the citizens of a polity appear in the public realm as members in equal standing of that realm; they are co-legislators as well as equal subjects of its constitutive law. According to Arendt's argument, while citizens are distinct and unique individuals, differentiated by their natural capacities as well as by their distinctive modes of realising these, all are equalised by their legal personas and equally entitled to participate in the political sphere and to be considered authors of its constitutive law. To be deprived of one's legal personality, then, means to be reduced to one's 'natural', pre-political status (Arendt 2006, 98). It means being relegated to the private sphere of 'the merely given' in which human laws of equality exert no influence and the natural world's 'law of universal difference and differentiation' is supreme (Arendt 1986, 301).

It is only because one is recognised as an equal subject of law that one can claim – from a position of equality, or as a matter of 'right' – that one is entitled to the particular rights accorded under the law. Participation in the constitutive law of equality is the condition precedent for presumptive recognition as a rights holder – or as a claimant in respect of any of those rights spelled out in accordance with the law. Describing such rights as 'natural' and 'inalienable' is anti-political because it ignores the political achievement involved in the constitution of individuals as equals and the assertion of equality in accordance with law. If 'equality' and 'equal rights' are seen as natural, we are inclined to forget that their recognition depends on political commitment and is defended against a background of natural difference that constantly threatens the rule of equality (see Arendt 1968, 301–2).

Arendt's assertion that equality is the product of political commitment and is secured by a constitutive law whose subjects are presumed to be its authors points to problems concerning the authority and status of that law, and its application to individuals who are not considered parties to its foundation. A constitutive law of equality – which is also the law of 'the state' as Arendt analyses it in her account of the birth and death of the nation-state – cannot consistently also treat some people as unequal. To retain its fundamental character, the law must apply generally and impartially and must be open to all who come before it. Yet if the subjects of law are also its authors, such that the authority of law stems from its subjects' commitment to recognise each other as equals, then the political outsider who has no claim to participation in this commitment or contract of mutual recognition cannot be recognised as an equal. There are echoes here of the situation identified by Habermas (2001; 2001a) as the 'co-originality' of popular sovereignty and of rights. My discussion begins prior to a commitment under law to any particular 'rights', taking the principle of equal legal subjectivity as its starting point, but this is in fact also Habermas' starting point. As he says:

> Citizens participate in legislation only as *legal* subjects ... Hence the legal code as such must already be available before the communicative presuppositions of a discursive will formation [i.e., the basis for popular sovereignty] can be institutionalized in the form of civil rights. To establish this legal code, however, it is necessary to create the status of legal persons who as bearers of individual rights belong to a voluntary association of citizens and can, when necessary, effectively claim their rights. (2001, 117)

In Habermas' account, as in Arendt's, 'the status of legal persons as rights-bearers' is the product of mutual recognition, which can be thought of as a constitutive and on-going commitment to an association in which all participate as equal legal subjects (Habermas 2001, 125–6). Importantly, however, the constituted quality of the community's founding law (and its principle of equality) appears to presuppose an exclusivity at odds with the capacity of the law to deal consistently with those who are not parties to the constitution. This problem is at the core of the modern nation-state, which – as Arendt's account of its evolution demonstrates, is committed to impartial rights recognition and thus to the equality of those who come before its law, but is also founded on the consent of its members. It is no surprise then, that in the international system of nation-states the legal standing of individuals is derived from their national membership, as I discussed in Chapter 1, and it is only on the basis of this membership that citizens are characterised as participants in the contract that founds and legitimates the nation-state's law. The implications of this contractarian account of legal standing appear to be that people without a nationality are also people without a legal personality.

In *Origins*, Arendt analyses the problem this poses for our conception of the nation-state as committed to an egalitarian rule of law in terms of a conflict between notions of law as an expression of the good – as expressed most starkly in Hitler's claim that '[r]ight is what is good for the German people', and older understandings of civil law as grounded in a divinely mandated order – as Plato put it: 'Not man, but a god, must be the measure of all things' (1968, 299). Although the account of politics Arendt develops in her later work is antipathetic to transcendental understandings of law, she argues in *Origins* that 'once the absolute and transcendent measurements of religion or the law of nature have lost their authority' we inevitably adopt a conception of law according to which 'the right' is conflated with 'the good' (1968, 299).[17] Deprived of its universal foundations, law becomes simply a contingent expression of cultural value, while the morality that might be seen to ground the authority of law appears in the guise of 'a set of *mores*, of customs and manners, which [may] be exchanged for another set with no more trouble than it would take to change the table manners of a whole people' (Arendt 2003, 43). Regardless of whether we speak of the good in terms of 'the individual, or the family, or the people, or the largest number' (Arendt 1968, 299), the fact that it is not tethered to any external standard means that it can be used to exclude and thus to politically annihilate. This is a form of annihilation that may well be a precursor to physical annihilation, as it was in the case of the German Jews. Extrapolating from the motto, '[r]ight is what is good for the German people', Arendt argues that even were we to replace 'the people' with 'mankind', 'it is quite conceivable … that one fine day … humanity will conclude quite democratically – namely by majority decision – that for humanity as a whole it would be better to liquidate certain parts thereof' (1968, 299). In 'The Great Tradition', Arendt returns to this issue. Here she points out that, according to the presuppositions of natural law:

> The standards of right and wrong as they are laid down in positive law have, as it were, two aspects: they are absolute insofar as they owe their existence to a

17 Arendt's later work makes clear that this is an 'inevitability' only insofar as we remain embedded within the philosophical tradition in which natural law has historically occupied a central place.

> universally valid law, beyond the power and the competence of man; but they are also mere conventions, relative to one people and valid within limitations, insofar as they have been posited and framed by men. (2007a, 720–21)

Habermas (2001, 115) similarly discusses the problem of law's legitimacy in the context of modern pluralist societies in which recourse can no longer be had to 'a religiously or metaphysically grounded natural law'. Habermas' identification of the legitimacy problem for positive law is, however, motivated not by the position of outsiders or refugees who may be excluded from recognition under the law, but by the fact that positive law is always open to revision. Habermas says that natural law in the past provided a moral foundation or a 'check' by which amendments to positive law could be judged and contested (2001, 115). Without, however, being able to fall back on the 'collectively binding ethical system' (2001, 115) that the natural law represents, modern nation-states have been forced to provide an alternative basis for the legitimacy of law. In Habermas' account, political theorists of the nation-state have produced 'a twofold answer to the question of legitimacy: popular sovereignty and human rights' (2001, 115). As I have stated already, this 'twofold answer' clearly has significant and troubling implications for refugees who are unwelcome in the liberal democratic state.

The account of politics developed in Arendt's later work – and with it, her invocation of a conception of law that draws on elements of the Greek pre-philosophical understanding of law (*nomos*) as well as on the Roman idea of law (*lex*) – provides her response to the problem of the legitimacy of modern law. I introduce Arendt's account of politics in the next chapter, and discuss the understanding of law integral particularly to Greek polis life in Chapter 4.[18] In *Origins* we are simply left with the legitimacy problem. According to Arendt, the lacuna it represents was masked to begin with by the original focus of the rights declarations. The proclamation of the rights of man responded to the breakdown of older social and religious structures, many of which were oppressive, but that had also provided a degree of security for individuals. Human rights seemed to provide an alternative source of security, a basis on which government could be held to account and constrained in its treatment of its citizens (1968, 293). It was taken for granted that the sovereignty of the people as one national body played a central role in this regard, with government empowered to act on the basis of the trust invested in it by the people, who continued to hold it accountable. Thus it was assumed that, as Arendt (1968, 291) puts it, 'the "inalienable" rights of man would find their guarantee and become an inalienable part of the right of the people to sovereign self-government'.

The result of the connection drawn between sovereign self-government – conceived in terms of national self-determination – and the realisation of individual rights was, Arendt says, that 'Man', who had only just 'appeared as a completely

18 See Breen (2012) for an account that also emphasises the Roman influence on Arendt's thought.

emancipated, completely isolated being who carried his dignity within himself without reference to some larger encompassing order … disappeared again into a member of a people' (1968, 291). Thus 'the people' as one national body supplanted individual man, while humanity itself – the 'idea of mankind' that Arendt suggests could have founded a genuine comity of nations – was supplanted by the sovereignty of nation-states. It was not, however, until the appearance of the refugees after World War One that the significance of the conflation of the rights of man with the rights of peoples in an international order based on the principle of sovereignty would become apparent (Arendt 1968, 291). Suddenly rights that had been described as inalienable disappeared into thin air and it became clear that the person deprived of the protection of a national government was deprived of protection altogether, and everywhere in danger of persecution.

Chapter 3
The Perplexities of the Rights of Man[1]

Introduction

By proclaiming the rights of man as the foundation of government, the American and French revolutions marked a crucial turning point in history. The announcement of the rights of man demarcated the political realm as an egalitarian and inclusive sphere distinct from the social and religious spheres. Henceforth law's coercive authority would not be justified as an emanation of divine justice, administered by the monarch, nor function as an instrument of inherited power, in the hands of the political classes. Instead, the law would secure a newly created political space, inhabited by the members of the body politic and constituted by the rights held equally by each. The state, as the institutional embodiment of this constitutive or basic law, would from now on protect a political sphere based on justice and rights. This much was implicit in the wording of the French and American Declarations.[2] But as I discussed in Chapter 2, the Declarations had other implications as a result of the fact that they simultaneously justified state power and the role of government – responsible for administering the law of the state – by reference to the sovereignty of 'the people'. Furthermore, Arendt argues that the announcement of natural rights as the foundation of governing power undercut the political potential of the American and French Revolutions. In her argument, there are no such thing as 'natural and inalienable' rights, and describing the rights of citizens in these terms masks the fact that rights are dependent on mutual recognition within the context of political communities committed to the principle of equality. This commitment precedes the attribution of particular rights, constituting individuals as legal subjects and thus potential bearers of rights, but also as equal participants in the public realm. In Arendt's view, while the particular rights recognised in the Declarations (and subsequently in the American Bill of Rights) may protect individual citizens from the overweening power of government, they are not of themselves a realisation of political freedom and nor do they consistently serve the interests of freedom.

In the following discussion I return to the account begun at the end of Chapter 2 of the nation's foundational role in the eighteenth century's rights declarations. I then consider the role played by the 'rights of man' – actually the rights of citizens – in

---

1 Arendt's title to Part II of Chapter 9 of *Origins*. In the German version of the book the title is 'Die Aporien der Menschenrechte', or 'The Aporias of the Rights of Man' (Menke 2007, 756 fn. 3).

2 See Chapter 1, 24.

the context of Arendt's distinctive understanding of politics and the public realm. This role is anti-political insofar as liberal accounts of political legitimacy assume that the primary purpose of government is to secure individual rights. Thought of in Arendtian republican terms as constraints on government power that protect the activities of individuals in the private sphere but are based on the same law of equality that demarcates a public realm within which politics takes place, recourse to the language of rights becomes increasingly anti-political when rights are conceived only as facilitating the autonomy of self-interested property owners and as government's sole concern. Against this liberal understanding of rights, and the inducement to sentimental nationalism that it represents, Arendt's invocation of a public sphere of action provides an appropriately political basis on which to establish solidarity among rights bearing citizens. The revitalisation of a public sphere of action requires recognition that the realisation of individual rights – although 'a condition of freedom' (Cohen 1996, 174), does not constitute freedom itself. Freedom is a political value that can only be realised in concert with others, and it provides a form of civic solidarity capable of both internal and external inclusivity. A flourishing public sphere and the realisation of freedom would allow the nation-state – in all the guises in which this political form now appears – to be conceived as a member of an international comity, with its interests qualified accordingly. This is a discussion to which I will return in my concluding chapter.

In my conclusion to the current chapter, I specifically relate these considerations to the position of refugees in the liberal democratic state. I pick up the themes I introduced in Chapter 2's critique of the claim that all individuals are born with rights to argue that those who are forced to fall back on their natural or human rights have been deprived of standing as subjects of law and thus – according to the modern nation-state's constitutive law – as equals. Their appeal to human rights reflects their loss of the grounds on which they may claim rights as a member of some state, and as such – their loss of the 'right to have rights'.

Sovereignty and the Nation

Instead of focusing on the political achievement of its rights-based constitution, France in the years before World War Two succumbed to the myth that rights are natural. Furthermore, it took for granted the role of the nation as the ultimate guarantor of these natural rights. As I discussed in Chapter 2, Arendt argues that the revolutionary politics on which the original nation-states were based was fatally undermined by nationalism and by connecting rights recognition to membership of the nation. And in fact, the sovereign role of the nation was enshrined in the French Declaration. Just as 'Man appeared as the only sovereign in matters of law', 'the people was proclaimed the only sovereign in matters of government' (Arendt 1968, 291). Arendt does not specify the manner in which the Declaration connects rights recognition to national belonging or membership of the people, but an analysis of its content vindicates her account. Article 3 states explicitly that '[t]he principle of all sovereignty resides essentially in the nation. No body nor individual may exercise any authority which does not proceed directly from the nation'; while Article 6 declares the impartiality of the law at the same time as it specifies the principle of equality before the law only by reference to citizens, describing law as 'the expression of the general will':

> Law is the expression of the general will. Every citizen has a right to participate personally, or through his representative, in its foundation. It must be the same for all, whether it protects or punishes. All citizens, being equal in the eyes of the law, are equally eligible to all dignities and to all public positions and occupations ...

The French Revolution's recourse to a concept of the nation as a sovereign unity – an expression of 'the general will' in Rousseau's sense, in which that will is undivided and speaks for the nation as 'one person' (Arendt 2006, 147; and see Habermas 2008, 315–16), can be historically explained, Arendt thinks, by the French history of sovereign absolutism. In effect, the Revolution put the sovereignty of the nation into the place vacated by the sovereign king, placing the nation above the law as the king had been above the law (146–7; and see Breen 2012, 19; Slaughter 2007, 69). The American Revolution, on the other hand, drew on the British tradition of limited monarchy and 'took its cue from the English constitution' (Arendt 2006, 147), thus it treated the separation of powers as an essential ingredient of its new constitution. This has certainly been very significant in American political history. Nevertheless – although Arendt fails in *On Revolution* to notice it – the American Declaration also posits 'the people' as a collective that pre-dates the constitution of the body politic.[3] It proclaims the right of 'one people' to 'dissolve the political bands which have connected them with another' and not only to institute a new government for their protection, but in doing so, 'to assume among the powers of the earth, the separate and equal station to which the laws of nature and of nature's God entitle them' (preamble). The body of the Declaration states that 'whenever any form of government becomes destructive of [the ends for which it was instituted], it is the right of the people to alter or to abolish it, and to institute new government', and it claims that the King of Britain has proved himself 'unfit to be the ruler of a free people'. It asserts the sovereign rights of each of its signatory states as 'free and independent states' both in the name of a collectivity, 'a free people', and in the name of the constituents of each of the states: 'in the name and by the authority of the good people of these colonies'. Slaughter (2007, 68) interprets this aspect of the American Declaration similarly, noting that 'the Representatives' of the USA named in the preamble

3 Arendt was nevertheless well aware of the problems involved in the foundation of any new body politic. In *Origins* she points out that historically, 'whatever political organization men may have achieved has its origins in crime' (1968, 10).

are 'already acting in the name of the "good people" whose incorporation [they] are about to declare'. Furthermore, over the course of its history, liberalism and market relations have defined the American polity, as have deep racial and social inequalities. The result has been social and political atomisation and cross-community fractures; and at the same time, resort to myths of organic nationhood and national unity. Thus while political culture in America has been relatively stable, restrained by federalism and constitutionalism, a strident nationalism has supported a belligerent attitude in global affairs and operated internally to dictate who counts as a 'genuine' member of the American nation.

As I discussed in Chapter 2, Arendt believed that sentimental nationalism was originally a Western European response to the atomisation of societies that embraced the values of liberal individualism and were at the same time divided by class interests. In such conditions, nationalism seemed to offer the only means of uniting the members of the polity and eliciting their loyalty to the state. While constitutional traditions recognising individual rights and providing checks on the power of the state served in the older nation-states to restrain the most virulent forms of nationalism and its personification of 'the people', there was a tendency in all to bow before the alter of the nation. Thus pseudo-mystical nationalism conquered political nationhood; the state was conquered by a sentimentalised version of the nation and was then personified in the same manner as it. Just as 'the sovereignty of the nation' was assumed to replicate the 'sovereignty of the individual', 'the sovereignty of the state as national state' became the representative of both and 'the supreme individual before which all other individuals had to bow' (Arendt 1994, 209). In 'The Nation', Arendt argues that the personification of the state, and the tendency to treat it as an 'autonomous individual', reflects in the sphere of practical politics a kind of Hegelian 'individualisation of the moral universal within a collective', although without any connection to Hegel's particular brand of idealism (1994, 209). As a result, 'right' can be conceived as an emanation of the undivided 'will of the people' ('right is what is good for the German people') rather than a standard of justice according legal personality equally to all individuals and a means by which the will of the majority can be constrained: '[w]hile the state as a legal institution has declared that it must protect the rights of men, its identification with the nation implied the identification of the citizen as national and thereby resulted in the confusion of the rights of men with the rights of nationals or national rights' (Arendt 1994, 208). This conceptualisation of the state as a sovereign national state continues to be tremendously influential.

We have seen that the rights declarations pronounced rights as the new provenance of politics, and also that they assumed these rights would be secured by the twinned sovereignty of the state and the nation. At the same time, as a result of the pronouncement of 'Man' as both the source and subject of rights, law was deprived of any claim to justification on the basis that it is an expression of divine or natural authority. So although the declarations expanded the political sphere, rejecting inherited sources of authority, they also restricted it by linking it to the nation. The nation's unifying role, and its legitimacy as the ultimate source of rights, was to a significant degree simply taken for granted. Occasionally, however, rights were successfully invoked by insiders against the power of the state – and by implication, the nation that the state was increasingly assumed to represent. When people who were not members of the nation appeared without invitation within the nation-state's borders, however, it proved incapable of treating them as the subjects of rights.

Political Freedom and the Rights of Citizens

The modern nation-state's failure to treat the inter-war refugees as subjects of rights related to the fact that rights that had hitherto been described as 'natural' or 'human' were in fact the rights of citizens. Rights recognition flows from a state's constitutive law of equality, and the enforcement of rights depends on a state's legal apparatus. But while rights are 'political' in the sense that we are not born with them and we cannot rely on their recognition outside the context of a political community that has agreed to secure just these rights, Arendt argues that they do not of themselves represent or ensure political freedom. In fact, their articulation may actually undermine political freedom – in part because they are pronounced as 'natural', but also because they are characterised as protecting the liberty of individuals to act in their own interests and it is then assumed that the realisation of rights constitutes the political association's primary aim and end. Where this occurs, a rights-based account of political legitimacy is an inducement to sentimental nationalism. Membership of a mythically united nation promises a form of solidarity otherwise very difficult to achieve in a society of autonomous rights holders whose political commitment is based on their desire to pursue their own interests, including their potentially conflicting conceptions of the good life.[4] My discussion to this point has emphasised the threat to the modern state's constitutive law of equality posed by nationalism. Arendt's account of political nationhood provides an alternative basis on which the solidarity of members of rights-based states might be forged – a basis that avoids the dangers for refugees, as well as for internal minorities, of nationalism. The forging of *political* nations requires recognition, however, that the end of government and *raison d'être* of political community extends beyond the securing of individual rights.

---

4 A liberal rights-based account of political legitimacy can be interpreted in numerous ways. One possibility is to assume the model that posits autonomous rights holders as the subjects of law is an accurate representation of individual subjectivity in liberal society. A slightly different interpretation assumes that the model misconstrues individual subjectivity, but nevertheless entrenches individualism and atomisation through its basic presuppositions. Either of these interpretations raises the anti-political implications that are my focus in this section. The distinction between these interpretations was suggested to me by Walzer's (1990) essay on the communitarian critique of liberalism.

When Arendt speaks about politics and its practise, she has a particularly demanding conception in mind. For a start, she derides the suggestion that political societies represent a collective response to the meeting of humans' physical needs, and she describes as 'politically pernicious' the idea that 'life is the highest good' (2006, 54). Arendt attributes the strengthening of this doctrine in modernity to Marx. In *The Human Condition*, however, she comments that materialism more broadly 'is not Marxian and not even modern in origin, but as old as our history of political theory', indeed, 'at least as old as the Platonic-Aristotelean assumption that political communities ... and not only family life or the coexistence of several households ... owe their existence to material necessity' (1998, 183 and 183 fn. 8). While it is true, Arendt says, that all human activities bear some relation to politics (1998, 7), in her view activities directed towards 'mastering the necessities of life' are pre-political and belong to the private rather than the public sphere (30–31; and see 2006, 99). Even given the likelihood that material necessity historically played a role in the founding of political societies, Arendt claims that such necessity has no bearing on how a genuinely engaged polity – such as arose in the pre-philosophical Greek city-states – perceives itself (1998, 197–8). She is equally dismissive of the Lockean claim – which is my focus in Chapter 5 – that the role of political communities lies in guaranteeing the physical security of their members and in securing equal spheres within which each may act without constraint (1998, 31).

In a genuinely engaged polity, action undertaken in the public sphere has a particular significance that is illuminated for Arendt by the fact that both Greek and Latin had two different but interrelated words designating the verb 'to act'. One word in each case implied beginning or setting in motion, and the other achieving or finishing. The classical understanding of action thus appeared to divide it 'into two parts, the beginning made by a single person and the achievement in which many join by "bearing" and "finishing" the enterprise, by seeing it through' (1998, 189; and see 2003, 46–7; 2007b, 947). Arendt's understanding of political activity – which in *The Human Condition* she defines as the sphere of 'action' as distinguished from the spheres of 'labour' and 'work'[5] – draws on these ancient roots.[6] It is not because material necessity plays no part in it that action is an

5 Labour is defined as the activity relating to the natural functioning of the human body – it produces those 'vital necessities' which sustain 'life itself' (1998, 7) and it 'assures not only individual survival, but the life of the species' (1998, 8). Work is the activity which separates humans from the natural world by constituting a created world, 'an "artificial" world of things, distinctly different from all natural surroundings' (1998, 7). Through the production of human artefacts, work 'bestow[s] a measure of permanence and durability upon the futility of mortal life' (1998, 8).

6 The Greek polity that Arendt invokes here pre-dates the polis of the philosophers. It is the city-state of Herodotus and Homer, rather than Plato and Aristotle, although some aspects of the former certainly survived in the latter (see 2007b, 943). Arendt's account of ancient Greek political life is not a call for the contemporary realisation of that life, even if

exercise of freedom – this freedom from material necessity is a precondition of action but has nothing to do with its content (see 2007b, 944–5). Rather, action is an exercise of freedom because it involves a new beginning (1998, 9). As such, action – which may include discussion or even thought,[7] is not predetermined, whether by history, nature, ideology or even the laws of logic. Thus there is always the possibility that it will take as its starting point a position that is entirely novel, or set in motion the unprecedented.

The outcomes of action are unpredictable because what is initiated by one person in the public realm is taken up by others and enters into a web of 'innumerable, conflicting wills and intentions' (1998, 184; and see 2007b, 947). Nevertheless, Arendtian politics paradigmatically involves individuals acting together in pursuit of a common concern (1968, 474): it is a constructive engagement as opposed, for example, to the common idea of politics as a constant mediation between conflicting interests, and its 'specific productivity' arises from its 'tremendous capacity for establishing relationships' (1998, 191). Arendt highlights the importance of the cooperative dimension of all political action by pointing out that history 'is full of examples of the impotence of the strong and superior man who does not know how to enlist the help, the co-acting of his fellow men' (1998, 188–9). In *On Revolution* she also quotes Mirabeau's claim that 'ten men acting together can make a hundred thousand tremble apart' (2006, 238).

This does not mean, however, that the political sphere is based on a common identity or on interest convergence or unanimity of opinion. Arendt refers, for example, to 'the decisive incompatibility between the rule of a unanimously held "public opinion" and freedom of opinion' (2006, 217). She also argues that in the Greek city-states, living as one of the small class of 'equals' had nothing to do with conformism – instead, the polis 'was permeated by a fiercely agonal spirit' (1998, 41).[8] Politics, for Arendt, 'corresponds to the human condition of plurality, to the fact that men, not Man, live on the earth and inhabit the world … this plurality is specifically the condition … of all political life' (1998, 7). As such, diverse perspectives are not cause for embarrassment but rather a source of tremendous vitality and creativity. The fact that individuals are unique explains the profundity of politics and allows the production of a lived world to which all

such a thing were possible, and she in fact discusses a range of different political forms in the context of discussing polis life, celebrating but also critiquing aspects of each.

7 'Thinking [when it is political] does not lose contact with the world of my fellow-men because they are represented in the self with whom I lead the dialogue of thought' (1986, 476). See also Arendt's discussion of Jaspers' peculiarly political mode of thinking (1995, 79), as well as her distinction between 'thinking', which is active and oriented toward the world, and the essentially wordless and a-political faculty of 'contemplation' (1998, 16 and 20).

8 See also the contrast she draws in *On Revolution* between the Jacobins' attempt to secure 'a unified public opinion, a "general will"' and what she calls 'the public spirit, [and] the diversity inherent in freedom of thought and speech' (2006, 237).

political actors contribute by providing their distinctive points of view. In Arendt's argument, even our experience of sensory data is made meaningful through our interaction with others and our openness to their perceptions. Without being able to refer to a 'common' sense – that is, to shared interpretations and perceptions – we would have to fall back on our 'own particularity of sense data', data which in itself is always 'unreliable and treacherous' (1968, 475–6). 'Only because we have common sense, that is only because not one man, but men in the plural inhabit the earth can we trust our immediate sensual experience' (1968, 476).

In the political realm, we also make sense of our experience by sharing it with others. This would be unnecessary if not for the fact of human difference. 'Action would be an unnecessary luxury, a capricious interference with general laws of behaviour, if men were endlessly reproducible repetitions of the same model, whose nature or essence was the same for all and as predictable as the nature or essence of any other thing' (1998, 8). Politics thus involves individuals appearing before each other in public and giving an account of themselves – and their vision of and for the world – through speech and action. In doing so, they shape and take responsibility for the world they share in common. By comparison to the earth or the natural environment, this world is the product of artifice, constituted both by the artefacts that humans produce and by human interactions. Living political communities, like the physical world created by work, allow individual mortality to be transcended – in this case not through a built environment that survives its creators, but through the legal constitution of an enduring public space within which each individual has the freedom to act. Without plurality we would be deprived of this common world of action, which for Arendt means to be made worldless; to retreat from a shared and publicly interpreted reality into a private and shadowy unworldliness.

The creation of a shared public world would, however, be impossible if human plurality was characterised only by natural difference. The ability to act politically presupposes equality as well as difference. Plurality – 'the *conditio per quam* … of all political life' (Arendt 1998, 7) – is defined not only by interaction between humans who are distinct from each other, but also by the fact that it arises among people who recognise each other as equals – that is, as holding equal shares of power in the public sphere. In this sphere, equality involves neither ruling nor being ruled – a relationship involving ruling is excluded altogether (2006, 20; and see 1998, 32, 33; 2007b, 943). It is only among equals that we can exercise our specifically political freedom, and among whom our actions are accorded weight by being seen, judged and remembered (2006, 21–2). If we do not act among our equals, our actions lose all significance insofar as a public, shared world is concerned: they make no contribution to the constitution of that world. According to Arendt (2006, 20; 1998, 32), the freedom of citizens in the Greek polis was based on equality in just this sense.

Clearly, Arendt's interpretation of the ancient Greek understanding of equality bears little resemblance to modern accounts of equality. The Greek polis understood equality as a political achievement and 'the very essence of freedom' (1998, 33), and it depended on restricting access to the political sphere and extreme inequality in the private sphere. This inequality, and in particular, the relationship between master and slave, allowed the citizens of the polis to cater to their material needs and thus to put necessity to one side when they were engaged in polis life (see 2007b, 944–5). Modern accounts of equality, on the other hand, take the claim that men are 'born equal' as their starting point.[9] While she is no defender of social or economic inequality, Arendt urges a return to a concept of equality that sees it in political terms as an essential precondition for the exercise of 'that freedom of action which is specifically human' (1968, 301); in other words, that enables individuals to act in and contribute to the creation of a shared world. Power in the public realm must, Arendt thinks, be equally shared, and the legitimacy of the institutions that structure and establish this realm depends on equality in this sense. This account of equality differs fundamentally from the liberal rights-based account of political legitimacy, according to which natural equality grounds a right held by individuals with potentially conflicting interests to equal spheres of freedom from interference. It is now 'almost axiomatic', Arendt says, to understand political freedom as 'the more or less free range of non-political activities which a given body politic will permit and guarantee to those who constitute it' (2006, 20). While Arendtian political equality invokes the freedom to engage constructively in community with others, political equality within liberalism is premised on securing the individual's freedom to act in isolation or without particular regard for one's fellow humans. The liberal conception is reflected in the French Declaration's claim that '[l]iberty consists in the freedom to do everything which injures no one else; hence the exercise of the natural rights of each man has no limits except those which assure to the other members of society the enjoyment of the same rights' (Art. 4).[10] This liberal brand of freedom – which Arendt calls 'liberty' – nevertheless represents an important recognition of individual autonomy. It is just that in Arendt's view, liberty 'can only be negative' – it is 'the condition of freedom' but 'by no means leads automatically to it' (2006, 19; see also Cohen 1996, 164).

While Arendt seeks to revive a version of the ancient Greek understanding of political equality, she does not sanction the levels of social disadvantage that co-existed alongside it. Instead, she thinks that we must secure political equality at the same time as we pursue social or distributive justice. Although for Arendt the achievement of social justice is – like the liberal recognition of individual

9 Arendt also argues that modern liberal capitalist societies 'equalise' 'under all circumstances', reflecting the fact, which I discuss below, 'that society has conquered the public realm, and that distinction and difference have become private matters of the individual. This modern equality, based on the conformism inherent in society and possible only because behaviour [conformable to "natural [biological] laws"] has replaced action as the foremost mode of human relationship, is in every respect different from equality in antiquity, and notably in the Greek city-states' (1998, 41).

10 See also Arendt's reference to Locke, who she justifiably describes as treating politics as a means to protect a society of property-owners (1998, 31).

liberty – pre-political, it is not for that reason insignificant. Social equality or 'equality of condition', is important in and of itself; it is a 'basic requirement of justice' (1968, 54). It is also important because a degree of social equality is a fundamental precondition for the establishment of an inclusive political sphere in which freedom is realised (and can only be realised) among political subjects who are equals. If individuals are preoccupied with attending to the necessities of life, they will have neither the inclination nor the ability to participate in the political sphere. Such participation requires both a basic level of personal autonomy and of material wellbeing. It is inevitable, Arendt thinks, that 'liberation from necessity, because of its urgency, will always take precedence over the building of freedom' (2006, 102).[11] But while freedom from want is a 'prerequisite' of freedom in the public realm, it is a prerequisite 'which, unfortunately, no political action can deliver' (2006, 234). Here Arendt seems to take her account of what constitutes 'political action' too far. As Christodoulidis and Schaap (2012, 111) suggest, her claim that political action must not aim for and can never deliver social equality has the effect of 'privatis[ing] social suffering'. Arendt's attempt to keep issues of material and economic distribution out of the political realm makes sense, however, in light of her reading of the failures of the French Revolution.

When, in Chapter 2, I discussed Arendt's account of the decline of the Western European nation-state, I mentioned her claim that the French Revolution's failure to secure basic social and economic equality allowed French society to fracture along class lines. In Arendt's view, there was a 'fundamental contradiction' between the concept of political equality initially championed by the Revolution and the social and economic inequality of the class system (1968, 12). But Arendt also claims that we must distinguish between these forms of equality and the realms within which their achievement should be sought. She thinks that the French revolutionaries committed a fatal mistake by abandoning the pursuit of political equality – as it was fleetingly experienced through the spontaneous uprising and involvement of the people in revolutionary action and popular councils;[12] focusing instead on social and economic conditions.[13] When this occurred, the leaders of the Revolution, who were economically and socially well-off, began to act out of

11 See also 1998, 30–31: 'it was a matter of course that the mastering of the necessities of life in the household was the condition for freedom of the *polis* [in Greek city-states]'.

12 Societies that 'spread all over France during the Revolution' (2006, 236), and in which 'an enormous appetite for debate, for instruction, for mutual enlightenment and exchange of opinion ... developed' (2006, 238). After the political aims of the Revolution were abandoned, the societies were infiltrated by Jacobin clubs and successfully transformed from non-violent popular initiatives into instruments of terror (2006, 239–40).

13 The 'deep concern with forms of government' that characterised the American Revolution was 'also very important in the initial stages of the French Revolution' (2006, 46), which began 'with the strictly political rebellion of the Third Estate' (2006, 98). When the French leaders of the revolution abandoned their concern with forms of government, 'they lost, together with the institutions and constitutions which are "the soul of the Republic" ... the revolution itself' (2006, 46). They could, however, hardly have done

what they described as 'compassion' for the lower classes, rather than in solidarity with them as equals (2006, 64–6). They 'had no conception of the [legal] persona, and no respect for the legal personality which is given and guaranteed by the body politic' (2006, 98). As a result, they 'were no longer concerned with the emancipation of citizens' (2006, 98), who must relate to each other as equals in the public realm, but believed instead that 'they had emancipated nature herself, as it were, liberated the natural man in all men, and given him the Rights of Man to which each was entitled, not by virtue of the body politic to which he belonged but by virtue of being born' (2006, 98). Natural man may be an object of compassion, but he is not a subject of politics – and mankind's failures in the sphere of compassion are notorious. Not only did the 'compassion' of the Jacobin government and its followers fail to achieve lasting social change, but it mutated remarkably quickly into rage and fear (2006, 100). Its role as the guiding ethos of the revolution spelled the sacrifice of political equality.

By comparison, the American Revolution achieved more success in establishing a public sphere based on political equality because there was a greater degree of material equality among the American revolutionaries than was ever the case in France. The American revolutionary leaders were not significantly economically or socially distanced from their fellow revolutionaries, and were also, politically speaking, 'among the oppressed', thus 'they felt they belonged to the people, and did not need to summon up any solidarity with them. If they became their spokesmen ... they spoke and acted as their representatives in a common cause' (2006, 64).

In *On Revolution*, Arendt argues that America's early bills of rights[14] were intended only as a form of restraint upon the power of government, 'and hence presupposed the existence of a body politic and the functioning of political power' (2006, 99). In Arendt's analysis, the American revolutionaries considered the bills simply the mechanism by which government would be constrained to recognise its citizens' rights. The French Revolution, on the other hand, ended in (and was usurped by) the characterisation of natural rights as the very 'foundation-stone of the body politic' (2006, 99). Because social and economic inequality did not play the role in the American Revolution that it played in the French, Arendt thinks that the American revolutionaries were able to focus more consistently on the creation and constitution of government – that is, on political questions:

> the main question for them certainly was not how to limit power but how to establish it, not how to limit government but how to found a new one ... the establishment of new power could not be based upon what had always been essentially a negative on power, that is, the bill of rights. (2006, 139)

---

otherwise, given 'the fight for public freedom' faced 'the overwhelming odds of private misery' (2006, 237).

14 Bills that were adopted by the pre-federated States and that influenced the drafting of the US Bill of Rights.

When their thoughts turned to the articulation of rights, Arendt argues they were quite clear that these were rights to be claimed by citizens against the power of their own government. Since the assertion of independence from Britain meant that rights could no longer be characterised as the rights or liberties 'of Englishmen', they were 'declared solemnly to be rights of all men' (2006, 139). Yet all this declaration was intended to imply was the virtues for all men of constitutionally limited government:

> The American version actually proclaims no more than the necessity of civilized government for all mankind; the French version, however, proclaims the existence of rights independent of and outside the body politic, and then goes on to equate these so-called rights, namely the rights of man qua man, with the rights of citizens. (2006, 140)

Ultimately, however, although the American revolutionaries may have been quite clear about the status of the rights they were declaring, those rights were still pronounced, as Arendt recognises in *Origins*, as every man's natural birth right, and as the only legitimate foundation and end of government (1968, 293).[15] And while the revolutionaries' constructive concern with forms of government led them to adopt a federal system based on the separation of powers, they did not take the further step of institutionalising the means by which citizens could continue to be actively engaged in government – through the establishment, for example, of local town councils to operate on a model of town hall meetings. Thus the American Bill of Rights would, like the French Declaration, eventually be interpreted not merely as securing individuals' autonomy rights, but in doing so, as enshrining the *raison d'être* of government.

The Declarations' failure to distinguish between political and non-political concerns, and to recognise the significance of the political, represented and foreshadowed what Arendt sees as a fatal blurring of the distinction between public and private realms. In *The Human Condition*, she argues that public life has succumbed to the realm of the social, which emerged in modernity and 'found its political form in the nation-state' (1998, 28). The social realm grew out of the modern tendency to conflate political power with economic power, and it is premised on a collective life 'devoted to production and consumption … [in which] economic concerns … dominate both politics and human self-consciousness' (Canovan 1998, xii). Arendt argues that the rise of the social realm has produced a situation in which we now perceive 'political communities in the image of a

15 See also her earlier essay, in which Arendt says the rights of man were 'solemnly proclaimed' by both the French and American revolutions 'as the new foundation stone of all civilized societies' (1949, 24). As noted in Chapter 1, the American Declaration states that men 'are endowed by their creator with certain unalienable rights' and that 'to secure these rights, governments are instituted among men'.

family whose everyday affairs have to be taken care of by a gigantic, nation-wide administration of housekeeping' (1998, 28).

For Arendt (2006, 136), the foundation of a government based on political freedom and equality can only proceed from a collective act by which the members of the polity empower themselves and establish the means by which they will continue to exercise power. While, as we saw in Chapter 2, this can occur through a process of constitution making or as the product of the 'progressive history' of a nation, it will be undercut by the failure to distinguish clearly between the private and the political spheres, and to recognise the political significance of freedom and equality. This failure is perpetuated in the rights declarations' claim that 'natural' rights are both the foundation and the end of government. Nevertheless, Arendt is wrong to think that a concern with material inequality must be strictly quarantined within the 'private' sphere. Like the more traditional liberty rights, economic rights are 'pre-political' in the sense that they secure the autonomy of individuals but do not guarantee the functioning of a public political sphere. The quest for such rights, however, and the determination to hold governments accountable in respect of a commitment to recognise and secure them, itself represents a form of political activity insofar as it is premised on constituting rights rather than on merely securing 'natural' rights.

Furthermore, while the blurring of private and public spheres in the modern realm of the social makes it difficult to appropriately characterise and value rights that play a constructive though pre-political role in relation to the constitution of a public and political sphere, this does not mean that such rights are insignificant – as Arendt herself makes clear. The recognition of certain key rights contributes to the maintenance of a sphere within which political freedom can be exercised. Such rights include rights to a basic level of distributive justice,[16] and rights to freedom of speech and association, all of which can facilitate the exercise of political freedom. As Canovan (1992, 212 fn. 38) points out, Arendt was quite willing to 'insist on the importance of [civil rights] when faced with left-wing dismissals of "bourgeois freedom"'. This is a point also made by Cohen (1996, 174), who says that 'liberation and the negative civil liberties that institutionalise and protect the non-political (private) sphere of action' are, for Arendt, 'a condition of freedom' although they are distinct from it and do not necessarily lead to it. Cohen thus describes Arendt as 'a republican thinker who understood the importance of rights in the liberal sense' (1996, 164). She points out that Arendt 'argued strongly for the constitutional articulation of rights to property, privacy, and personal autonomy, even though her main focus was on the problem of how to establish and protect public spaces for the exercise of political freedom

16 Arendt (in Young-Bruehl 2004, 210) believed American constitutionalism guaranteed 'that minimum of social justice without which citizenship is impossible'. While her faith in the American system's ability to deliver social justice was unjustified, the point here relates to her characterisation of social justice as a necessary precondition for engagement in the constructive sphere of politics.

and action' (1996, 164). Not only do rights allow individuals to pursue their own projects, representing a 'legal bulwark for the private realm against public power' (Arendt 2006, 244), but they may also make it easier for individuals to join together and to act politically. Arendt argued, for example, that the First Amendment's protection of freedom of association was an important aid to the protest movement against the Vietnam war, without which there would have been nothing standing between the protestors 'and tyranny' (in Young-Bruehl 2004, 427). Rather than relying solely on grassroots mobilisation and hoping for 'the good will of the government' in response to such mobilisation, she said 'I would much rather have a legal leg to stand on' (in Young-Bruehl 2004, 427).[17]

Human Rights are the Rights of Those Who are Not Equal in the Eyes of the Law

The refugees currently going crazy with fear, boredom and uncertainty in the immigration detention centres of the liberal democratic world, whose predicament I describe in Part III, do not have 'a legal leg to stand on'. Instead, they are forced to fall back on their human rights, and in ironic recognition of what this entails some have noted that is better to be a pet in the Western world than to be merely human. As I demonstrate in Chapter 7, refugees are denied legal standing at the same time as they are subject to the full force of the state's coercive power. Their appeal to human rights, if they make such an appeal, reflects this fact and is at the root of their predicament. They are objects of the law but not its subjects, and they are neither free nor equal.

For Arendt, an appeal to human rights is an appeal to 'the paradoxical rights of the private, poor, unpoliticised individual' (Rancière 2004, 298). While such an appeal may have moral or humanitarian force, it is not made in the public sphere by a person who is a subject of law or politics, thus it is not a claim made on the basis of justice or right. Human rights are proper to what Lefort (1986, 243) describes as 'the sanctuary of morality, a sanctuary that each individual carries within himself'. In Part II, I elaborate upon the significance of the distinction I am drawing between the realm of justice or right and the realm of morality, arguing that political equality, and thus public recognition and action, is possible only in the former. At the end of the previous chapter, I discussed Arendt's identification of a conflict between notions of law as an expression of 'the good' and older understandings of law as grounded in a divinely mandated law of nature. If, in modern pluralist societies, it is no longer possible to have explicit recourse to the idea of a natural moral law that founds and legitimates the law of the state, this would seem to

17 In *On Revolution*, Arendt describes the right to assemble as now 'the most important positive political freedom', but because it does not directly allow citizens to engage in the process of government, it remains 'essentially negative; … the result … of liberation but … by no means the actual content of freedom' (2006, 22).

imply that law is answerable only to its authors, who are the citizens of the modern state. On the contrary, however, the achievement of the modern nation-state has been – like the less inclusive but, in Arendt's terms, more politically successful achievement of ancient polis life, to forge a political community grounded in a law of constituted equality. Although this law is based on mutual recognition and disavows transcendental reference points, its consistency and integrity depends on its capacity to constitute everyone whom it coerces as an equal. This means that all who are subject to the coercive power of the state must be entitled to recognition under its constitutive law – including those whom its current subjects would prefer to exclude. The difficulty of reconciling popular sovereignty and open and equal access to the law is something that I take up in Chapters 8 and 9, at which point it should be clear *why* the consistency and integrity of the law must be preserved.

In Part II, I locate the tension between the egalitarian, open law of the state and the closed law of the nation within the theoretical foundations of liberalism, and elucidate it with reference to much older traditions and understandings of law. I want to conclude Part I, however, by returning to the significance of the fact that the person who holds nothing more than the 'rights of man' is reliant on rights supposed to spring automatically from human nature. Arendt (1968, 441) reminds us that human nature has proved an unreliable source and inconsistent respecter of rights. In the face of the Nazi concentration camps and their 'mass production of corpses' (1968, 441), she says, 'we are perhaps better qualified to judge exactly what this human "nature" amounts to; in any event it has shown us potentialities that were neither recognized nor even suspected by Western philosophy and religion, which for more than three thousand years have defined and redefined this "nature"' (1968, 298). Rather than positing humans as the natural subjects of rights, then, we need to focus on the political conditions that make the attribution of rights possible, and to recognise rights as dependent on a political commitment to a constitutive law of equality.

PART II

Chapter 4

Natural Law and the False Promise of a Universal Community of Equals

Introduction

In Part I, I discussed the anomalous position of Europe's inter-war refugees. The refugees were treated with impunity in the constitutional democracies of Western Europe but had no basis upon which to challenge their treatment or to obtain recognition under the laws of those democracies. I considered the historical commitment in Western European nation-states to rights, and discussed the tension between the universalism of the law underpinning rights and reliance on an organic conception of the nation as the ultimate source of law. I situated this tension in the context of the conceptual tension between rights and popular sovereignty – thus demonstrating that the issue also arises in pluralist nation-states. I argued as well that these states continue to resolve the tension in favour of a form of popular sovereignty underpinned by myths of nationhood. I outlined the manner in which rights have been articulated and conceptualised in modern nation-states, demonstrating the failure to recognise the artificial, constituted character of rights, and the significance of this failure. And I introduced Arendt's account of action in the public realm as an alternative mode of civic solidarity – a mode that, unlike nationalism, should be capable of according full recognition to newcomers under its constitutive law of equality.

In Part II, I consider in greater depth the lineage of our concepts of political legitimacy, law and rights. I begin in this chapter by discussing the idea of natural law – an idea to which explicit resort is no longer possible in pluralist secular democracies, but which nevertheless remains central to the understanding of rights and political obligation enshrined in the Western European nation-state and globalised through early modern and contemporary international law. I argue in this chapter that positing a universal natural and moral law has allowed liberal rights theorists and their natural law predecessors to obscure and ignore the constituted character of individual equality within the democratic community. As a result, they have failed to acknowledge that the political inequality of outsiders who are denied standing under a community's constitutive law is not remedied nor ameliorated by recognition of the outsiders' innate equality under a universal law of nature. This is especially the case given the secular assumptions of modern liberal democracies and the consequent privatisation of all matters related to morality. Despite the rhetoric of moral equality, the reality of political inequality induces a form of moral amnesia, allowing political inequality to act as a marker of moral inequality. The perverse result – as should be clear from the treatment of the inter-war refugees and that applies as well to contemporary refugees – is that those forced to rely on their natural or human rights are actually recognised and treated as *unnatural* and *inhuman*.

The idea that rights are held by all individuals in accordance with a universal law of nature did not develop until around the fourteenth century, but the concept of the natural law itself has roots in classical thought and refers to a universal code embodied in the 'natural order of things' (Jones 1994, 74) and binding for all people. Characterised as a manifestation of divine reason and of the principles governing the rationally ordered universe, the natural law is discernable by all reasoning beings, and it is common to speak of it as constituting a universal community of mankind. Arguably, the association drawn here between moral law and a universal community originally reflected quite a different understanding of law – that found in the 'pre-philosophical Greek political experience' to which Arendt refers in 'The Great Tradition' (2007a, 716) and which I mentioned in Chapters 2 and 3. According to this pre-philosophical understanding, laws are the artificial or constituted 'boundaries [that] men establish between themselves and between city and city' (Arendt 2007a, 716). The establishment of law is the means by which power is limited and confined – and at the same time, allowed to flourish within these confines. Although the power of each individual is limited by the law, individuals acting together in the public sphere engender power.[1] Law in the pre-philosophical experience both constitutes the public realm and ensures the equality of men within that realm. According to this way of thinking, if we posit a universal law, this law must constitute a global community whose members are equal subjects of law with equal shares in power. My account in this chapter demonstrates, however, that this is not how the concept of natural law was understood or has since been interpreted.

Although classical natural law theorists took for granted that a 'law' properly speaking constitutes a community of equals, they did not conceptualise natural law as constituting political or legal subjects. Rather, they thought of the natural law as establishing a spiritual community of the gods and those men who have fully developed their rational nature – thus who are both wise and virtuous. Because all men have the capacity for reason, each has the potential to enter this illustrious community and to realise its principle of lawfulness within himself (women were not considered rational subjects at all). As a matter of fact, however, most men fail to fully develop their natural reason and thus cannot hope to enter the divine kingdom of perfect reason and happiness. Nevertheless, natural law theorists assumed that the capacity for reason provides a basis for communication between strangers – whose differences of background and experience might otherwise render each unintelligible to the other. And because the capacity for reason allows

1 See my discussion in Chapter 3 and also Arendt's discussion of Montesquieu's 'great discovery that power is not indivisible' (2007a, 721) and 'is not *one* instrument to be applied to *one* goal' (2007a, 722).

all rational beings to participate – even if only partially – in the divine law of reason, it provides the basis for some form of equality and universal community. Regardless of this, however, natural law theorists continued to treat civil law as decisive insofar as political and legal recognition was concerned.

These theorists, including eventually natural rights theorists such as John Locke and Immanuel Kant, whom I discuss in Chapters 5 and 6, take for granted that different forms of obligation arise in the spheres of natural and civil law, and that membership of a lawfully constituted political community is a necessary precondition for recognition under the founding law of that community. For natural law theorists, the natural law is a rule of moral equality that provides a reference point and grounds of legitimation for civil law but does not ensure recognition under that law. The concept of a law of nature is used by these theorists to posit a universal moral or spiritual realm that exists outside the sphere of mundane life and the political obligations proper to it. While natural law precepts may be relied on either to sanction the immoral conduct of individuals or to critique civil law, the universal and egalitarian implications of natural law are assumed to be consistent with the bounded commitments that arise within particular political communities and with the refusal of these communities to accord equal standing to outsiders.

In the discussion that follows I describe the content and anomalous character of a law 'of nature' in the context of the pre-philosophical understanding of law, and consider the implications of positing a natural law for how we think about law as such. I examine the Stoic idea of natural law as constituting a global 'cosmopolis' and note the use of natural law as a justification for the expansionist policies of Alexandria and imperial Rome. In the final section of the chapter I briefly discuss the role of natural law in the thought of Thomas Aquinas and the subsequent development of the doctrine of natural rights.

Two Concepts of Law: Social Artefact and Natural Order

The 'pre-philosophical Greek political experience' that Arendt discusses in 'The Great Tradition' (2007a) understood law as constituting and protecting a public realm within which men relate to each other as equals. In this conception, the role of law is to establish and protect an enduring space within which natural differences of status and power do not influence relations between individuals. Within this legally constituted public sphere individuals are accorded the *persona* of equals, and in the guise of equals share the task of governing themselves (neither ruling nor being ruled) (Arendt 2006, 20; 1998, 32 and 33; 2007b, 943). Law not only establishes a common space of interaction free from the influence of brute power, it also fences the activities of individuals within that space. It establishes a boundary within which each person is equally free to act – not in pursuit of his own ends, as in Locke, but in the public realm. Without recourse to law, the inequalities naturally distinguishing human beings and allowing some to exercise power over others will prevent that distinct form of collaboration that can arise only between equals.

Although part of the 'pre-philosophical' experience of polis life, this understanding of law appears, Arendt says, in Plato – who 'evokes Zeus as the God of boundaries' (2007a, 717), as well as Aristotle – who 'expressly states that political science deals with things that are *nomô* [lawful] and not *physei* [natural]' (2007a, 717–8). The philosophers also continued to assume that citizens form a 'partnership' or association (*koinōnia*) within which no one has a stronger claim to exercise power than anyone else. But at the same time as the pre-philosophical Greek experience supported an understanding of law as a social artefact, designed to ensure the stability of the polis and the flourishing of its political life, there developed in the work of the philosophers 'another, altogether different understanding of law' – an understanding based on the idea of 'an order inherent in the universe and [which] governs its motion' (Arendt 2007a, 718). According to this conception, law is not an artefact that contains power within certain bounds, allowing it to flourish and grow within these bounds; instead, law is the aim or end of all life – both political and moral – and power the instrument through which law is enforced.

According to Douzinas (2000, 26), probably the first fully developed reference to the concept of a law *of nature* is in Aristotle's *Rhetoric*. Here Aristotle distinguishes between particular law ('defined by each group in relation to itself') and 'general law'. Aristotle continues:

> For there is something of which we all have an inkling, being a naturally universal right and wrong, even if there is no community between the … parties nor contract, to which Sophocles' Antigone seems to be referring, in saying that it is just, though forbidden, to bury Polynices … (*Rhetoric*, 1373b)[2]

Sophocles refers, in the extract from *Antigone* cited by Aristotle, to 'unwritten and certain laws of the gods' that 'command always', but he does not refer to nature as embodying those divine laws (Douzinas 2000, 26). From Plato and Aristotle onwards, however, Western philosophy is increasingly characterised by its understanding of nature as a law-governed order distinct from – although ideally mirrored in – the order established within particular communities. In this understanding, law regulates the rationally ordered universe and humans and gods may together participate in this law. What is lawful is what is rightful and just (as we see in Aristotle), and also what is in accordance with reason (see, with particular reference to the Stoic tradition, Annas 1993, 303; Nussbaum 1997, 30). This association between law, justice and reason would later be emphasised by Cicero:

2 I have quoted the section at greater length than Douzinas.

> Since nothing is better than reason, and this exists in both man and god, man's first association with god is in reason. But those who have reason in common also have right reason in common. Since that is law, we men must also be reckoned to be associated with the gods in law. But further, those who have law in common have justice in common. (*de legibus* I 23, in Schofield 1991, 67–8)

The perfectly ordered law governed universe exists apart from the conflict ridden world known to man, and is also at odds with mankind's experience of the material world as one of flux, decay and destruction. The perfectly ordered universe stands outside or beyond 'the changing world of ordinary experience', and its law is 'grasped by reason rather than by observation' (Stalley 1995, ix). What reason was said to dictate coincided with what natural law theorists deemed best.[3] Thus, in distinguishing between natural justice and conventional or man-made justice, Aristotle in *Ethics* (1134b, 8–24) defines both as forms of 'political justice', which is justice that 'obtains between those who share a life for the satisfaction of their needs as persons free and equal', and that is 'defined by law, and is found in communities where law is naturally accepted: those whose members share equally in ruling and being ruled'. Aristotle says natural justice can, however, be distinguished from civil justice on the basis that natural justice 'has the same validity everywhere and does not depend upon acceptance'; its laws are 'immutable'. Conventional justice, on the other hand, is a variety of political justice that 'can take one form or another ... but which, once laid down, is decisive'. Its laws 'are not the same everywhere, because forms of government are not the same either'. Notably, however, there is 'everywhere ... only one natural form of government, namely that which is best'. Political communities approach the ideal of political justice to the extent that they enshrine the principles of natural justice. But Aristotle has already defined political justice as that justice which obtains between those who share a life based on freedom and on equality, and who share equally in ruling and being ruled. These principles, then, must also be mandated by the natural law.

The idea of natural law means that individual equality can be posited on the basis of participation in the principle of reason enshrined in that law. Every reasoning being is theoretically capable of partaking in the law and of independently ascertaining its dictates. Nevertheless, both Greek and Roman natural law theorists assumed that law constitutes political community. Thus in the citation above, Cicero continues, 'those who have these things [reason, law,

3 While Annas (1993, 162) thinks that some of the later Stoic writers, such as Aurelius and Epictetus, rely on 'ethical strategies which seem to be derived directly from the idea ... we are all simply parts of a larger whole', she argues that in this respect these writers are 'distinctively different' from their Stoic predecessors, who generally do not derive their ethics from their account of nature, but simply claim the ethics they articulate are, by virtue of the fact they have been characterised as ethical, therefore also 'in accordance with nature' (1993, 163). Annas' point applies equally to Aristotle's characterisation of natural law.

and justice] in common must be held to belong to the same state (*civitas*)' (*de legibus* I 23, in Schofield 1991, 68). Similarly, Marcus Aurelius says: '[i]f reason is common, so too is law; and if this is common, then we are fellow citizens. If this is so, we share in a kind of organized polity. And if this is so, the world is as it were a city state' (*The Meditations*, Book IV, 4, in Nussbaum 1997, 31).

Hutchings (1999, 12) argues that the concept of natural law has served 'to institutionalise a split between moral and political orders'. In the political realm, laws are publicly proclaimed and enforced, and membership of the political community is a prerequisite of recognition as an equal under its constitutive law. In the moral realm, all individuals are subjects of natural law, but they must determine the dictates of the law in accordance with their own reason and conscience, binding themselves to obey the law, whose dictates cannot be publicly coerced. From Arendt's point of view, however, rather than forcing a wedge between moral and political orders, the idea of law as 'inherent in the universe' breaks down the distinction between moral and political, private and public realms (2007a, 718). Law can no longer be conceived of 'as a wall or boundary erected by men' (2007a, 718) in order to constitute a public space of action and equality. Instead, any laws based on the natural order must have

> a validity … not restricted to one community, nor to the public realm as such, nor generally to matters that happen between men as distinguished from those that happen within men. The cosmic law [is] universal in every respect, applicable to all things and to every man in every situation and condition of life. (2007a, 718)

While it is true that natural and civil law have always been presumed to impose distinctive obligations, Arendt is correct that the distinction between public and private realms has been thoroughly obscured in the natural law tradition. Within this tradition, 'law' cannot be thought of purely as a manufactured boundary, constituting the equality of participants in the political realm and – in this realm alone – overcoming their natural differences of strength and power. Any law manifest in the divine order of the universe and applicable to all communities and all individuals is clearly pre-political. Yet the use of the language of 'law' obscures this pre-political status, at the same time as it blinds us to the political achievement involved in the constitution of a law-governed community of equals. This assimilation of the moral and the political – at the very same time as the force attributed to each diverges (and does so dramatically in modern secular societies) – means that any person who appears in the community and is not recognised in accordance with its constitutive law of equality appears as an aberration – a person beyond the reach not just of the civil law but also of the moral law: an alien in the global cosmopolis.

In the natural law tradition, the universal community governed by natural law shares common possession of the earth's surface. Within this perfectly law-governed community there is no private property and nor are there separate polities or wars. Clearly this is a community unknown in human history, yet while ancient accounts of the role of natural law converge in assuming it establishes a universal community of equals – 'as it were a city state', they do not as a consequence assert the desirability of one global polity. Instead, they treat the natural law as the basis of an idealised and other-worldly community, whose inhabitants are both men and gods. The existence of this ideal community provides a foundation for communication between strangers. While it was also considered the source of obligations to strangers, as one would expect of any political community, these obligations – unlike those arising in actual political communities, were private and could not be enforced. Within the political realm, laws are publicly proclaimed and enforced. In the realm of morality, however, every rational individual has the authority to interpret and apply the natural law. Historically there has been widespread agreement concerning the fundamental precepts of natural law, including its universality and rule of common possession, but as a 'law' it has always been anomalous because its proscriptions cannot be authoritatively proclaimed nor compelled, and it does not constitute political subjects.

At the same time as they posited a law of nature, early natural law theorists recognised law as the artifice through which inevitable inequalities of power are overcome. They were, however, also able to characterise civil law as a realisation of divine principle by imagining the divine and law governed universe either as a *telos* towards which the mundane world of men could evolve, or as an ideal template existing outside or beyond the actual universe. When they spoke of a universal city-state governed by the law of nature, they invoked a community of gods and men as an ideal that could provide a reference point for particular communities, but that could not match the political achievement of a polity constituted by civil law and committed to equality in the public sphere. The subjects of natural law were participants in a divine realm, but they could not claim the constituted subjectivity on the basis of which citizens of the Greek and Roman polis related to each other as equals. It is not surprising, then, that civic law would be considered decisive – as Aristotle says – in determining the recognition accorded to individuals under law. Furthermore, while superficially the existence of discrete polities and the institution of private property would seem to be at odds with recognition of a universal community based on common possession of the earth's surface, the natural law tradition almost always treats the two realms as consistent and even mutually supporting. It does so by emphasising the spiritual and 'other-worldly' dimensions of the 'community of mankind' while at the same time treating civil communities as necessary mechanisms for the protection of their members and the enhancement of life in the mundane world. The best political communities can then be conceived as earthly instantiations of the ideal and perfectly law governed universe.

The Universal City

The Stoic tradition, which accords the concept of natural law a central place, is widely regarded as an early exemplar of cosmopolitanism (Nussbaum 1997; Pangle 1998, 240), but the universalism it promotes is often a private ethic rather than a political ideal. Where it has political dimensions it is either, as I have said, assumed to support the existence of discrete polities, or, as I discuss in the next section, used in support of imperialist or expansionary policies.

The early Stoa were influenced by the Cynic school.[4] The Cynics were not reformists, proposing a positive program of political change; instead they championed the independence and integrity of the wise individual. Thus when Diogenes, the founder of the Cynic school, famously described himself as '*kosmopolitês*' – a 'citizen of the world' (Diogenes Laertius VI, 3, in Nussbaum 1997, 53 fn. 11), he was only in a very flimsy sense affirming his membership of a universal community. More emphatically, he was expressing his scorn for the mundane affairs of men and any claim to allegiance made upon him by the city-state in which he lived. Cynic philosophy did not advocate a global society but instead encouraged individuals to distance themselves from their own societies.[5] The Cynic influence on the Stoa is significant because of its individualism and disregard for the realm of the polis. It treated individual virtue as the sole good for human beings. Insofar as all humans have the capacity to seek virtue, Cynic philosophy assumed a basic commonality between humans everywhere, but insofar as most people lack virtue, it assumed most are fools, madmen or slaves. For the Hellenic Stoa, as for Aristotle, the *telos* of all human life – thus the end at which it rightly aims – is *eudaimonia*: happiness or well-being. The Stoa broke with Aristotle, though, in claiming, along with the Cynics, that 'only what is morally good is good' and thus that *eudaimonia* is a product of virtue alone (Erskine 1990, 15–16; Annas 1993, 166–7). Humans have free will, so they may choose to ignore the law of nature, but they act rightly or justly, and at the same time consistently with their own nature, when they act in accordance with the natural law. According to the Hellenic Stoa, the divinely, harmoniously and rationally ordered universe is a community 'in which there is no internal strife nor the possibility of defeat by external forces, but

---

4 Erskine (1990) claims the Cynic influence on the early Stoa, and particularly Zeno, the school's founder, has been overstated (see, for example, 1990, 9). Erskine's objection is part of his broader argument that the Greek Stoa were more politically engaged than is generally realised. I discuss this characterisation below.

5 Nussbaum (1997, 53 fn. 11) says of Diogenes: 'His life was strikingly apolitical and defiant of all earthly authority'. Pagden (2000, 4) goes further, arguing that Diogenes' 'famous claim to be a "citizen of the world" was … intended as a challenge to all forms of civility'. Erskine (1990, 27) says the claim to be citizens of the world 'merely means that Cynics recognised no city as their own'.

"a dance of happiness danced with understanding and supreme wisdom"' (Schofield 1991, 63, citing Dio Chrysostom, 36th *logos*, §22).[6]

This ideal universe clearly transcended the known world of experience. Nevertheless, it was described both as 'natural' and as law-governed: 'the universe ... is in the proper sense a city, but ... those here on earth are not – they are called cities, but they are not really. For a city or a people is something morally good, an organization or a group of men administered by law which exhibits refinement' (Clement, *Strom.* IV, 26, in Schofield 1991, 61).[7] The human citizens of the cosmic city are wise men and sages, the perfectly virtuous, of whom Socrates was considered to provide the only known historical example. Thus 'only the wise exercise true citizenship of the universe' (Schofield 1991, 77), and 'a share of law and constitution [is given] not to any living being whatsoever, but to those who have a share in reason and wisdom' (Dio Chrysostom, in Schofield 1991, 85). Echoing their Cynic predecessors, the Hellenic Stoa argued that while the perfectly wise are citizens, friends and free, the morally bad are aliens, enemies and slaves (Schofield 1991, 95; Erskine 1990, 19).

The early Stoic invocation of the natural law was, Bloch (1986, 13) argues, an 'appeal to a golden age', to a commune of men (as I have said, women were excluded) and gods 'without private property, states, or war' (see also Douzinas 2000, 60; Erskine 1990, 43; and re property: Erskine 1990, 103; Schofield 1991, 52). The Stoa asserted no man is a slave by nature (Erskine 1990, 46) and all are naturally equal (Bloch 1968, 13). But all of this was premised on each man achieving his full potential as a perfectly rational and therefore perfectly virtuous being. It was only when this occurred that each would be able to take his place next to the gods in 'the rational empire of love' (Bloch 1968, 13). Furthermore, individual virtue was to be achieved through a life of contemplation, and its cultivation had little if anything to do with engagement in the public realm.

Although the political quietism of the early Stoa is assumed by many commentators, Erskine (1990) and Schofield (1991) both argue that this quietism has been overstated and that Stoicism's ideal city was intended to provide a spur to change. This appears to be true in the case of some Stoic thinkers. For example, Zeno, the founder of Stoicism, provided a model in his *Republic* for the reform of earthly city-states along the lines of a Spartan republic (see Schofield 1991). Schofield (1991, 52 fn. 47) also claims that early Stoicism 'developed an account of how the wise man should conduct himself in existing circumstances, where the conditions necessary for the emergence of the ideal community were not satisfied'. Thus while generally opposed to any form of violence, the Stoa accepted that individuals might have a duty to defend their city against external attack. They thought the wise man might hold office in or seek to influence either a

6 Dio was a sophist and 'is not regarded as a prime source' for Stoic doctrine, but Schofield (1991, 64) argues he nevertheless provides a 'reliable witness [in respect of] orthodox Stoic views on the city and the cosmos'.

7 Here Clement is describing the views of the Stoa.

constitutional government or a monarchy (Stobaeus, in Erskine 1990, 66), and that he would have the skill to be a king, general, politician, householder and 'acquirer of property', knowing 'from what sources one should acquire property and when and how and to what extent' (Stobaeus, in Schofield 1991, 95–6). They suggested that as well as making laws and educating men, the truly wise would be prepared to suffer and even to die for their city (Stobaeus, in Erskine 1990, 66).

Neither Schofield nor Erskine suggest, however, that the early Stoa relied on the concept of natural law to argue against the existence of separate polities or in favour of a global state. On the contrary, most Stoic writers assumed that the constitution of diverse civil societies was an essential mechanism for improving the life of men given the challenges posed by the mundane world of experience, and the degree to which this world diverges from the harmonious and perfectly ordered universe of natural law. Furthermore, the establishment of appropriately constituted and law governed polities could be used to realise the principles of natural law within these societies. As Cicero put it: 'nothing of all that is done on earth is more pleasing to that Supreme God who rules the whole universe than the assemblies and gatherings of men associated in justice which are called states' (*De Re Publica*, 3.6.13). It was taken for granted, however, that the realisation of freedom and equality in the political realm could apply only to the select few – as all political experience to that point attested.

The Roman Stoa, like their Hellenic predecessors, interpreted the natural law as a law of freedom and of common possession of the earth's surface (Tuck 1979, 18), while at the same time assuming civil laws could justifiably enshrine hierarchical relations. The Roman Stoa simply regarded such relations of dominion – whether over people or property – as conventionally rather than naturally mandated. Again, according to Cicero, '[n]othing is private by nature but rather by long occupation … or by conquest … or by law, by agreement or by allotment' (in Erskine 1990, 105). There is no reason, in Cicero's account, for impugning the institution of property simply because it is conventional rather than natural, and there is no necessary incompatibility between natural possession in common and private property. While Cicero also refers in *On Duties* to 'the produce of the earth' as existing 'for the sake of men and common to all men', Erskine (1990, 109) claims 'he always adds the qualification that one should not imagine that this affects private property': '[a]ll things which nature has produced for the common use of men should be kept as common, with the proviso that those things which are assigned by statutes and civil law should be held as laid down by those laws' (*On Duties*, 1.51, in Erskine 1990, 109). Seneca also argues that private property is consistent with the claim 'everything belongs to the wise' (Esrkine 1990, 110), while Ulpian says '*dominium* over other men (slaves) or goods' is not natural but a product of convention which reflects what men have agreed upon for their mutual benefit (Tuck 1979, 17–18). Cicero frequently speaks of the unity and interdependence of the human race, but he also believes one's strongest obligations are to one's family, friends and fellow citizens (Pangle 1998, 260–61). He argues that we should not harm those who are strangers to us, or take from them what is theirs, and that we have an obligation to provide assistance where it is needed, but only in cases in which providing assistance does not involve a cost to ourselves, our family, our friends, or our compatriots (in Pangle 1998, 253; and see *On Duties*, 1.51–52). The recognition of our common humanity under the natural law is thus presumed to be consistent with the fact that each man's primary attachments and responsibilities are to those closest to him.

Consistently with this, Nussbaum (1997, 32) argues that the Stoic invocation of 'universal citizenship' does not mean one must 'give up local identifications and affiliations, which can be a great source of richness in life'. She says Cicero and other Stoic authors employ what was even then a familiar metaphor when they compare our attachments to self, family, friends, neighbours, fellow citizens, and humanity to a series of concentric circles, with humanity comprising the outermost circle. 'In general, we should think of nobody as a stranger, as outside our sphere of concern and obligation' (1997, 33); and we should seek, through our own actions and orientation towards them, to draw each circle towards us. Nevertheless, we are still entitled to 'give what is near us a special degree of attention and concern' (1997, 33). But Nussbaum argues that this justified partiality must be qualified, in the Stoic conception, in two ways: 'first, we should always remember that ... our most fundamental allegiance is to what is human. Second, we should consider that even the special measure of concern we give to our own is justified not by any intrinsic superiority in the local but by the overall requirements of humanity' (1997, 33). This resonates with the account provided by Annas (1993, 262–72) of the Stoic theory of *oikeiōsis* – the natural impulse towards bringing others closer into one's sphere of care and concern: which Annas calls 'familiarisation':

> The root idea is that of making one person or thing oikeion to another. *Oikeion* in turn comes from *oikos*, the house or household. People are *oikeioi* if they are related to you, or in some other way attached to your household; so *oikeion* comes to mean both 'akin to' and 'what belongs to you or is on your side', as opposed to what is *allotrion*, alien, not belonging. (1993, 262)

The theory of *oikeiōsis* makes two claims: the first that nature makes us familiar to ourselves; and the second that it makes other humans familiar to us (1993, 262). What follows from the first claim is that we are born with a natural instinct to preserve ourselves, but, given our rational nature, we are capable of learning that virtue is the sole good, and thus 'the only thing to be sought for its own power and status' (Cicero, *De Finibus* III, 16, in Annas 1993, 264). The person who is fully familiarised to himself will act in accordance with his rational nature, and will be guided by reason even where the result does not further his own projects or superficial desires. Other humans become familiar to us by the rational extension of our instinctual concern for our families.

The plausibility of the idea that partiality towards 'our own' can be justified by 'the overall requirements of humanity' was defended by the Roman Stoa in a manner that remains popular in the arguments of contemporary liberals. Nussbaum

(1997, 33) points out that the Roman Stoa diverged from their Greek predecessors, who were said to be in favour of abolishing the nuclear family, by suggesting that the best way to care for children is to allow their parents to look after them. By allowing parents to nurture their children, and to focus their concern upon them, the Roman Stoa argued that all children would be better cared for than if the duty of raising children rested on unattached and impartial carers. But Nussbaum claims that parents' 'intense' concern for their own children should not reflect a sense that their children 'are really more worthwhile than other people's children' (1997, 33). Instead, it should be based on the recognition 'that it makes most sense for me to do my duties where I am placed, that the human community is best arranged in this way' (1997, 33). 'This', she concludes, is what, for a Stoic, 'local and national identities should be like, and that is how they can be fortified and encouraged without subverting the primary claim of humanity' (1997, 33).

This burden-sharing or assigned responsibility account of partiality is plausible if the obligations being considered – towards self, family, friends, polis, and humans universally are all of the same order. But this is not the case. Civil law may – as in the classical Greek experience – constitute a community within which power is distributed equally, but in all cases it compels in a manner quite unlike the internalised compulsion of the natural law. Recognition of shared membership of a naturally ordered universe might lead to a sense of fellow feeling among individuals, but this is a private, spiritual matter and it cannot be publicly determined or enforced. When the precepts of natural law are rendered determinate and binding through civil law, the compulsion of this law, that was said to uniquely enshrine natural law, could be imposed on other societies without their consent.

Philosopher's Dream Versus Conqueror's Reality

It is widely accepted that the Roman Stoa moved away from the more individualistic spiritual elements of Hellenic Stoicism, and many defended Roman imperial law as instantiating natural law. But Stoic doctrine also informed the development of the body of law holding between different Greek city-states which 'had already begun to develop before the time of Alexander', and which 'descended upon the world as the ideology of the Alexandrian Empire' (Bloch 1991, 14). Pagden (2000, 5) argues many proponents of Stoicism traded on the assumption that Hellenic law uniquely enshrined the universal law of mankind. Similarly, while Plutarch's account of the universalism of early Stoic natural law in his essay on Alexander is often cited by contemporary cosmopolitans, it is less common to draw attention to the contrast drawn by Plutarch between the 'philosophers' dream' and its imperial realisation:

> The much admired *Republic* of Zeno, who founded the Stoic sect, is aimed at this one main point, that our arrangement for habitations should not be based on cities or peoples, each one distinguished by its own special system of justice, but

> we should regard all men as citizens and members of the populace … This Zeno wrote, picturing as it were a dream or image of a philosopher's well-regulated republic, but it was Alexander who gave effect to that theory. (Plutarch, *de Alex. Virt.* 329 A-B, in Schofield 1991, 104)

Schofield (1991, 110) thinks Plutarch misrepresents Zeno in this passage, and that Zeno's aim was not the creation of a universal society, but instead the recognition of a common law of nature as 'the source of moral authority in any city of the good and wise'. But even if Plutarch's account is a misrepresentation of early Stoic doctrine, it is a telling one. The universal natural law of the Stoa was an otherworldly ideal that could nevertheless be adapted to the interests of regimes with imperial aspirations.

After arguing that there is 'but one eternal and unchangeable law', Gaius Laelius proceeds, in Cicero's dialogue, to enunciate the rules by which war may be waged in accordance with justice. He observes that '[o]ur people … now holds sway over the whole earth through defending its allies', and then adds the rhetorical flourish, '[d]o we not observe that dominion has been given, by nature herself, to what is best – with the greatest consequent benefit to those who are weaker?' (*Republic* 3.33–35). While this is not a position that Cicero himself – critical of Rome's 'emerging despotism' (Pangle 1998, 240) – unequivocally endorses, he does portray Roman expansionism, at its best, as a noble enterprise benefiting all of mankind: 'as long as the empire of the Roman people was maintained through acts of beneficence rather than injustices … our rule could more truly be called a paternal protectorate of the entire earth rather than an empire' (*On Duties*, 2.26–29, in Pangle 1998, 256). Cicero is well known for combining the idea of mankind's shared participation in a natural and divine order with an account of the natural law as underwriting a universal civil law. As Pangle (1998) and Pagden (2000) note, however, this civil law is assumed to be the law of 'civilised' nations and although it admits of cultural variants, its model is Roman law. Within this framework, it was taken for granted that the political sphere of freedom, equality and republican citizenship must be limited to the select few, and supported by the hierarchical ordering of society outside this specially constituted space. While all men have a share in reason, and thus the divine law of nature, the universal community constituted by the natural law is either a spiritual and ideal realm set apart both from the mundane world and the constituted realm of the polis, or it is used to support and justify the imposition of a particular society's rule over other communities. As a spiritual ideal, the natural law provides a basis for communication between all men on earth and potentially the grounds of moral obligations between them, but these obligations are of a different order to those arising under civil law, and they cannot be externally enforced.

Aquinas and the Neo-Thomist Account of Natural Rights

The Stoic conception of the natural law as a universally applicable rule of reason was adapted by Christian thinkers including, in the thirteenth century, Aquinas, who characterised natural law as an embodiment of divine reason inscribed in the conscience of every individual: '... all men know the truth to a certain extent, at least as to the common principles of natural law' (*Summa Theologie*, ST I-II, Q.93, 3d Art. 38, in Douzinas 2000, 58). In Aquinas' account, the natural law provides a standard of justice, rationally discernable by all individuals in accordance with which each must govern his behaviour for his own good and the good of humanity. Aquinas echoes the Roman Stoa in claiming that private property and hierarchical relations, including slavery, are 'not the products of nature, but made by human reason for the advantage of human life' (Tuck 1979, 19). Like his Stoic predecessors, he does not impugn such distinctions simply because they are conventional in origin – if they could be characterised as in accord with 'the dictates of reason' then they could be presented as grounded in the natural law. Aquinas also suggests that '[t]he common possession of all things, and the equal liberty of all' is 'according to the *ius naturale*'; but he explains that in this context 'according to the natural law' means simply that 'nature does not prescribe the opposite' (in Tuck 1979, 19). In the same way, Aquinas says, 'we can say a man is naked under the *ius naturale*, since he received no clothes from nature but invented them himself' (in Tuck 1979, 19).

The universalism of natural law is perfectly consistent, for Aquinas, with obligations to particular political communities, which he viewed, following Aristotle, as the natural product of man's innate sociability. For Aquinas, there is no conflict between acting to preserve one's fellow man, one's political community, and humanity generally, and virtue requires that we do each of these. The precepts of natural law on the basis of which one should act were, however, uniquely enshrined in societies governed by Christian precepts and these societies were entitled to enforce natural law precepts beyond their borders. Thus war could be 'justified by the iniquity of the adversary' (Ward 2006, 694), with such 'iniquity' including 'practices perceived to be contrary to natural reason such as idolatry, cannibalism, human sacrifice, and even violation of the rights of hospitality' (Ward 2006, 694, citing both Augustine and Aquinas). Thus the Christian natural law tradition, like the Hellenic and the Roman rendering of natural law, licensed a distinctively imperialist universalism.

When Aquinas speaks of natural justice, law or right, he invokes an idea of fairness – or that which is in itself fair (Finnis 1996, 206), and a measure against which rulers along with other individuals can be judged, but he does not recognise a natural framework of individual entitlements or rights.[8] The concept of individual

8 While Tuck (1979, 19) argues that Aquinas did at times draw on 'at least the basic concept of a right' in relation to property, his 'general theory', as was 'true of all other thirteenth century theorists' 'was not a genuine natural rights theory'. In the fourteenth

dignity, and recognition of the importance of individual conscience that grew in significance during the Renaissance and the Reformation, provided a basis upon which natural law theory could be interpreted by neo-Thomists such as Francisco Suarez as according individual entitlements (Vincent 1993, 251). While the natural law would continue to be characterised as setting rightful limits on the pursuit of individual aims, individuals were also said to have natural rights of control or mastery over their own property, including their bodies. Thus for Suarez, natural right or justice is 'a kind of moral power ... which every man has, either over his own property or with respect to that which is due to him' (Vincent 1993, 251; Finnis 1996, 206–7). To suggest that the natural law supports individual rights is not yet, however, to say anything about how these rights may be interpreted. This is a topic to which I turn now.

---

century, however, theories of property rights underwent a transformation that Tuck argues paved the way for the natural rights theories of the seventeenth century (18–19).

Chapter 5
Liberalism's False Promise I: Locke

Introduction

Written towards the end of the seventeenth century, John Locke's *The Second Treatise of Government* purports to provide a universally applicable account of political legitimacy. Locke's model commonwealth, based on a contract forged between free, equal and independent men and designed to secure the natural rights with which each is born, exemplifies what is now the standard way of theorising the legitimacy of the democratic nation-state.[1] Its presuppositions are also apparent in international law, within which the characterisation of human rights and the importance of sovereign states as mechanisms for securing these rights has a distinctively Lockean flavour. Locke's account relies on the idea of a universal law of nature, and like many of his natural law predecessors Locke assumes what is in effect a burden-sharing or assigned responsibility model to characterise the role of political communities.[2] At the same time, however, he implicitly accords states more significance than is warranted by a model that establishes them as institutional functionaries protecting rights held universally and equally by all individuals.

Like the early natural law theorists, Locke takes for granted that law constitutes community and that the natural law founds a universal community of equals. But also consistently with his natural law predecessors, Locke characterises natural and civil law very differently, and while civil law is justified as an instantiation of the universal but unwritten law of nature, membership of the universal community of mankind does not translate to equal standing under the civil law of states other than one's own. Individuals outside the civil community are the subjects of natural law and rights, but they are not recognised as subjects of justice within the community itself constituted on the basis of natural law and rights. Instead, recognition of equal political status depends on participation in a society's founding contract, which constitutes members as authors as well as subjects of the state's law. The law of nature remains – in Locke's theory as in the accounts of the earliest natural law theorists – an anomaly in legal terms; it is individually interpreted and cannot be publicly enforced. This means that the force of the natural law is personal and moral rather than public and juridical. As with his natural law predecessors, Locke's use of the concept of a *law* of nature obscures the politically constituted status of citizens: the fact that the subjects of civil law are citizens who have

1 See Introduction, 8.

2 See Chapter 4, 78.

mutually agreed to recognise each other as equals and to establish a community based on this mutual recognition. While the particular laws of the community may accord rights to non-citizens, the non-citizen has no standing under the community's constitutive law of equality. It is true that Locke assumes many people within the political community, including all women, will also be excluded from full citizenship, but the implications of his model of legitimacy mean that these members are able to contest their exclusion on the basis of their social membership as well as their participation in the universal law of nature. Because of the qualitative difference between civil law and the universal but unenforceable law of nature, the outsider who cannot point to social membership as a ground for recognition of equal status will not succeed on the basis of 'natural right' alone.

Within civil society, Locke characterises political equality as a largely apolitical right to autonomy. Autonomy for Locke involves control over one's person and possessions, and freedom of conscience. Because he defines equality in terms of the right to private autonomy, Locke's model political society is very different from the pre-philosophical Greek polis that I discussed in Part I of this book. While the Greek experience saw law as establishing boundaries between men in order to assure to each an equal sphere of freedom, this was the freedom to act in concert with one's equals in the public sphere. The freedom secured by the Lockean state and its constitutive law is the liberty to act in pursuit of one's private ends. Locke's model was revolutionary insofar as it expanded the membership of the polis to potentially include all rational beings, but this revolutionary potential was undercut by the anti-political nature of the Lockean polis. It is also notable that Locke's reliance on the concept of a universal law of nature obscured the partisan and imperialist uses to which that concept continued, in his own day, to be put.

In the next section, I describe Locke's account of natural law and the rights and duties that flow from it, as well as his reasons for arguing it is in individuals' interests to move from a state of nature to civil society. In the following section, I discuss the distinctive status of individuals as members of civil society and subjects of conferred rights, and I spell out the differences in Locke's theory between, on the one hand, the sphere of morality, natural law and natural rights; and on the other hand, the sphere of justice, civil law and conferred rights. I also discuss the role played by the public good in the *The Second Treatise*. I argue that the concept of the public good grounds a more substantive notion of political community than Locke's status as a forefather of classical liberalism would imply. This anomaly is, nevertheless, a consistent feature of the liberal tradition and it continues to inform contemporary understandings of the role of the state and the sovereignty of the people, providing a basis for the nationalistic discourses that would – at face value – appear to be at odds with rights-based justifications of the coercive power of the state. In the final section of this chapter I consider the imperialist implications of Locke's account of political legitimacy.

Natural Law and Natural Rights

In the *The Second Treatise of Government*, Locke tells us that in order '[t]o understand political power right and derive it from its original, we must consider what state all men are naturally in' (1952, 4).[3] This is the state of nature, which is a universal society of mankind constituted by common subjection to the natural law (1952, 128; and see 172). Unlike the classical conception, Locke's community of natural law is not a divine realm of perfection but rather a primeval society located within the mundane natural world. Similarly to the classical conception, however, the rule of natural law is one of common possession of the earth's surface and of individual freedom and equality. As in the classical conception, freedom and equality for Locke relate to man's rational faculties and his capacity to divine for himself the dictates of natural law – which is the 'right rule of reason' (1952, 10; and see 172), but equality for Locke also has a more political component. Locke suggests that men's natural equality follows from the fact that all are 'creatures of the same species and rank, born to the same advantages of nature and the use of the same faculties' (1952, 4), and God has refrained – as Locke claims to have established in the *The First Treatise* – from setting 'one above another' (1952, 4; and see 2003, 67). As equals, Locke says that no man has an innate or natural right of domination over other men – in the state of nature 'all the power and jurisdiction is reciprocal, no one having more than another' (1952, 4; see also 7 and 44).

While this conception appears capable of grounding an account of collaborative political action along the lines of the pre-philosophical Greek experience, the connection that Locke draws between equality and an individualistic or privatised understanding of autonomy undercuts this potential. Locke characterises man's natural freedom as the ability to act and to dispose of his person and possessions according to his own will, although 'within the bounds of the law of nature' (1952, 4 and 128). The natural law is a rule of universal preservation dictating for every man preservation of self and – insofar as it is consistent with self-preservation – preservation of others (1952, 6). After the institution of civil society, the natural law also dictates preservation of the society of which one is a member (1952, 129). Self-preservation is a right and a duty, and from the right of self-preservation flows a right 'to meat and drink and such other things as nature affords for [man's] subsistence' (1952, 25). Locke argues that this logically presupposes original ownership in common of the earth 'and all that is therein' (1952, 25 and 26). He also argues, however, that the institution of private property is necessary in order to allow individuals to enjoy the natural products of the earth, so the right to acquire property by mixing one's labour with common land is, he says, a natural right (see 1952, ch. 5). The right of self-preservation also (and as a consequence) accords a right – limited only by other individuals' equal rights – to control and preserve one's property, defined as including one's life, liberty and estates (see,

---

3 All references to the *The Second Treatise* are to paragraph numbers that are standard across all editions.

for example, 1952, 87 and 123). All individuals also have the executive right to enforce the law of nature. The executive right itself founds 'two distinct rights' – the right of punishing breaches and the right of taking reparation where one has directly suffered as a result of a breach (1952, 11).

Although itself characterised by 'peace, good-will, mutual assistance, and preservation' (1952, 19), a 'state of war' can intrude upon the state of nature because of 'degenerate men' who refuse to be bound by its law (1952, 128). Furthermore, the law of nature has no common authority to judge and enforce it (1952, 19). Given there is no 'standing rule and common judge' (1952, 91) in the state of nature, and given all individuals share equally in the law of nature with none having a natural right of domination, every individual must be 'judge for himself and executioner' (1952, 87) of the natural law. Locke describes the executive right of nature as flowing from the right every man has 'to preserve mankind in general' (1952, 8). It is a form of juridical power, and it is presumably for this reason that Locke also characterises it as 'political' (1952, 171). Like the law of nature itself, this 'political' power is anomalous because it is innate to and exercised by individuals. Locke cautions that because every individual is equally entitled to interpret and enforce the law of nature, self-interest is likely to influence the manner in which it is interpreted and disputes to arise concerning its dictates (1952, 13). Thus a universal rule of self-preservation within the boundaries of the law of nature cannot be the best means of ensuring the preservation of mankind.

Civil Law and Conferred Rights

The Institution of Civil Society

Civil government is, Locke says, 'the proper remedy for the inconveniences' that flow from living in a state in which men 'may be judges in their own case' (1952, 13; and see 91, 123, 127). The purpose for which individuals enter civil society is the apolitical goal of self-preservation: the 'fundamental, sacred and unalterable law of self-preservation' is that for which men enter society (1952, 145). Similarly, government is created 'for this end, that men might have and secure their property' (1952, 138; and see 139). Political societies thus allow their members to live together comfortably, safely and peacefully, 'in a secure enjoyment of their properties and a greater security against' outsiders (95). Admittedly, Locke claims that civil society provides 'communion and fellowship' as well as a mechanism to rationalise productive and exchange processes (see 1952, 15). He thinks, however, that its most significant advantage, aside from its productive benefits, is that it leaves individuals free to pursue, within the boundaries necessary to ensure others' equal rights, their own conception of the good life.[4] Civil law protects equal spheres of individual freedom (1952, 17), but it does so not primarily to facilitate the collaborative exercise of power, as in the ancient Greek political experience, but rather to ensure individual security (1952, 17 and 23) and to allow the pursuit of private ends: it is 'a liberty to follow my own will in all things where the rule prescribes it not' (1952, 22).

Locke provides an account of the institution of political societies in two chapters in the *The Second Treatise*, in Chapter 5, 'Of Property', and in Chapter 8, 'Of the Beginning of Political Societies'. Chapter 8 opens with a reiteration of Locke's admirably universalist claim that men are 'by nature all free, equal, and independent' (1952, 95). As there is no 'natural' political subjection the only legitimate way for men to become subject to the power of government is by their own consent. In the state of nature, where standing government does not exist, men 'put ... on the bonds of civil society ... by agreeing with other men to join and unite into a community' (1952, 95). Through this agreement or social contract a 'political' or 'civil' society is established (1952, 87, 89).

Notably, Locke claims that the social contract precedes the establishment of government or the positing of positive law – it is only once 'thus incorporated' that parties to the contract 'set up what form of government they [think] fit' (1952, 106; and see 132) and accord the legislative the authority to make laws (1952, 134, 136). Thus the forging of the body politic through the social contract is a foundational act that precedes the institution of civil law and creates the conditions within which civil law will function. The parties to the social contract not only constitute a political community but – on the basis of the mutual recognition embodied in the contract – also constitute their civic identities, recognising each other as lawmakers as well as equal subjects of law. Only once they have constituted their political society and in doing so, their identity as equals within it, do the parties to the contract invest the legislative with authority. The constitution of the legislative is itself, Locke says, 'the original and supreme act of the society, antecedent to all positive laws in it and depending wholly on the people' (1952, 157). Here it is clear that the authority of all civil law rests ultimately on 'the people' who found the body politic and who invest government with authority to act on their behalf. The government thus constituted is directly answerable only to its own citizens, who established it solely for their own ends. Locke repeatedly emphasises that all legislative and executive power comes from the community established through the forging of the original contract (1952, 21 and ch. 13). Although Locke does not speak of it, it is true that his model implies that government may have duties to outsiders derived from the natural duties of its citizens – who entrust government with the task of discharging these duties as well as securing their rights. Locke certainly assumes that any legitimately constituted government is obliged to operate in a manner consistent with the natural law in

---

4 Freedom of conscience was a central concern for Locke by the time he wrote the *The Second Treatise*. See Shapiro 2003, x; Tully 1993, 12 and 55.

its relations with outsiders, but any obligations here are – as I discuss further below – moral rather than juridical. As Ward (2006, 702) claims in the context of discussing whether Locke's theory implies that states have duties to provide humanitarian intervention, 'Locke clearly establishes that the overarching moral purpose of each society is the security and welfare of its own people, and thus any moral duty on states to intervene can never be more than an imperfect duty qualified by the danger involved'.

In his chapter on property, Locke claims that border agreements are negotiated between separate communities when land becomes scarce in some parts of the world. Around the same time that territorial boundaries are settled, the distinct communities 'by laws within themselves, regulate ... the properties of the private men of their society, and so by compact and agreement, settle ... the property which labor and industry began' (1952, 45). But the border agreements by which different communities relinquish 'their natural common right' to land and the agreements forged by individuals to establish civil societies are different in kind. Only the latter establish a political or civil society and institute standing law and a judicial system, thereby removing the parties from the state of nature (1952, 14, 20, 87). The state of nature continues to characterise interactions between states and those still living in the state of nature (1952, 145), between the subjects of civil society and those still living in the state of nature (1952, 14, 145) and between states themselves. As Locke says, 'it is not every compact that puts an end to the state of nature between men, but only this one of agreeing together mutually to enter into one community and make one body politic' (1952, 14).

Locke repeatedly stresses that the legitimacy of 'the body politic' depends on its foundation in consent: all men remain in a state of nature 'til by their own consents they make themselves members of some politic society' (1952, 15); man being 'naturally free', nothing can 'put him into subjection to any earthly power but only his own consent' (1952, 119; and see 95–7, 122). Nevertheless, he also claims that civil societies are legitimated not on the basis of a consensus among all individuals living within a territory but on the basis of the decision of the majority: in his words – 'that which begins and actually constitutes any political society is nothing but the consent of any number of freemen capable of a majority' (1952, 99). Locke implies that the majority's decision to establish civil society is consistent with the claim that only an individual's consent can bind him to recognise the authority of civil government because he suggests that any individual who objects to the institution of civil society is free to leave the territory where that society is established and outside its borders to remain as he was before, 'in the liberty of the state of nature' (1952, 95; and see 115).[5]

5 Locke does not engage with the issue of the loss a person may suffer by being forced to leave behind property that is now within the jurisdiction of the legitimately constituted commonwealth.

The Status of Individuals as Members or Residents of a Commonwealth

Having provided an account of the institution of civil societies, Locke deals with the status of individuals born into pre-existing civil societies. Consistent with his thesis of natural freedom and equality, he says that no one is automatically bound to acknowledge the authority of the society in which he is born, but upon reaching adulthood each is considered a 'freeman', 'at liberty what government he will put himself under, what body politic he will unite himself to' (1952, 118; and see 73). This sounds as if legitimately constituted civil societies have an obligation to allow anyone willing to abide by their laws to join their society on equal terms. But although Locke does not engage with the implications of his account for individuals denied membership of societies other than their own, his account of the social contract as the foundation of civil law presupposes that if the current parties to the contract do not want to admit a newcomer, then they have no strong obligation to do so. Miller suggests that Locke's approach to territorial rights in *The Second Treatise* 'has nothing directly to say about … the right to control the movement of people and goods across borders' (2011, 103). This is not true in respect of exit rights – as I have said, when they become adults men may choose to reject the authority of their political society and leave its territory; but it is true in respect of the entry of non-citizens. Given Locke's silence in this regard, there are those who have argued that his theory is consistent with complete freedom of movement (see, for example, Steiner 1992). Such accounts fail, however, to recognise the independent standing and authority of the political community and its partisan commitments. In Locke's account, outsiders are the subjects of natural rights, but as I show in the ensuing discussion, these rights are privatised moral claims that carry less weight than the conferred rights accorded and recognised by civil society. The outsider does not have a 'right' in any meaningful sense to enter a legitimately constituted state unless invited to do so by its current members.

In relation to those born into a particular commonwealth, Locke says that the decision to remain constitutes tacit consent to its authority (1952, 117, 119, 121). This tacit consent may be withdrawn at any time, allowing the individual to leave the political association. On the other hand, if the individual provides his express consent to unite with a particular 'body politic', this consent cannot subsequently be withdrawn (1952, 121). It is this express consent, and only this, that makes a man a 'perfect member' (1952, 119) and 'perpetual subject' of a commonwealth (1952, 122). Anyone within the territory of a lawfully constituted commonwealth, including visitors who are the subjects of other political societies or who live elsewhere in a state of nature, can be considered to have provided their tacit consent to the authority of its government and on this basis are bound to obey its laws (1952, 119, 122). But living within a society and submitting to its laws does not make foreigners 'subjects' or 'members' of the commonwealth (1952, 122). It does not accord the political and legal subjectivity that is associated with full membership of the state and that alone entitles an individual to be considered an equal among his fellows – not merely an object of law but an author of the state's constitutive law.

According to this account, many individuals born within a legitimately constituted commonwealth – like foreigners living within its jurisdiction – will not be regarded as parties to its founding contract, and thus would similarly appear to be denied the equal recognition afforded by that contract. But being born into the community accords these individuals (or at least those who are considered rational beings) the right to join its founding contract when they reach adulthood. Outsiders have no such right. Thus Locke says that the 'alien' who lives within the commonwealth and is punished for a crime is only rightfully punished in accordance with natural law – strictly speaking, the laws of the state 'reach not a stranger; they speak not to him, nor, if they did, is he bound to hearken to them' (1952, 9). This suggests that natural law persists in civil society, and indeed, Locke explicitly says that, '[t]he obligations of the law of nature cease not in society but only in many cases are drawn closer and have by human laws known penalties annexed to them to enforce their observation. Thus the law of nature stands as an eternal rule to all men' (1952, 135). As a moral rule, however, it does not have the publicly binding status of civil law. Locke also claims that civil law is valid only insofar as it conforms to the dictates of natural law (1952, 12). But this does not mean that civil equality is the same as equality under natural law. While Locke emphasises that all people within the territory of a state are – by virtue of their tacit consent to its authority – subject to the laws of that state, his claim that civil law does not 'reach' or 'speak to' the alien implicitly references the founding contract and the mutual recognition of equality that it enacts.

The legal subjectivity and political status that one acquires as a party to the polity's founding contract provides a form of standing within the state that is denied to outsiders. It is on the basis of this standing that one is recognisable as a full subject of justice. It is also on this basis that one is entitled to claim the rights conferred and secured by the state. Subjects of natural rights may make a claim, founded in the law of nature, on the members of the rights-based state – but the force of this claim is personal and moral rather than public and juridical. It is possible that at the time of writing Locke conceived moral obligations as potentially carrying more force than public obligations of justice, or as requiring recognition by the state regardless of the implications for the property rights it secures. As I discuss in the next section, many theorists argue that Locke treats the duty to render charity to those in desperate need as overriding property rights (see the discussion in Lamb and Thompson 2009). Regardless of whether they are correct about this, it is clear that Locke assumes it is government, once legitimately constituted, that has the power to adjudicate property rights and claims to public welfare within the state. Citizens are bound by the outcomes of this adjudication, and any 'welfare' rights accorded by the state acquire the same status as other conferred rights. Locke takes for granted that any such adjudication must be undertaken by government in the interests of its own citizens, ignoring the claims or interests of outsiders. Individuals may have a moral justification (and indeed, obligation) to proffer charity outside the framework of their civic obligations, even though they are legally entitled to refuse to surrender their property, but they have no basis for requiring their fellow citizens to do the same, and instead must defend their fellow citizens' conferred rights against any incursion from outsiders – regardless of the nature of the claims made by these outsiders.

Although Locke recognises the possibility of conflict between preservation of self, preservation of mankind and preservation of the society of which one is a member (he says, for example, that each man ought to 'preserve the rest of mankind' only insofar as 'his own preservation comes not in competition' (1952, 6), the plausibility of his claim that civil law rests on the law of nature relies on the compatibility of all three forms of preservation. Thus Locke argues that the institution of civil government serves all mankind: '[t]he end of government is the good of mankind' (1952, 229). His account implies that the preservation of states serves to advance the preservation of the individual members of each state and thereby individuals universally.[6] On the other hand, however, Locke also characterises the state, like the individual, as an autonomous actor with a fundamental interest in preserving its freedom and autonomy (1952, 145). Territorial rights replicate individual property rights (1952, 45, 117), and states – like individuals – have a natural right to defend themselves against attack (1952, 3 and 145–7). Unlike individuals, however, states cannot rely on a framework of civil law to protect their freedom (1952, 14, 145), and Locke nowhere advocates the institution of such a framework (Simmons 2001, 183–4; Ward 2006, 692, 694). While Locke characterises civil law as the essential means of securing individual freedom, the freedom of states is achieved by enhancing their power vis-à-vis other states.[7] The result is that the preservation of individual states will at least sometimes conflict with the aim of preserving all mankind. This is particularly the case given Locke specifies that the executive's exercise of power in respect of outsiders and other states is unconstrained by the framework of civil law and right that limits its power in respect of its own citizens (1952, 145–7). This means that the subjects of civil law are accorded a status and recognition very different from the status and recognition accorded to individuals (and analogously to states) as subjects of natural law.

6 Simmons (2001, 183) similarly suggests that Locke 'appears to want to deny the *possibility* of conflict between our legitimate political obligations (owed to our local political communities) and any larger responsibilities (under natural law) to persons generally'.

7 Arguably, Locke intended his account of political legitimacy to answer to conditions in a world of emerging mercantile or 'welfare-warfare' states – 'a zero sum, balance of power system of military and commercial rivalry with other European states over the conquest, colonization and exploitation of the non-European world' (Tully 1993, 85. The phrase 'welfare-warfare state' is taken by Tully from Lawrence Stone).

Conferred Rights versus Natural Rights

I have argued that equality within the Lockean commonwealth is a product of mutual recognition – it is a feature of the founding contract. On the basis of their constituted equality, citizens are the subjects of conferred rights. They may also be the subjects of natural rights, but these rights are different in kind to conferred rights. To the extent that natural rights can be enforced by individuals in the state of nature (using what force they can muster either individually or in league with others), such rights are surrendered upon entry to civil society. Locke says that men in civil society 'give up the equality, liberty, and executive power they had in the state of nature into the hands of the society, to be so far disposed of by the legislative as the good of the society shall require' (1952, 131). Elsewhere he says that individuals give up their natural political power 'into the hands of the society and therein to the governors whom the society has set over itself' (1952, 171; and see 136).

The natural executive right or 'the power of punishing' breaches of the law of nature is, in Locke's words, 'wholly' surrendered, and each man now 'engages his natural force ... to assist the executive power of the society, as the law thereof shall require' (1952, 129). Natural liberty is relinquished to the degree required by 'the good, prosperity, and safety of the society' (1952, 130). While the natural liberty of man 'is to be free from any superior power on earth', the 'liberty of man in society is to be under no other legislative power but that established by consent in the commonwealth' (1952, 22). The 'freedom of men under government is to have a standing rule to live by, common to every one of that society' (1952, 22).

Not only are the general liberties and the executive right of nature surrendered in civil society, but property rights acquired in the state of nature are also transformed. The impact on natural property rights of the institution of civil society is the subject of debate. Locke himself says that 'every man, when he at first incorporates himself into any commonwealth ... by his uniting himself thereunto, annexes also, and submits to the community, those possessions which he has or shall acquire that do not already belong to any other government' (1952, 120). Simmons (1992, 310) argues that the parties to the social contract give up those natural rights which 'must be surrendered for effective government to be possible'. In his view, this means that Locke's various references to property being 'fixed', 'settled', 'secured' and 'regulated' in civil society have different implications for chattels and for land. While natural rights to chattels will generally be recognised in civil society, rights to land will be recognised only insofar as this is consistent with preserving the territorial integrity of the state – as Locke says, the commonwealth will not permit 'any part of [its] dominions to be dismembered' (1952, 117).[8] Tully argues, on the other hand, that the institution of civil society involves a fundamental reconstituting of property rights, with the state responsible for redistributing property in accordance with the relative contributions made by each member of society to the public good (1993, 119 and ff.). He recognises, however, that

> there would be some continuity between the possessions held in the state of nature and those protected in political society, at least for the industrious and rational, and this because the legislators are bound by natural law to ensure property in the product of one's labour insofar as this is consistent with the public good. (1993, 121, citing Locke, *The Second Treatise*, 45)[9]

My argument is that the legislators are directly bound only by the trust invested in them by the parties to the original contract. While this trust requires the legislature to respect the general tenets of natural law, so that the content of conferred rights as a general rule replicates the content of natural rights (this is, after all, what motivated citizens to contract with each other in the first place) the 'public good' now, as Tully agrees, determines the issue.[10]

My claim that conferred rights are not continuous with natural rights in Locke's taxonomy, and that the sphere of civil law and justice establishes relationships of obligation different in kind to moral obligations, is contentious. Most commentators agree with Hutchings (1995, 5) that 'Locke's citizens as members of, and participants in, a particular political order are first and foremost

8 In Steiner's view, there is no sound basis for this prohibition on individual secession within the context of Locke's theory of rights – as he puts it, it 'flies in the face of basic Lockean … property right principles' (1992, 93). While this is correct, the prohibition is perfectly consistent with the moral significance that Locke implicitly attributes to the political body and its territorial home.

9 Contrast this with Miller 2011, 96.

10 Although they disagree about the effect on natural property rights of the transition from the state of nature to civil society, both Simmons and Tully assume that property rights in civil society will be limited by the claims of needy individuals. Tully argues there are natural limits on individual property rights which in civil society are converted to charitable claims and the limits imposed by reference to the public good (1993, 113). For Simmons, limits on natural property rights are a consequence of positive duties that he says stem from the natural law of preservation, but like Tully, he thinks these limits will be recognised in civil society in the form of claims to charity (1992, 326–7). In Tully and Simmons' reading of Locke, then, the claims of justice and of right will not necessarily trump the claims of charity and morality. There is some support for this position in comments made by Locke in *The Second Treatise* and elsewhere (see, for example, *The First Treatise* 2003, 42 and *The Second Treatise* 1952, 183), but in cases in which Locke envisages principles of charity overriding principles of justice, this is a matter of individual conscience rather than of enforceable law or right.

individuals who are members of, and participants in, a universal moral order'. Jones (1994, 76) also rehearses a widely accepted argument when he suggests that 'the establishment of political authority [does] not mean the disappearance of natural rights. On the contrary, men carr[y] their natural rights forward with them into political society'.

This is a position defended by Waldron (1984) in a well-known article attacking Tully's claim that Lockean natural property rights are surrendered when individuals enter civil society. Such interpretations suggest that the political realm is a subset of the moral realm, and that the rights and obligations proper to the moral realm do not disappear in the political realm but instead are more effectively secured. It is also implicit in these interpretations that because all humans (or at least, all rational individuals) are the subjects of natural rights, these rights will be recognised in any society founded on recognition of man's natural freedom and equality. This is not, however, the case for Locke. Natural rights are purely moral rights, and as such, they are not recognised as binding in a constituted political community. They are heard as appeals to charity or compassion that may register in the conscience of individuals but are not publicly enforceable appeals to justice.

Despite what I have just said, there is certainly explicit support in *The Second Treatise* for a reading that assumes the continuity of natural and conferred rights. As we saw earlier, Locke claims repeatedly that natural law persists in civil society and that man enters civil society in order 'to preserve his property' (see Waldron 1984, 98 fn. 2) – thus implying that conferred rights are simply an enforceable form of natural property rights. According to Waldron, Locke's claim that government 'is obliged to secure every one's property by providing against those ... defects ... that made the state of nature so unsafe and uneasy' makes sense only if 'we assume that the property entitlements which are to be secured under government are the same as the property entitlements whose enforcement was so insecure in the state of nature' (1984, 98, citing Locke, *The Second Treatise*, 131). But while the property that is the object of rights may be the same, I have shown that the rights themselves are different in kind. The distinctions between natural and conferred rights can be summarised as follows: firstly, conferred rights are determinate. Natural rights conform to and are recognised by the natural law, but despite the fact the natural law is 'the common rule and measure God has given to mankind' (Locke, 1952, 11), 'it serves not, as it ought, to determine the rights and fence the properties of those that live under it' (1952, 136). Secondly, conferred rights are socially mediated – the standard to which they must conform is 'the public' or the 'common' good (131). Thirdly, and as a result of the fact that conferred rights are socially mediated, they cannot be universal. When a man enters society, Locke says that he gives up the natural right 'of doing whatsoever he thought fit for the preservation of himself *and the rest of mankind* ... to be regulated by laws made by the society, so far forth as the preservation of himself *and the rest of that society* shall require' (1952, 129, my emphasis).

Close attention to the distinctions that Locke draws between natural and conferred rights, as well as to his defence of sovereign states and his account of the public good within states, demonstrates that there is a fissure in his theory between the realm of natural law and rights, and that of civil law and conferred rights. Because of this divide, governments constituted in accordance with Locke's account of political legitimacy have only very limited obligations to recognise the natural rights of outsiders. These obligations are derived from the moral or natural obligations of their citizens. They are weaker, and of a different order, to the obligations of justice owed by the state to its citizens and by citizens to their compatriots.

Locke's Account of the Common Good

In Locke's account, the public or common good is more than simply an amalgamation of individual rights. Because it founds a more substantive conception of the political community than Locke's account of political legitimacy justifies, it pulls against the universalism of his theory, and bolsters the distinction I am pointing to between conferred and natural rights. It also demonstrates the distinctive standing that Locke accords to members of the political community. Although the role of the community and the 'public good' in Locke's theory has been widely ignored or downplayed, 'the people' in fact functions implicitly as a national body whose unity is to be preserved even at the cost of individual rights, and always against the claims and intrusions of outsiders.

When Locke says that men give up their natural liberty and equality in civil society, he cautions that each does so 'only with an intention … the better to preserve himself, his liberty and his property', thus 'the power of the society, or legislative constituted by them, can never be supposed to extend farther than the common good' (1952, 131). Here the common good sounds like nothing more than the sum of all individual rights. Elsewhere, however, Locke refers to the community as a discrete entity that can be distinguished from its members: for example, he says that the legislative is entitled 'to direct how the force of the commonwealth shall be employed for preserving the community *and the members of it*' (1952, 143, my emphasis). Furthermore, the community created by the agreement of its individual members is repeatedly individuated – it is sometimes 'one body politic' (as in 1952, 95), often simply 'one body' (see, for example, 1952, 87, 89, 96, 242), and in respect of outsiders, it functions as an organic unity: 'though in a commonwealth the members … are distinct persons still in reference to one another … yet, in reference to the rest of mankind, they make one body which is … still in the state of nature with the rest of mankind' (1952, 145).

As I have emphasised already, the community is united through the agreement of its members and only subsequently invests its government with power, thus the unity of the people as 'one entire and independent body' precedes the establishment of the state (1952, 211). Locke also says that we must

> distinguish between the dissolution of the society and the dissolution of the government. That which makes the community and brings men out of the

> loose state of nature into one politic society is the agreement which everybody has with the rest to incorporate and act as one body, and so be one distinct commonwealth. The usual and almost only way this union is dissolved is the inroad of foreign force making a conquest upon them. (1952, 211)

Thus governments may be unseated and new governments instituted without the dissolution of the body politic, which in these circumstances retains 'the native and original right … to preserve itself' (1952, 220).

Within civil society, the natural law of universal preservation becomes a law first for the preservation of society and only secondly for the preservation of its individual members. The rule that all members must be preserved is subordinate to the rule that society must be preserved: 'the first and fundamental natural law which is to govern even the legislative itself is the preservation of the society and, *as far as will consist with the public good*, of every person in it' (1952, 220, my emphasis). The preservation of the body politic is identified as an end in itself and the basic constitutive principle of the political community: 'a constituted commonwealth' acts 'according to its own nature' when it acts 'for the preservation of the community' (1952, 149). Furthermore, the right to dissolve the legislative or rebel against the executive, although traceable to the ends for which government was originally constituted – thus the preservation of each individual's liberty and property, is a *collective* right:

> there remains still *in the people* a supreme power to remove or alter the legislative when they find the legislative act contrary to the trust reposed in them … *the community* perpetually retains a supreme power of saving themselves from the attempts and designs of anybody, even of their legislators. (1952, 149, my emphasis)

> Whenever the legislators endeavour to take away and destroy the property of *the people* … by this breach of trust they forfeit the power the people had put into their hands for quite contrary ends, and *it devolves to the people*, who have a right to resume their original liberty and, by the establishment of a new legislative … provide for their own safety and security. (1952, 222, my emphasis)

As noted above, Locke routinely implies that the preservation of the community and the preservation of its individual members – like the preservation of distinct political communities and mankind generally – is not only compatible, but can be assimilated (see, for example, 1952, 239). The coherence of his model of political legitimacy depends on this being true. On occasion, however, he acknowledges that the preservation of society may conflict with the preservation of some of its members. This is implied in his discussions of the power of the majority (1952, 95–9). Everyone is bound 'to be concluded by the majority' (1952, 96); if political action were only possible with the consent of all citizens, the body politic would soon dissolve, given 'the variety of opinions and contrariety of interests which unavoidably happen in all collections of men' (1952, 98). The possibility of conflict between 'the public good' and individual interests is also evident when Locke attaches some form of limitation to the claim that the end of society is the preservation of each of its members, as when he says that it is a 'fundamental law of nature and government' that '*as much as may be*, all the members of society are to be preserved' (1952, 159, my emphasis).[11]

Self-preservation conditions the legitimate ends of civil society in the very limited sense that individuals retain the right to 'appeal to heaven' (1952, 20, 168, 176, 241), that is, to publicly argue for their rights and their interpretation of them against the excesses of government. This does not mean, though, that repressive treatment in the name of the public good is unjustified – if the individual chooses to oppose a government that is supported by the majority in the belief that the government's actions breach natural law, his only hope is for justice in heaven, he cannot expect to be vindicated on earth. Locke makes it clear that society does not have an overriding duty to defend the rights of individuals when he dismisses the suggestion that the right to appeal to heaven – and thus to appeal to the natural law against the dictates of civil law – is a threat to the stability of government. He reassures his readers that attacks on individual rights will not move citizens to rebel against their government until the rights of the majority are threatened: that is, until 'the inconvenience is so great that the majority feel it and are weary of it' (1952, 168; and see 230). Locke concludes his discussion of the people's collective right to dissolve government by emphasising:

> the power that every individual gave the society when he entered into it can never revert to the individuals again as long as the society lasts, but will always remain in the community, because without this there can be no community, no commonwealth, which is contrary to the original agreement. (1952, 243)

Thus the 'original agreement' forges a community not simply of individual rights holders but of common purpose – a people or a nation whose unity transcends and outlasts its individual members, promising a degree of stability that Locke's account of individual rights is – on its own terms – patently ill-equipped to provide.

Natural Law in the Service of Empire

Beyond the boundaries of this 'independent community' (1952, 133), Locke's universal community of mankind is either ignored by civil law – outsiders having been left in a state of 'perfect freedom' to devise their own rights protecting arrangements, or it is treated as a community of natural competitors, with whom

11 In a different context, Simmons (1992, 94 fn. 75) cites Locke's claim in 'An Essay on Toleration' that considerations of the common good 'limit and alter the obligation even of some of the laws of God'.

peaceful relations are possible, but likely to be fraught. For British and European thinkers, the Americas represented an expansive horizon for development, and the prospect of access to almost unlimited natural resources. Competition to secure this access was fierce, however, and faced determined resistance from indigenous peoples. Locke's account of property rights and political legitimacy is an intervention in a political and theoretical debate that, in Tully's words, 'raged across Europe and America from the early sixteenth century to well after 1690' (1993, 146). Arguably, it represents a calculated challenge to the indigenous Americans' claim to be 'self-governing nations exercising sovereign authority over their people and their territory' (Tully 1993, 147–8). Waldron suggests it is more likely that the punitive features associated with Locke's international 'state of nature' were primarily directed against European autocrats (2002, 148–50, in Ward 2006, 701), but in my reading these features could nevertheless be relied on to support British colonialism.[12] Locke was well versed in what Europeans knew of Indigenous American peoples[13] and he was centrally involved in the development of English policy concerning the Americas. According to Tully (1993, 140), in his role assisting Lord Shaftesbury, who was secretary of the Lord Proprietors of Carolina between 1668 and 1671, and secretary to the Council of Trade and Plantations between 1696 and 1700, Locke was 'one of six or eight men who closely invigilated and helped to shape the old colonial system during the Restoration'. Locke's public role was also supplemented by a personal, entrepreneurial interest, as an investor in the 'slave-trading Royal Africa Company (1671) and the Company of Merchant Adventurers to trade with the Bahamas (1672)' (Tully 1993, 140–41).

Throughout *The Second Treatise*, Locke uses America as a point of contrast with 'civilized' society, and refers to the 'inland, vacant places of America' as an example of the state of nature (1952, 36). At the close of his discussion of the state of nature, Locke dismisses the supposed 'mighty objection' that there never were 'any men in such a state' by claiming not only that international society remains a state of nature, but also that the Swiss and Indian confronting each other in 'the woods of America' are 'perfectly in a state of nature with reference to one another' (1952, 14). His chapter on the institution of property is full of references to America. It is in the context of these repeated references that Locke says 'there are still great tracts of ground to be found which … lie waste, and are more than the people who dwell on it do or can make use of, and so still lie in common' (1952, 45). In the following section he uses 'Americans' as an example of people still participating in the 'global common' whose activities continue to be

12 For a more qualified reading of the 'colonial implications' of Locke's argument, see Ward 2006, 700–701.

13 Tully (1993, 140) says that 'Locke had extensive knowledge of and interest in European contact with aboriginal peoples. A large number of books in his library are accounts of European exploration, colonization and of aboriginal peoples, especially Amerindians and their ways'.

based on subsistence, rather than the monetary exchange system (1952, 46). And in subsequent sections he refers to 'the middle of the inland parts of America' as 'the wild common of nature' (1952, 48), claiming that 'in the beginning all the world was America' (1952, 49). When he turns, in Chapter 8, to a discussion of the inception of political societies, he comments that America yet remains 'a pattern of the first ages in Asia and Europe' (1952, 108). In his discussion of conquest, Locke says that a conqueror in a just war is entitled to fair reparations, but does not thereby acquire a right to any significant portion of the land of those he has conquered because the value of land is so great. Locke is, however, careful to limit his discussion to land that is 'cultivated'. Echoing his earlier account of the trifling value of uncultivated land by comparison to cultivated land (1952, 43), Locke considers the possible extent of reparations that may be due to a conqueror and concludes that even 'five years product is not worth the perpetual inheritance of land', but qualifies this with the phrase, 'where all is possessed and none remains waste' (1952, 184). On the other hand, 'half a year's product is more worth than the inheritance [that is, the right to inherit the land itself], where, there being more land than the inhabitants possess and make use of, any one has liberty to make use of the waste' (1952, 184).

As Locke's pointed comparisons make clear, the relationship to land, and the property claims asserted on the basis of this relationship by indigenous American peoples against Europe's colonial ambitions, do not conform to his account of property rights. Nor did indigenous governance structures conform to his account of constituted political societies based on established institutions of justice that administer written laws. Locke suggests, for example, that the kings of Indians 'are little more than generals of their armies' whose power devolves in peacetime to a 'plurality of governors' (1952, 108; and see 102). Locke was well aware that his account of property rights based on settled agriculture and continuous cultivation of land, and civil society based on standing laws for the regulation of property and disputes between citizens, could be challenged – and had been challenged – by alternative accounts of political community. Tully (1993, 150, 154, 156–7) cites contributions to the colonial debate that opposed the characterisation of America as a wasteland open to appropriation by referring to evidence of systematic and careful land management by the Amerindian nations, often involving seasonal cultivation, as well as land clearing and hunting. Locke would also have been aware of the 'unwritten yet orally transmitted system of [Amerindian] customary law' and of the 'national, clan, and family systems of community property and distribution' recognised by the Amerindian nations (Tully 1993, 153).

The significance of Locke's portrayal of America as still in a state of nature, and thus part of the 'global common', extends beyond legitimating the colonial appropriation of indigenous lands; it also allowed attacks by indigenous peoples on colonial interests to be characterised as breaches of the natural law, invoking the right of war, and the attendant right to punish, destroy and enslave. While, in his opening discussion of the state of nature, Locke emphasises the need to punish breaches of natural law in a measured and proportionate manner (1952, 8), he also suggests, using the example of a thief, that the threat of imminent violence gives rise to a right to put someone to death (1952, 18). In his discussions of the state of war (1952, ch. 3), which may intrude upon the state of nature as it may upon civil society; of despotical power (1952, 172–4); and of conquest (1952, ch. 16); Locke makes it very clear that any use of 'force without right', including taking another's possessions, accords to the victim or victims 'the right of war', which is the right to put the violator to death or instead to enslave him. While Locke's account of conquest is generally couched as a discussion concerning confrontations between sovereign powers, it applies equally to confrontations between a constituted body such as a colonial power and individuals in the state of nature, as he characterises indigenous American peoples. Thus attacks by these peoples on colonists' persons or property – including land to which the indigenous peoples claimed title – were a breach of the law of nature and were punishable by death or enslavement:

> slaves ... being captives taken in a just war, are by the right of nature subjected to the absolute dominion and arbitrary power of their masters. These men, having ... forfeited their lives and with it their liberties, and lost their estates, and being in the state of slavery not capable of any property, cannot in that state be considered as any part of civil society. (1952, 85)

As in classical times, the universalism of the 'law of nature' provides an excuse in Locke for a politics of imperialism whose reality could not seem further from the stirring claim that man's natural state is one 'of perfect freedom' and equality (Locke 1952, 4).

Chapter 6
Liberalism's False Promise II: Kant

Introduction

More than a century after the publication of Locke's *The Second Treatise of Government*, Immanuel Kant published a series of works concerned with politics and the role of the state that echoes Locke in many respects.[1] Like Locke, Kant affirms the freedom and equality of all men under a universal law of nature, and bases political legitimacy on the idea of a social contract that secures the freedom of each in a manner consistent with the freedom of all. Kant also characterises the international sphere as a state of nature, but he goes beyond Locke in his articulation of the conditions necessary to the achievement of international peace and in his identification of 'cosmopolitan right'. Kant is thus widely considered to have inaugurated a new era of liberal cosmopolitanism – an era in which liberalism's universalist commitments are more clearly articulated and the supra-national obligations these commitments imply recognised.[2] But while Kant was undoubtedly more concerned than Locke to theorise the conditions that would lead eventually to global peace, like Locke he characterises the civil sphere within a legitimately constituted state as the exclusive arena of justice, law and right. Outside this sphere, natural law and its extensions, including cosmopolitan right, require 'promulgation' in order to bring about a rightful condition (1996, 89) – but prior to promulgation the language of law is anomalous. The natural law is not grounded in mutuality, and obedience to it cannot be publicly compelled.

As I argued in relation to Locke, Kant's recourse to the language of natural law obscures the distinction he draws between a universal sphere of morality and a limited sphere of law, justice and rights. This distinction is, however, further muddied in Kant because he explicitly opposes the sphere of virtue, in which individuals bind themselves to act in accordance with natural law precepts, to the sphere of justice or right, in which he locates *both* civil law (which is the law of the

---

1 See, primarily: 'The Contest of Faculties' [1798] (1970); 'The Metaphysical Elements of Right' (in *The Metaphysics of Morals*) [1797] (1996); 'Perpetual Peace' [1795] (1963); 'Theory and Practice' [1792] (1970a); 'What is Enlightenment?' [1784] and 'Idea for a Universal History with a Cosmopolitan Purpose' [1784] (1963a).

See also Simmons' discussion (2001, 190 and ff.) of the 'quite extensive' similarities between Locke and Kant's theories of political legitimacy, as well as Kant's departures from Locke.

2 See the contributors to Bohman and Lutz-Bachmann (1997), and in particular Nussbaum.

legitimately constituted people and their state), and natural law precepts that relate to external relations between people but that have not been recognised in civil law. These precepts include those falling within what Kant calls the 'right of nations' (dealing with relations between neighbouring states) and 'cosmopolitan right' (concerning relations between nations globally) (1996, 89, 114, 121). Natural law principles sit uneasily within Kant's sphere of justice, however, and his account makes clear that they are not principles of justice or of right 'strictly speaking' (1996, 25). While Kant assumes that legitimate civil law is an instantiation of the natural law, and all states and their members operate within the universal ambit of the natural law, he also characterises the state as securing a distinctive political realm in which citizens are constituted as authors of the community's founding or basic law. Within the state, principles of natural law that have to do with ownership and external relations are rendered determinate and enforceable, and thereby transformed into principles of justice and right.

Like Locke, Kant relies on the 'state of nature' as a device for thinking about the role of political society, although in his penultimate work of political philosophy, *The Metaphysics of Morals*, he makes it clear that the state of nature is conceptual rather than historical. *The Metaphysics* represents Kant's most coherent and developed thinking on the question of political legitimacy and the conditions necessary to securing global peace, and it is my focus in this chapter. Because every individual is naturally free, none has an innate or inherent right to govern. In a theoretical state of nature all individuals would, Kant says, be vulnerable to attack and thus prevented from acting in accordance with their natural freedom. On this basis, all individuals have an obligation to enter into civil society or to recognise the authority of the civil society in which they are born. The institutional arrangements of the state can be considered just, Kant tells us, insofar as individuals can conceive of themselves as authors of its founding law – thus to the extent that they would be able to give their consent to the arrangements under ideal conditions of freedom. For Kant as for Locke, the purpose of political societies is to secure individuals' property, and thereby that degree of autonomy that is, in theory, consistent with other citizens' equal autonomy. As a result, Kant's account of political legitimacy is similarly apolitical – not only because it is based on the assertion of *natural* freedom and equality, but also because it assumes that individuals' interests are inherently opposed and it is premised on the need to secure to each individual a sphere of autonomy free from interference. As with Locke, there is no part of Kant's account that is concerned with establishing or sustaining a space for collaborative action.

In what follows, I discuss the universal moral framework within which Kant locates his 'doctrine of right' and explain how he distinguishes principles of virtue and principles of right. I consider how Kant characterises the state of nature, including his theory of property, before turning in the following section to discuss the sphere of civil law and conclusive rights. In the final section of the chapter, I engage with Kant's 'right of nations' and 'cosmopolitan right', drawing into question the supposed universalism of his political philosophy.

The Universal Moral Sphere

The Metaphysics of Morals sets out the framework within which Kant positions his account of political legitimacy. It is divided into two parts, the first dealing with 'the doctrine of right' (concerning external relations between individuals) and the second with 'the doctrine of virtue' (concerning internal states of mind). Both are part of the broader 'doctrine of morals' (1996, 3), dealing with the sphere within which human behaviour is governed by duty (1996, 145). This is the sphere of natural law, in which *a priori* moral laws are laws revealed by reason alone. As such, they can be distinguished from natural laws of causality. Because they are founded on principles revealed by reason, and do not pander to natural or animalistic impulses or vary according to empirical contingency, Kant describes them as laws of freedom. The freedom of individuals under a universal moral law can be contrasted with the unfreedom of individuals who are governed by appetites or desires rather than by reason and moral principle.

In Kant's account, the morality of an action depends on it being based on principles that are universalisable.[3] All rational beings have an innate dignity and equal standing as moral agents capable, through the exercise of reason, of ascertaining and upholding the universal moral law. The true nature of the human being is as a member of 'a kingdom of ends' – to be taken into account equally, and treated always as an end in himself – never *merely* as a means to further someone else's ends (1948, 97). Women are not excluded from the universal sphere of moral law and reason – they, too, have a share in reason, but Kant consistently employs the masculine pronoun. As I discuss below, he also assumes that most women will be excluded from the political sphere. No one has an innate right to govern (1996, 30), and simply by virtue of his humanity, each has an 'innate freedom' limited only by the fact that this freedom must 'coexist with the freedom of every other in accordance with a universal law' (1996, 30). 'Equality' is defined as an 'aspect' of this innate freedom and consists in 'independence from being bound by others to more than one can in turn bind them; hence a human being's quality of being his own master'.[4]

All moral laws are 'imperatives' and therefore obligation-imposing (1996, 14), but Kant argues that they can be differentiated according to whether they require compliance merely through external action or compliance for the right reasons, that is, right motivation. External action in conformity with moral law can be publicly enforced, and here '[r]ight and authorization to use coercion …

3 Kant's categorical imperative is a principle of moral universalisability: 'act upon a maxim that can also hold as a universal law' (1996, 17); 'Act only on that maxim through which you can at the same time will that it should become a universal law' (1948, 84). A 'maxim' is defined by Kant (1996, 18) as 'a *subjective* principle of action, a principle which the subject himself makes his rule (how he wills to act)'.

4 '… as well as being a human beyond reproach … since before he performs any act affecting rights he has done no wrong to anyone' (1996, 30).

mean one and the same thing' (1996, 26). It is legitimate, Kant says, to coerce action in conformity with right because this does not involve enforcing a particular mental state, and nor does it infringe the principle of universal freedom given it merely prevents the exercise of freedom by one person from impinging on another person's equal right to freedom (1996, 25). The doctrine of right is 'the sum of the conditions under which the choice of one can be united with the choice of another in accordance with a universal law of freedom' (1996, 24). Internal compliance with law, or a motivation to obey the precepts of morality because it is right to do so, must, on the other hand, be self-imposed. While Kant's doctrine of right concerns the possibility – through external lawgiving – of the outward or external conformity of actions to moral law, his doctrine of virtue deals with internal states of mind. The doctrine of right is concerned 'only with the external ... relation of one person to another' (1996, 23–4). It is '[t]he sum of those laws for which an external lawgiving is possible' (1996, 23; and see 31, 145), and it is divided into 'private right', dealing with property relations in the state of nature (1996, 37 and ff.) and 'public right', dealing with the right of a state in its relation to its individual members, right of nations, and cosmopolitan right (1996, 89). The aim of the entire doctrine of right is the achievement of peace and an end to war between individuals and between states (1996, 123).

The right of nations (dealing with relations between neighbouring states) and cosmopolitan right (concerning relations between nations globally) are, along with individual proprietary rights that have only been 'unilaterally' asserted, all part of Kant's doctrine of right; but the right of a state (concerning the state in its relations with its individual members) is the only sphere within which right has actually been realised. In the absence of the institution of external law and right, Kant posits a 'state of nature' distinguished by 'an unceasing threat of war' (1963, 92). The potential for violence in the state of nature 'lies *a priori* in the rational idea of such a condition' as it is a condition within which each is entitled 'to do *what seems right and good*' in accordance with his own reason (1996, 90). Accordingly, even well motivated individuals may come into conflict with each other as a result of conflicting judgments at which each has, in good conscience, arrived. There is no way out of this impasse in the state of nature because there is no public law to which the parties can appeal and 'no judge competent to render a verdict having rightful force' (1996, 90). So despite the fact that the natural law can be grasped 'from the decree of sound reason alone' (1996, 80), in the state of nature it is judged according to 'the private will of each' (1996, 82) and represents the expression of a 'unilateral' will (1996, 45). As a consequence, the precepts of natural law in the state of nature constitute 'private law' or 'private right' (1996, 34, 86; 1963, 131). Kant is quite clear, however, that 'lawful force ... can be found only in a general will' (1996, 45), thus any judgment in the state of nature, even those made in accordance with natural law, has 'little lawful force' (1996, 45). Kant suggests that the state of nature is not necessarily one of '*injustice*', but rather a state which is '*devoid of justice*' (1996, 90, emphasis in original).

In Kant's account (1996, 50), as in that of Locke and the early natural law theorists, all humans are in 'original possession in common' of the earth. The thesis of original possession in common allows Kant, like Locke before him, to reject an argument widely deployed by monarchists and aristocrats that a divine or natural right to govern can be traced via titles to land that has been owned since 'time immemorial'. The thesis of innate freedom is similarly a rejection of any attempt to claim a right to govern on the basis of innate superiority. On the basis of humanity's original common possession of the earth's surface (distinct from the possession in common of the civil condition, which I discuss in a moment), every individual is equally free to acquire land not already the subject of a property claim, and thereby to exclude others from the use of that land. Such acquisition is 'original acquisition', and 'any piece of land can be acquired originally' (1996, 50). The concept of freedom of choice would be senseless were original acquisition impossible, Kant says, because there would be no 'objects of choice' available in respect of which individuals could exercise their freedom to choose (1996, 41; and see 46). Kant defines an 'object of choice' as 'something that I have the *physical* power to use' (1996, 41), and he argues that possession is a precondition of use because individuals' interests are inherently opposed, thus mutually beneficial use of common land is impossible (1996, 54). If land is to be used, it must be subject to individual title.

Kant acknowledges in passing the possibility of collective land ownership and use rights that are held in common: 'in Mongolia ... since all the land belongs to the people, the use of it belongs to each individual' (1996, 53). While this land is not owned by any one person, Kant appears to accept that it is not thereby rendered unusable. Kant may be relying here on a distinction between land that is held 'in common', and land that is the subject of a collective claim or title. While 'original common possession' of the earth's surface means no one has any greater right than anyone else to the use of particular areas of land, a claim to collective possession is a claim by a specific group of people in respect of a specific area, and it allows that group of people an exclusive right to use that area, as well as the right to exclude others from it. Recognition of collective land ownership may, therefore, sit quite comfortably within a broader framework of ownership based on private title, but Kant's reference to Mongolia nevertheless undercuts his claim that the use of land depends on the ability of individuals to assert an exclusive title to it. While the act of taking original possession is an expression of a 'unilateral will', Kant claims 'its possibility is ... an immediate consequence of the postulate of practical reason' (1996, 51) which specifies that 'it is a duty of right to act towards others so that what is external (usable) could also become someone's' (1996, 42).

Because it is based on an individual's unilateral will, original acquisition only establishes a provisional right (1996, 52), but Kant claims that under certain conditions this provisional right can nevertheless be characterised as 'true' or 'valid' and in conformity with universal laws of freedom (1996, 54). Original acquisition will be consistent with universal freedom, Kant says, if the land in question has not previously been claimed by anyone else; if the person asserting a claim to it has the capacity to bring it under his control and to use it; and if his 'will' to make it his own is 'in conformity with the idea of a possible united *will*' (1996, 47, emphasis in original) – that is, if he asserts his title provisionally, with 'a view to' 'the establishment of the civil condition' (1996, 54). The way in which a person takes possession is by exercising control over the land (1996, 48, 51), where control is equated with the ability to defend the land (52 and 56). Although in the earlier 'Theory and Practice' Kant implies that rightful acquisition is at least partially dependent on a proprietor's ability to cultivate the land with his own hands (1970a, 78), in *The Metaphysics* he explicitly rejects the Lockean principle that original acquisition is only achieved through the development or cultivation of land – the assertion of control is, Kant says, all that is required (1996, 52 and 55). Possession of land will also accord a provisional right, without needing to do anything in particular to assert that right, to the corporeal things found on the land (1996, 55).

Civil Law and Conclusive Rights

Individuals move from empirical possession to intelligible (and thus rationally defensible) possession through entry into a civil condition within which each agrees to respect his compatriots' possessions. Despite Kant's claim that all individuals have an 'innate freedom' under a universal moral law, he states that 'freedom in accordance with universal laws' is only possible in civil society (1996, 45). Physical possession of property in the state of nature is 'in anticipation of and preparation for the civil condition' (1996, 45; see also 52). The acquisition and its defensibility necessarily remain provisional until the institution of the civil condition; without the sanction of public law or the possibility of institutional enforcement, there are no conclusive rights (1996, 90). The concept of ownership in accordance with right, combined with the impossibility of defending the rightful status of ownership in the absence of a coercive legal framework, provides the grounds on which a person can compel another to enter the civil condition. Given, Kant says, that we must assume the possibility of ownership, we must also posit 'a right to constrain everyone with whom we could have dealings to enter with us into a constitution in which external objects can be secured as mine or yours' (1996, 45).

As I discuss below, however, this is not a 'right' properly speaking, and it does not provide a basis for outsiders to obtain entry to and equality within a legitimately constituted state. It is only within a constituted community based on mutual rights-recognition that natural rights which individuals hold provisionally under a universal moral law are rendered determinate and enforceable. The civil condition is, Kant says, 'the only state in which men can possess rights' (1970a, 81); without the sanction of public law or the possibility of institutional enforcement, there are no conclusive rights (1996, 90). Kant actually defines 'a right to a thing' as a right 'to the private use of a thing of which I am in ... possession in common with all others' (1996, 49). Here the concept of 'possession in common' refers to an institutional framework or community of rights holders within which the private possessions of each are recognised in accordance with laws that hold for all (1996, 50).[5] Only such a community allows, according to Kant's reasoning, a person to move from asserting a claim to an object on the basis of physical control to having that claim recognised regardless of whether or not the object is in his physical control at any particular time. Even rights in respect of one's own body depend upon a community of rights recognition. This community ensures that the potential for violence inherent in a condition in which every person is entitled to do 'what seems right and good' in accordance with his own reason is ameliorated, and the physical integrity of each is equally protected.

Kant's legitimately constituted community thus ensures that rights are impartially adjudicated and enforced. My argument goes beyond this claim, however, to suggest that it actually constitutes its members as the bearers of the rights that it secures. As such, it accords them a distinctive legal personality that is not shared by outsiders. This legal persona is not simply a creature of positive law – it is founded on a broader conception of justice, as can be seen from the fact that Kant characterises the social contract as an ideal. He says that the 'act by which a people forms itself into a state is the *original contract*',[6] but he adds: '[p]roperly speaking, the original contract is only the idea of this act, in terms of which alone we can think of the legitimacy of a state' (1996, 92–3). In ideal terms, the original contract is an emanation of what Kant calls a 'lawgiving will' that is united 'not contingently but *a priori* and therefore necessarily' (1996, 51). This idea of a state based on 'pure principles of right' 'serves as a norm ... for every actual union into a commonwealth' (1996, 90).

Every 'actual union into a commonwealth' falls short of the ideal, however, given that it is an 'acquired' right. This must be so given Kant's thesis of humanity's original ownership in common of the earth's surface. Because acquired rights are 'strict' rights that can be publicly compelled and do not involve any appeal to individuals' internal moral reasons for acting (1996, 25), it would be impossible in a genuine state of nature governed only by the natural law to motivate a move by individuals from that state to the civil condition. Kant acknowledges as much when he says that in actuality, all civil constitutions are founded in violence, and when he denies that members of civil societies are entitled to enquire into the legitimacy of the founding of those societies (1996, 95; 1963a, 15). Rather, the legitimacy of

5 While Kant's account of humanity's original possession in common of the earth's surface maps very closely his account of the civil community of possession within which rights are secured, in the former case individuals' possession is in conformity with right but 'prior to any act of choice that establishes a right' (1996, 50).

6 Strictly speaking this involves two acts: the mutual agreement (or social contract) among members of 'a people' in which they agree to enter into rightful relations with each other – this act establishes the 'civil condition'; and then the act by which the people establishes the institutions of government and state (see 1996, 89).

all actually constituted societies depends on the degree to which their basic law conforms to the concept of the social contract as a law of equal freedom.

While Kant describes the social contract as an 'omnilateral' acquisition[7] derived from the particular individual wills of everyone who is party to it (1996, 48), not all members of Kant's legitimately constituted community are full parties to this founding contract. Kant draws a distinction in *The Metaphysics* between 'active' and 'passive' citizens. Active citizens have three rights that are attributes of citizenship, and 'inseparable' – in Kant's words – from the individual's 'essence as a citizen' (1996, 91). Kant's identification of these rights demonstrates clearly the constituted character of the active citizen's legal persona. The first right is to 'lawful freedom': 'the attribute of obeying no other law than that to which he has given his consent' (1996, 91); the second is to 'civic equality', or the right to be bound in matters of right only to the same degree as a person can in turn bind others (1996, 91); and the third is reflected in the concept of 'civic independence', which implies 'owing [one's] existence and preservation to [one's] own rights and powers as a member of the commonwealth' (1996, 91). Kant adds that civic independence accords an individual 'civic personality', which is the 'attribute of not needing to be represented by another where rights are concerned' (1996, 91; and see 94; 1970a, 74). Through these rights active citizens are constituted as equals within a sphere of mutual rights recognition. They adopt the legal persona of equals and on this basis claim rights that are grounded in justice and mutuality.

The constituted character of the active citizen's freedom, equality and civic independence is obviously significant not only for people outside the state, but also for those insiders described by Kant as 'passive' citizens. Active citizenship accords a right to vote and is based on being financially self-supporting (1996, 91–2). Thus the 'passive' citizens in a state include, Kant says, women, children, apprentices, domestic servants and indentured labourers (1996, 92). But while passive citizens do not share the rights of active citizens, and so are not entitled to be self-legislating contributors to the management of the state nor to be viewed as equals under its constitutive law, they are nevertheless *potentially* equals in a manner in which outsiders are not. The regulative ideal of the social contract is one of equality among all members of the community established by the contract. Kant supports his claim that the inequality of passive citizens is 'in no way opposed to their freedom and equality *as human beings*' by explaining that passive citizens, along with their active compatriots, 'together make up a people' (1996, 92). Furthermore, active citizens cannot, through legislation, exclude passive citizens from the possibility of working their way up from the 'passive condition to an active one' (1996, 92). Passive citizens as members of the people are entitled to become active citizens through the acquisition of property, and subsequently to be thought of as participants in the social contract. Outsiders, who are not part of

7 As such, it is distinguished from 'unilateral' acquisition through individual action in the state of nature.

the people on which the state and its law are based, do not have the same standing from which to claim participation or recognition under the state's basic law.

The concept of the social contract thus invokes more than an ideal of individual self-legislation and consent to the coercive power of government. As I've said already, in ideal terms it is based on a necessarily united lawgiving will. In practice, this *necessarily* united will appears, in Kant's account, in the form of a 'general will' emanating from 'a people' that – he says – has 'an original right to unite itself into a commonwealth' (1996, 119). 'The people' exists independently of the institution of government and membership of the people is inherited; it is for this reason, Kant says, that 'a state is also called a nation' (1996, 89). The 'natural' unity of the people is also indicated by Kant's claim that even if internal discord among a people in the state of nature does not induce them to institute a social contract among themselves, the necessity of defending themselves against other peoples will do so, because 'nature has placed each people near another which presses upon it, and against this it must form itself into a state in order to defend itself' (1963, 111).[8] Within the lawfully constituted state, 'the people' are the source of law and authority: the state's basic law, Kant says 'can come only from the general, united will of the people' (1970a, 77; and see 75),[9] and legislative authority within the rightful state can 'belong only to the united will of the people' because '*all right is to proceed from it*' (1996, 91, my emphasis; and see 54). A 'public law', Kant claims, 'contains in its very concept the public announcement of *a general will which assigns to each his rights*' (1963, 131, my emphasis).

It is true, as I have mentioned already, that Kant claims that all individuals have a natural right to constrain others with whom they may have dealings to enter into civil society with them (1996, 45), thereby ensuring that their claims to property or to physical integrity will be secured and mediated by public law. Like other natural rights in Kant's taxonomy, however, this is only a 'provisional' right, and it doesn't provide a basis for outsiders to obtain entry to and equal recognition within the Kantian state. This fact becomes clear when we consider that the Kantian state not only unites all individual wills within one 'general will'; it also unites individuals' provisional rights to land in the territory of the state. The sovereign is to be conceived as the 'supreme proprietor' or 'lord of the land' from whom all property rights are derived (1996, 99). This conception serves, Kant says, 'to represent the necessary union of the private property of everyone within the people under a general public possessor' (1996, 99). Thus, as we saw in Locke, while the object of property rights may be the same under the law of nature and in civil society, the rights themselves are different in kind. The natural right of an individual to constrain others to enter into a civil constitution is designed to ensure

8 Flikschuh (2010, 474) characterises the people differently. In her view, Kant assumes that the constitution of the sovereign state also serves to constitute the people. Nevertheless, once constituted, she suggests that Kant treats 'state sovereignty [as] itself an expression of the will of the people'.

9 Kant nevertheless supports majoritarian decision making (1970a, 79).

that provisional rights to external objects are secured. Refugees who seek entry to and equality within the legitimately constituted state are not asserting a proprietary interest in the territory of the state (they have no basis for doing so), and nor can they assert that their proprietary interests in their own bodies depends – in their relations with the state in question – on it recognising their rights. The state poses no direct threat to the physical integrity of the outsiders; it simply wants nothing to do with them. The natural right to compel others to enter into a social contract for the establishment of a law-based society is a moral right shared by all human beings to be subject to *some* 'lawful civic' constitution (1963a, 18). In abstraction from the institution of particular civic constitutions, it would in theory provide a moral basis for compelling another 'to enter with me into a state of civil law or to remove himself from my neighbourhood' (1963, 92 fn. 1), but where a constituted society already exists, it does not provide a basis for an outsider to *move into* the 'neighbourhood', or to claim a right to enter.

Within communities other than their own, the rights claims made by outsiders have moral force, but they are not justice claims and they cannot be heard by the law that founds the community. Furthermore, insofar as the individual members of that community are concerned, while they may register in their conscience that an outsider's claim imposes an 'obligation in accordance with [a universal moral] law', this cannot, Kant says, 'be appealed to as an incentive' for action, because in the realm of 'external right' only external constraints provide motivations for action (1996, 25). If this were not the case the public law of the community would attempt to induce internal motivations, thus intruding on freedom of conscience. So outsiders as bearers of moral or natural rights are excluded from recognition in the political sphere, and because for members of the state the moral sphere is a privatised, apolitical realm, the claims that outsiders make from within this sphere mark them out as unequal. Refugees may be recognised as objects of compassion or of moral concern, but they cannot be conceived as subjects of justice.

Justice Beyond the Borders of the State?

Although a global state based on a contract of mutual rights recognition between individuals universally would in theory constitute all humans as free and equal, Kant does not advocate it. He claims in 'Perpetual Peace' that a global state would invariably degenerate into 'a soulless despotism' and then into anarchy (1963, 113).[10] Given the empirical reality of global ethnic and cultural diversity, the imposition of a single political institutional structure could only be oppressive. Despite his rarefied starting point of abstract and universal morality, then, Kant is

---

10 In 'Idea' (1963a), Kant argues in support of 'a global state' – but despite his recourse to this phrase, he also explicitly advocates here for a federation of independent states. In 'Theory and Practice' (1970a), Kant occasionally appears to support a world state but here as well he cautions against the danger of such a state descending into tyranny.

deeply committed to sustaining global pluralism. Byrd and Hruschka (2008, 631) point out that in 'Religion Within the Limits of Pure Reason' Kant describes a global political society as one in which 'all freedom and with it (which it entails) all virtue, taste and scholarship must disappear'. The standard reading of Kant's political theory is that it is based on universalist and individualist premises. Given this, Kleingeld (2012, 26) says that 'most political theorists take it to be a defining problem of Kantian theory that it leaves no theoretical space for special duties toward one's own state'. Flikschuh (2010) is an outlier in this regard, arguing directly against the founding individualism of Kant's political philosophy. In her view, because Kant claims in *The Metaphysics* that justice, law and right can only be universalised through different categories of subject within distinct spheres, Kant is not committed 'to universal moral individualism from the outset' (2010, 470). As noted already, Kant identifies 'three possible forms of rightful condition' in *The Metaphysics*: right of a state in relation to its individual members; right of nations, dealing with the relationship between neighbouring states; and right for all nations or cosmopolitan right, concerning relations between all of the world's nations (1996, 89). In the earlier 'Perpetual Peace', Kant also includes under the rubric of cosmopolitan right an individual 'right to hospitality', as I discuss further below. Flikschuh argues that Kant's doctrine of right is a systematic account of global justice whose component parts – the three spheres of right – cannot be disaggregated (2010, 470). While Flikschuh is correct to emphasise the systematic nature of Kant's conception, however, she fails to acknowledge that this conception extends beyond the doctrine of right. Kant's founding commitment to moral individualism is evidenced by the fact that *both* his doctrine of right and his doctrine of virtue, dealing with ethics, are part of the broader doctrine of morals, dealing with the realm within which human behaviour is governed by duty (1996, 3). Nevertheless, Flikschuh's reading points to why the perception that 'Kantian theory ... leaves no theoretical space for special duties toward one's own state' is incorrect. Despite his starting point of 'universal moral individualism', I have argued that Kant treats the state as a distinctive realm within which membership of the people provides the grounds for recognition as a subject of law and justice. Kant is correct to worry about the loss of political plurality and the spectre of global tyranny in a world in which an abstract moral individualism is politically enforced. We need to be clearer, however, about the implications of his attempt to navigate this concern by realising 'right' within distinct spheres – particularly for refugees in the world as we know it.

Right of Nations

In 'Perpetual Peace' and *The Metaphysics*, Kant argues for a global federation of states. Global peace, he says, and conformity to the doctrine of right, is best achieved by establishing a federative union of states. Within such a union peace does not follow from the erosion of each state's power but 'is, on the contrary, produced and maintained by their equilibrium in liveliest competition'

(1963, 114). Here the 'spirit of commerce, which is incompatible with war' (1963, 114) plays a central role within and between states. Eventually this 'spirit of commerce' is bound, Kant says, to 'gain the upper hand in every state' (1963, 114) and when it does so it will ensure that the interests of the state are to be found in the promotion of 'honourable peace' between states (1963, 114).

This is Kant's answer to the conundrum posed by the fact that all individuals, given they invariably threaten their fellows' freedom, must be subject to the compulsion of public law (they 'require a master'), but the only master available who can 'force [mankind] to obey a will that is universally valid, under which each can be free' is 'the human race' itself (1963a, 17). Man, who is incapable of self-mastery, must learn how to master himself. In 'Idea' and 'Perpetual Peace', Kant suggests that humanity can move towards a situation in which it becomes fit to 'be its own legislator' through gradually accepting 'the idea of the authority' of a law that governs everyone equally, despite the fact that it does not conform to Kant's account of civil law because it is not backed by an external coercive power (1963, 120). If individuals and states recognise that their self-interest lies in conformity to law, Kant suggests – a situation which he thinks is possible in a world of lively commercial activity – then they will begin to act as if the law that governs them is backed by physical power even though it is not. In this way, 'universally valid public laws which restrict the freedom of each' (1963, 101) will apply globally, and ensure peace and justice between states. The content of these 'universally valid public laws', as with the content of rightful legislation internal to states, is justified by reference to *a priori* principles or the 'natural law as a model presented by reason' (1963, 119).

Although justified by the same *a priori* principles, in 'Perpetual Peace' Kant envisages two forms of public law: the first applying within states and the second applying in relations between separate states. Thus public law requires 'first, an internal constitution of the state erected on pure principles of right, and, second, a convention of the state with near or distant states (analogous to a universal state) for the legal settlement of their differences' (1963, 126). While 'analogous to a universal state' this convention would not create such a state – thereby avoiding the danger of tyranny that Kant associates with a truly universal civil society, because its subjects would be discrete and self-governing states. Furthermore, while the contract among individuals to found a civil state is validly 'founded on laws of compulsion' (1963, 131), the compact that establishes public law at the international level must be voluntarily adopted by independent states. These states, like individuals within civil society, bind themselves to recognise the valid law that holds between them; but, unlike individuals, they are not forced to obey this law through the imposition of an external coercive apparatus.

In *The Metaphysics*, Kant continues to argue in favour of a federation of separate states but, as we have seen, he amplifies on the theme that the doctrine of right can only be universalised by applying it to different categories of subject within distinct spheres. Kant argues that 'the principle of outer freedom limited by law' must be enshrined in all three spheres: right of a state, right of nations, and cosmopolitan right, in order for it to be reliably secured in any of them (1996, 89). Before forging a federation of states, all states exist in an international state of nature and relate to each other as autonomous entities. The state is 'a moral person' (1996, 114) and insofar as it is legitimately constituted it relates to other states as an equal (1996, 117). The condition of natural freedom between states is, as with the state of nature between individuals, a condition of war (1996, 114) in which each state acts as judge in its own case (1996, 119). Thus each state is under an obligation to enter into civil relations with neighbouring states (1996, 114). Prior to the forging of an alliance between states, natural law principles applicable to the international state of nature (hence those principles that fall under the rubric of the right of nations) deal with the declaration and conduct of war, and require that in both cases nothing is done that will preclude the possibility of future peace and a lasting alliance between states (1996, 115). While Kant posits the need for 'a league of nations in accordance with the idea of an original social contract' (1996, 115), the contract that he calls for between states differs fundamentally from the civil contract. It should preserve the autonomy (and thus moral personality) of independent states – it serves 'not in order to meddle with one another's internal dissensions but to protect against attack from without' (1996, 115), and unlike a civil constitution based on the sovereignty of the general will, the international contract does not constitute a new law or a new society – it is instead an alliance or 'voluntary coalition' that can always be dissolved (1996, 120).

Cosmopolitan Right

The fact that 'the earth's surface is not unlimited but closed' (1996, 89) means that contact between humans globally is inevitable and thus, Kant says, the idea of cosmopolitan right becomes an imperative. Cosmopolitan right follows from the fact that all nations 'stand *originally* in a community of land' (1996, 121). As discussed already, Kant conceives of 'original possession in common' in abstraction from individually willed action. It is antecedent to the establishment of external rights or the assertion of exclusive titles to land (1996, 50–51). While 'originally no one had more right than another to a particular part of the earth' (1963, 103), the natural right 'to be wherever nature or chance' has placed a person should be distinguished from 'residence [which is] a chosen and therefore an acquired *lasting* possession' (1996, 50). Consistently with Kant's account of the state of nature and natural rights, humanity's original possession in common of the world provides a framework compatible with the institution of rights; it does not provide a right to a place in the world that is recognisable outside the context of a law-governed civil society.

Kant claims that humanity's original 'community of possession' founds a 'right' to propose commercial relations between nations: 'each has the right to make this attempt [of offering to engage in commerce] without the other being authorised to behave toward it as an enemy because it has made this attempt' (1996, 121). Kant describes this natural right of commerce or 'cosmopolitan right' as providing a potential basis for a lawfully regulated union between nations (1996, 121) – it is not a relationship between individuals as such (Kleingeld 2012, 86). Nevertheless, on the basis of cosmopolitan right individuals should, Kant thinks, be able to '*visit* all regions of the earth' (1996, 121). While the right does not provide an excuse for settlement or colonisation against the will of a land's current inhabitants, Kant claims that there exists a right to settle in any case in which land is uninhabited and the settlement does not impinge on another people's established use of the land (1996, 122). Unlike Locke, however, he is not prescriptive concerning what constitutes 'use' of land. Even where a people are nomadic or are hunters and so traverse 'great open regions' – as is the case, Kant specifically says, of 'most of the American Indian nations' (1996, 122), 'settlement may not take place by force but only by contract, and indeed by a contract that does not take advantage of the ignorance of those inhabitants with respect to ceding their lands' (1996, 122).

In 'Perpetual Peace', Kant argues that humanity's original 'common possession of the surface of the earth' founds a right to hospitality, or 'the right of a stranger not to be treated as an enemy when he arrives in the land of another' (1963, 102–3). As Kleingeld (2012, 84) argues, the right may also be based on the innate right to freedom, which Kant claims implies the authorisation to 'do to others anything that does not in itself diminish what is theirs … such … as merely communicating [one's] thoughts' (1996, 30–31). Also described as 'a right of temporary sojourn', 'a right to associate' and 'the privilege of foreign arrivals' (1963, 103), the right to hospitality is limited to 'seeking to communicate with the prior inhabitants' of another land (1963, 103). Correlating to this natural right is the duty to abstain from attacking the visitor. The correlative duty may also require an offer of temporary hospitality where turning the visitor away would result in his destruction.

Kant appears to be thinking here of a situation in which people arriving by boat, for example, cannot immediately set sail because of dangerous conditions at sea, but the principle clearly has relevance to the case of refugees. While Kant's articulation of a right to hospitality implies that such people have a right to at least temporary refuge, this is not an enforceable right. It is, like the right to be 'wherever nature or chance has placed one' more generally, a precept of natural law that does not itself accord rights properly speaking or recognition in publicly established law. Although Kant claims that hospitality 'is not a question of philanthropy but of right' (1963, 102; and see 1996, 121), its status as a precept of natural law means that it remains a non-compellable moral obligation until translated into civil law. Given the parties to the civil contract are members of the state and the state's basic law does not engage outsiders, this cannot occur at the behest of the outsider until a form of civil law is established globally, but this is an extension of civil law that Kant himself was ultimately unwilling to support.

As I noted in my introduction to this chapter, Kant's articulation of cosmopolitan right has been hailed by many as inaugurating a new era of liberal cosmopolitanism. In *The Rights of Others*, Seyla Benhabib suggests that 'Kant's discussion of cosmopolitan right … delineates a new terrain in the history of political thought' (2004, 49). Cosmopolitan right, particularly as Kant articulated it in 'Perpetual Peace', for Benhabib 'signalled a watershed' that has 'paved the way for the transition' from a Westphalian conception of sovereignty to a conception that might be called 'liberal international sovereignty' (2004, 40). In my reading, however, Kant's cosmopolitan right is indebted to a natural law tradition that, despite its use of the language of moral universalism, accords distinctive status to political communities and to their members. In addition, Kant's reliance on 'the people' as the ground of rights within the state echoes Locke and reflects liberalism's implicit recourse to the nation as a source of solidarity among autonomous rights-bearing citizens. Benhabib herself is well aware of these tensions in the liberal democratic tradition, and in *The Rights of Others* she is actively engaged with a version of Habermas' co-originality thesis, which she calls 'the paradox of democratic legitimacy' (2004, 43).

As well as identifying the tension arising from the democratic state's dual sources of legitimacy in the constitutive mutual recognition of 'rights-bearing consociates' on the one hand, and 'universal principles of human rights' on the other (2004, 44), Benhabib links this tension to 'the juridical and moral ambivalence that affects discussions of the right of asylum and refuge to this day' (2004, 29). In Benhabib's view, Kant's account of the right to hospitality 'provides no clear answer' as to whether this is a right 'in the sense of [a] *reciprocal moral obligation* ... grounded upon our mutual humanity' or 'in the legal sense of being [an] *enforceable norm* ... of behavior which individuals and groups can hold each other to and, in particular, force sovereign nation-states to comply with' (2004, 29). While no mechanism currently exists under which a right to hospitality might be enforced, Benhabib suggests that it is nevertheless part of 'a sphere of right – *in the juridical and moral* senses of the term – *between* domestic constitutional and customary international law' (2004, 49, my emphasis). While this reading is consistent with Kant's terminology and his inclusion of cosmopolitan right within his doctrine of right, it fails to recognise the distinctive status that I have shown Kant accords to civil law and to citizens as the subjects and authors of this law.

PART III

Chapter 7
Scum of the Earth II: Contemporary Refugees

Introduction

In Chapter 1, I argued that Europe's inter-war refugees were forced outside the pale of the law. Arguably, their predicament arose because the idea of human rights carried very little weight in international law before World War Two. Individuals were entitled to claim rights directly only against the state of which they were citizens. Where states recognised the rights of visitors or non-citizen residents, they did so on the basis of inter-state treaty obligations or principles of reciprocity, or in accordance with provisions of domestic legislation such as naturalisation laws that they were free to limit or change at will. These principles and legislative provisions afforded no comfort to refugees. Without a legal identity protected and secured by their national state, and denied a right to remain by their host state, the presence of the refugees was anomalous. The refugees could be treated with impunity, and had no legal standing on which to contest their treatment nor recognised political avenue through which to seek redress.

Things are different now. An international refugee regime is administered by the Office of the United Nations High Commissioner for Refugees (UNHCR) and supplemented by an international human rights regime that proclaims and supports the universalism of human rights. States remain the main duty bearers with respect to rights protection and realisation, but they now have international obligations to accord rights to all individuals within their jurisdiction regardless of nationality or citizenship status, and individuals are accorded standing and recognition in international law to a degree unknown prior to World War Two. Protection for individual rights has also increased within many liberal democracies and at the regional level.[1] Nevertheless, I demonstrate in this and the following chapter that many refugees continue to be forced outside the pale of the law. The conflict that I have been discussing between the universalism of rights and the sovereignty of the nation in the history of Western European nation-states, as well as in classical liberalism, is writ large in our current world order. Despite the changes wrought by globalisation, this order continues to be structured on the basis of state sovereignty and the sovereign autonomy of states is presupposed by international human

1 See, for example, Canadian Charter of Rights and Freedoms 1982; Human Rights Act 1993 (NZ); Human Rights Act 1998 (UK); Convention for the Protection of Human Rights and Fundamental Freedoms 1950 (Council of Europe).

rights law. In Chapter 8, I discuss the claim that human rights are progressively 'humanising' international law and tempering the influence of sovereignty. While this claim has merit insofar as states' treatment of their own citizens and lawful residents is concerned, it has little bearing in the arena of migration policy. States' sovereign rights remain largely unfettered in respect of those who are unlawfully present or whose legal status is qualified by reference to their arrival without legal authorisation, and the supplementary status provided by international law does not bring these refugees within the purview of the liberal democratic state's law. Instead, it marks them out as unequal and unworthy of full recognition under that law. In this chapter, I introduce this argument by demonstrating how the international human rights regime, including the international refugee regime, sanctions the punitive treatment of refugees. I show that it takes for granted the sovereign right of states to regulate entry and matters related to citizenship and nationality, including through the militarised protection of territorial borders. The regime also specifically qualifies the rights of refugees unlawfully present in a state's territory. Although even these refugees should, according to the rhetoric of human rights, be afforded some basic rights, they do not have standing as subjects of justice who are able to demand their rights. Instead, their capacity to access and to enjoy even their most basic rights is undermined by the reality of their unlawful or legally qualified presence, which exposes them to arrest and detention or deportation. Within liberal democracies, legal provisions that specifically exclude refugees from rights protection and from the protection of the law have also multiplied. Domestic courts have been unwilling to impugn these laws. In the main, they uphold the government's capacity to make and enforce immigration policy through draconian measures, and defer to its claim that in doing so it is defending 'the nation' and the 'sovereignty of the people'. The result is that refugees within liberal democracies, or detained in camps funded by these countries, may be denied legal status altogether or be accorded some form of qualified status, but in no case can they be considered to exist within the privileged pale of the law.

In the next section of this chapter I describe how refugees are treated when they attempt to access the territory of liberal democracies. In the following section I analyse the legal status of refugees in international law and within the legal framework of liberal democracies. I argue that liberal democracies are deeply hostile to the rights claims of refugees. In the final section of the chapter I discuss the impact that this hostility has on the rule of law and institutional rights protections within liberal democracies.

Denigrating and Punishing Refugees

The parallels between our current treatment of refugees and Western Europe's response to the inter-war refugees are striking. Also striking, however, is the fact that the measures now taken by many states to exclude, deter and punish refugees go beyond the actions of the inter-war democracies and have been more comprehensively institutionalised. As I detail below, refugees are repelled at the borders of states, but they are also actively intercepted and repelled en route to liberal democracies. They are incarcerated in third countries at the cost of liberal democracies, and smuggled across borders by officials from liberal democratic states who collaborate with abusive regimes and have been quite willing to stoop to illegal acts (see Arendt 1968, 283). Refugees are denied access to the courts and like Europe's inter-war refugees, 'driven underground' and forced into breaking the law. They are imprisoned – often for years at a time – and brutally treated. For many the search for freedom or a better life has ended in death. Unknown thousands have died in the effort to obtain access to or asylum in a Western democracy. Many others have committed suicide after months or years in detention. As in the inter-war years, there is a vast gap between the rhetoric – where it does exist – of concern for refugees and the reality of the treatment inflicted upon them.

In detailing this treatment my focus is on Australia. Since 2001, Australia has been notable for the extreme nature of its refugee policies, but its approach reflects a more general tightening of border controls across the wealthy liberal democratic world since the 1970s (Wilsher 2012, 57, 121), and the increasingly punitive nature of these controls since the early 2000s. While Australia along with the USA can be considered a world leader in draconian border policing,[2] it differs from other wealthy liberal democracies only by degrees (Gibney 2004, 192). For example, while Wilsher (2012, 58 and 107–18) argues that since World War Two France has shown more restraint towards refugees on its territory or at its borders by comparison with common law countries, he acknowledges that from the early 2000s 'French governments have followed other countries in expanding detention facilities and powers to meet expulsion targets'.

Australia has a detention regime mandating the incarceration of all non-citizens without valid visas.[3] The year 2001 marked the inauguration of its 'Pacific Solution', involving naval interception of boats carrying asylum seekers and off-shore detention and processing of protection claims (see Marr and Wilkinson 2003; Dauvergne 2008, 51–3). Both Australia and the USA, however, have long-standing mandatory immigration detention regimes.[4] In the early 1980s, the USA began intercepting Haitian and Cuban asylum seekers at sea (Wilsher 2012, 67) and since 1991 it has used its naval based at Guantánamo Bay, Cuba as an immigration detention facility (Dastyari and Effeney 2012; Wilsher 2012, 239–43).

Throughout the Western world, immigration detention centres look and function like prisons, although without the framework of legal accountability within which prisons generally operate (see Burnside 2007, 23). In Australia, refugees are incarcerated behind electrified razor wire, under constant video surveillance and

2 Dauvergne (2008, 51; and see 53, 58–9) claims that since 2001, 'Australia has been the global leader in the refugee law race to the bottom'.

3 Migration Act 1958 (Cth), s.189.

4 Dating from 1980–81 in the case of the USA (Wilsher 2012, 67) and from 1989 in Australia's case (Brennan 2002, 13).

subject to the control of private security guards whose authority is 'akin to [the] police or army' (UN Working Group 2002, 11). Official expressions of concern for human dignity and rights appear frankly craven in light of the culture in Australian detention centres and in regional detention centres funded by Australia and managed under agreement with it. Most of these centres are in remote locations where physical conditions such as heat, over-crowding and lack of access to water make living conditions for detainees very difficult (see, for example, UNHCR 2013b). Public and media access, and other forms of independent oversight, are highly restricted and often refused altogether.[5]

These factors contribute to an environment in which psychological and physical abuse of detainees by detention centre staff is widespread and has at times been endemic (Burnside 2007, 23–7, 40–41, 49–52; Curr 2008; Davies 2013; 2013a; Hunter 2013; Isaacs et al. 2013; UN Working Group 2002, 8, para. 35).[6] Detainees are referred to by number rather than name, deprived of privacy, forced to queue endlessly for meals, telephone access and medical supplies, regularly placed in solitary confinement, and subjected to bizarre punishment regimes (Australian Human Rights Commission 2013; 2012;[7] 2011; 2010; Curr 2008; Davies 2013; 2013a; Hunter 2013; McKenna 2014; UNHCR 2013a; 2013b). Burnside (2007, 37–41) notes the case of a woman whose five year old son was placed in solitary confinement while she was held in a containment cell with two other of her cshildren for 15 days. For the first two days they were refused access to a toilet: '[t]he children had to use a plastic bag which I found in the cell as a toilet. I starved myself for two days as a protest before the guards would allow the children to use the toilet [outside the cell]'.[8] In an interview with the Australian Broadcasting Corporation (2008), former guards at a detention centre on Australian territory

5 Regarding lack of media access to the detention camp funded by Australia on Manus Island, Papua New Guinea, see Laughland 2014. Australia's Human Rights Commission has also been refused access to detention centres funded by Australia in Nauru and Papua New Guinea (Cullen and Woodley 2014).

6 Abuse within Australian detention centres was particularly severe in the period 2001–2005. After a short-lived period of reform, reports of abuse are again proliferating. For a brief history of Australia's mandatory detention regime, see Australian Human Rights Commission 2013, pp. 4–5 and appendix 2.

7 In its report of its 2012 visit to Christmas Island Detention Centre, the Australian Human Rights Commission notes (2012, 19) that almost all the detainees it spoke to said they had been treated respectfully by centre staff. This is at odds with the allegations of abuse cited above, including testimony from centre staff and Australian government personnel (Davies 2013a; Hunter 2013). It is unlikely that detainees aggrieved by their treatment were allowed to speak to the Commission. Nevertheless, there are undoubtedly detention centre employees who treat detainees respectfully. Regardless of this, conditions in the centres ensure serious abuses can and do occur, and mean that a culture of abuse becomes entrenched very quickly.

8 This is just one among a number of cases detailed by Burnside. Other cases are discussed at 49–52 and 113–15.

described baton attacks on detainees as an application of 'black panadol' – Panadol is the brand name of a widely used headache tablet in Australia – and the quelling of dissent by 'Emergency Response' teams as 'gas and bash'.[9] It is not surprising that detention centres are breeding grounds for abuse and brutality given 'the strong relationship between incommunicado detention and torture' (HRLRC 2008b, 3). Refugees are sent mad by the isolation, the boredom, the fear of return to countries in which they may be killed or persecuted and the 'wracking uncertainty' of their position.[10] Suicide attempts are frequent and self-harm is rife (Australian Human Rights Commission 2013, 10; Flitton 2014). Children who enter detention without behavioural problems stop eating, stop talking and begin self-mutilating as well as attempting suicide.[11] There have also been repeated eruptions of violence in detention centres run by Australia both on its own territory and in the Pacific Island states of Nauru and Papua New Guinea (Aly 2014). As I noted in the introduction to this book, attacks on detainees held on Manus Island, Papua New Guinea in February 2014 left the 23-year-old Iranian asylum seeker Reza Berati dead, another asylum seeker wounded by gun shot, and more than 60 others seriously wounded, including with slashed throats. Detainees claimed that following a non-violent protest they were attacked by detention centre staff as well as members of Papua New Guinea's mobile police squad, who were the only people carrying guns at the time (Cullen and Woodley 2014; Gordon and Ireland 2014; Gordon and Whyte 2014; Wroe and Callinan 2014; Wroe, Whyte and Wen 2014). Although it accepted that detention centre staff employed by its contractor G4S had attacked detainees, the Australian government 'stood by' its 'tough offshore processing regime' (Wroe, Whyte and Wen 2014). In defending his Immigration Minister, Prime Minister Tony Abbott declared that 'you don't want a wimp running border protection' (Wroe and Swan 2014).

Australia is alone in detaining refugees throughout the entire visa application process and after it pending removal if the application is rejected, but other liberal democracies routinely detain asylum seekers and other people who are unlawfully present (American Civil Liberties Union 2009; UNHCR 2012a; Phillips and Millbank 2005, 3; Roberts 2009; UNHCR 2012a; Wilsher 2012). As a result, detention in the twenty-first century has been 'normalised' 'to an extent only

9 The 'gas and bash' technique involved 'blow[ing] gas on people and beat[ing] them'.

10 A bi-partisan parliamentary committee noted in 2001 the 'despair and depression' of the people held in Australia's immigration detention facilities and referred to 'immigration detention syndrome' (in UN Working Group 2002, 12). In 2008 psychiatrists identified a new mental illness suffered by Australian immigration detainees, with clinical features 'similar to post-traumatic stress disorder, major depression and anxiety disorders' (Miller 2008).

11 In one well documented case a 12 year old repeatedly attempted to hang himself (see UN Working Group 2002, 11 and 12; Zifcak 2006). According to a case-worker on Nauru interviewed by Davies in 2013, a four-year-old child who was then in detention had 'become catatonic and [was] refusing to eat'.

previously seen in wartime' (Wilsher 2012, xxi). Asylum seekers in the UK and other EU countries whose protection claims are considered 'manifestly unfounded' or who have travelled through another 'safe' country en route to the country in which they claim asylum are automatically detained while their claims are considered under a fast track regime (Phillips and Millbank 2005, 4). Many EU countries also detain asylum seekers whose protection claims have been rejected pending deportation (Phillips and Millbank 2005, 4; Wilsher 2012, 115). The numbers affected by these policies are huge – as Wilsher suggests, immigration detention is now occurring globally 'on a vast scale' (2012, ix). The UK, for example, has an average daily immigration detention population of between 2,000 and 3,000 (Silverman and Hajela 2013). Immigration detention is also a thriving business in the US, where the average daily detention population is 34,000 (Urbina and Rentz 2013) and the industry is worth US$1.72 billion (Wilsher 2012, 59) – a figure that is striking in itself but dwarfed by the more than AUD$8 billion (US$7.18 billion) projected cost of Australia's detention regime over the three year period 2013/14–2016/17 (The Greens, Australia 2013). Not only are more people being incarcerated around the world, but they are being incarcerated for longer periods (Wilsher 2012, xii). Among those detained in the US, more than 4,000 have been incarcerated for at least six months and some for more than five years (American Civil Liberties Union 2009, 4; Roberts 2009).

All Western countries construct complex physical and legal barriers and use force to prevent refugees entering their territory (Carens 1987, 251; Wilsher 2012, 123). The result is death by drowning, starvation or heat exposure for hundreds of thousands of people (Hill 2013; Kumin 2007; Mills 2008; Shenker 2013). The militarised defence of Western borders and policing of access routes into these states forces refugees to rely on exploitative and abusive criminal smuggling networks (Dummett 2001, 43–4; Stevis and Ball 2013). It also licences and encourages the punitive treatment of refugees by other countries – thus Malaysia detains and canes Burmese Rohinga refugees and then deports them to Thailand, which smuggles the refugees back across the border into Burma, ignoring the fact that the Burmese military refuses the refugees a right to enter (Staples 2012, 147–9). Wilsher (2012, xii) points out that while the practise of incarcerating refugees began in Western states, it is now 'widespread' in other countries as well. In Indonesia many refugees whose ultimate destination is Australia are detained in appalling conditions (Taylor 2009; Human Rights Watch 2013). Australian Federal Police have also engaged for many years in joint 'People Smuggling Disruption' programmes in Indonesia, and Australia pays Indonesia and the International Organisation for Migration to pressure refugees resident in the country to return home (Taylor 2014). Many Western countries are party to 'containment' agreements with undemocratic and repressive governments. Australia has agreements with Afghanistan and Sri Lanka to ensure that potential asylum seekers are prevented from leaving home and can be forcibly repatriated when they do escape (Irin News 2013; Mogelson 2013). Stevis and Ball (2013) also point out that '[b]efore the Arab Spring, North African leaders such as Muammar Gadhafi kept a lid on [people ...] smuggling in exchange for billions in aid from Italy and other European countries'.

As part of its current military led border protection regime – promoted by the government under the label 'Operation Sovereign Borders' and headed by an Australian Defence Force Lieutenant General, Australia intercepts vessels carrying refugees from Indonesia and tows the boats back into Indonesian waters. The navy has also begun forcing refugees into lifeboats specifically purchased for this purpose. The lifeboats are towed into Indonesian waters and then abandoned (AAP/theguardian.com 2014). Under legislation passed with bi-partisan support in 2013, Australia excised its entire coastline and all off-shore territories from its migration zone. The result is that even when boats carrying asylum seekers land on Australian territory, the asylum seekers cannot lodge a protection claim under Australian law except with leave from the Minister for Immigration. Since 2013, leave has been denied wholesale, and almost all asylum seekers forcibly transported to the detention camps on Nauru or Manus Island. Nauru and Papua New Guinea have entered agreements with Australia to process refugee protection applications, but regardless of the outcome of these applications Australia has said it will not resettle the refugees. Other wealthy liberal democracies have created 'non-arrival' or 'non-migration' zones within their territory – for example, at airports and other entry points, and refugees who are detained upon arrival within these zones are denied access to the law of the state on whose territory they are detained.

Deportation operations are also conducted on a massive scale by wealthy liberal democracies. France alone deports around 30,000 people a year (Global Detention Project 2009) – although Wilsher (2012, 115) claims that many of these deportations are 'voluntary' in the sense that detention is not required in order to guarantee that individuals present themselves for removal. When deportations are involuntary the force used may involve shackling and blindfolding, and in Australia intravenously administered 'chemical restraints' (Australian Broadcasting Corporation 2005; Nicholls 2007, 139). Government employees in Australia's departments of immigration and foreign affairs have also engaged in identity fraud, for example by providing stateless asylum seekers with false passports, and have conspired with officials in autocratic countries to facilitate the deportation of asylum seekers (Australian Broadcasting Corporation 2005; Glendenning et al. 2004). Many people have been 'disappeared' after being forcibly returned by Australia to countries such as Afghanistan, Iran and Iraq; others are known to have been killed.[12]

The Legal Status of Contemporary Refugees

How is the treatment of refugees that I describe here possible, given the authority of government in liberal democracies is based on rights protection – to restate the

12 See Burnside 2007, 72; Corlett 2005; Glendenning 2004.

question with which I began Chapter 2, and given that these liberal democracies are parties to a whole gamut of international human rights instruments, including the Convention Relating to the Status of Refugees (Refugee Convention)?[13] In this section I discuss the international rights provisions relevant to refugees and how these provisions apply within liberal democracies. Rather than using the expansive definition of 'refugee' that I have employed to this point, I draw distinctions where necessary for the sake of clarity between asylum seekers seeking protection under the Refugee Convention whose status as Convention refugees has not been determined, and other 'unauthorised' immigrants who arrive in a country without prior permission.

According to Amnesty International, '[a]ll immigrants, irrespective of their legal status, have human rights' (2012, 12). Nash argues along similar lines that 'distinctions between citizens and non-citizens with respect to fundamental human rights are not permitted in international law' (2009, 17). Nash and Amnesty are supported by the claim in Article one of the Universal Declaration of Human Rights (UDHR) that 'all humans are born free and equal in dignity and rights'. The universality of human rights, and the importance of these rights as protections for individual freedom and equality, is consistently expressed in the international human rights system. The same language appears in the preamble to the UN Charter, in the UDHR, in the two major Covenants that provide a legally binding articulation of the rights contained in the UDHR – the International Covenant on Civil and Political Rights (ICCPR) and the International Covenant on Economic, Social and Cultural Rights (ICESCR), and in all of the major international rights instruments that have followed. The implications of this language – and of what I am calling the myth of human rights – is that these rights 'are universal, indivisible, interdependent, mutual reinforcing, and as relevant to refugees and stateless persons as to nationals in their own country' (UNHCR 2008, 129).

The ICCPR recognises rights to life (Art. 6); to liberty and security of the person (Art. 9); not to be subject to arbitrary arrest or detention (Art. 9); and to equality before the law (Art. 14). The ICESCR recognises a range of economic, social and cultural rights, including the rights to work (Art. 6) and to an education (Art. 13). Both Covenants also bind parties to protect the rights that they contain without discrimination of any kind, including discrimination on the basis of national or social origin (Art. 2(1) ICCPR; Art. 2(2) ICESCR).[14] The Human Rights Committee

13 The vast majority of Western liberal democracies are parties to the Refugee Convention and/or its Protocol, and to at least some of the core human rights treaties. The USA is notable for its historical unwillingness to ratify human rights treaties but even so, it is a party to the Refugee Convention and to the International Covenant on Civil and Political Rights. It has signed but not ratified the International Covenant on Economic, Social and Cultural Rights.

14 An exception is Article 25 of the ICCPR, which restricts the right of political participation to citizens. Article 2(3) of the ICESCR also recognises that developing

(HRC) and the Committee on Economic, Social and Cultural Rights (CESCR), responsible for overseeing the ICCPR and the ICESCR respectively, argue that the non-discrimination requirement extends to non-citizens (HRC 1994, para. 1), including immigrants whose presence is unlawful (CESCR 2009, para. 30). In fact, however, discrimination against unauthorised immigrants is justified in, and indeed assumed by, the human rights system. This is explicit in the International Convention on the Elimination of All Forms of Racial Discrimination, which – although prohibiting discrimination on a range of grounds including 'national or ethnic origin', also clearly states that this prohibition does 'not apply to distinctions, exclusions, restrictions or preferences ... between citizens and non-citizens' (Art. 1(2)). More broadly, it is evidenced by a striking absence in the list of ICCPR rights – the right to universal freedom of movement.

Despite constant reiteration of the claim that humans are born free and equal and are the subjects of human rights and fundamental freedoms, as well as recognition within the human rights system that liberty of movement is, as the HRC puts it, 'an indispensable condition for the free development of a person' (1999, para. 1), the system nowhere recognises a right to international freedom of movement. The UDHR accords rights to freedom of movement and residence *within* the borders of states (Art. 13(1)), and a right 'to *leave* any country' as well as 'to return to' one's own country (Art. 13(2)). As noted above, the right to leave one's own country is now frequently curtailed by repressive states acting under agreement with liberal democracies. Although arguing for its continued relevance, Goodwin-Gill (2011, 443) recognises that even to speak of such a right now 'probably sounds dated'. In any event, the UDHR does not contain a right to enter countries other than one's own. Article 14(1) of the Declaration accords a right 'to seek and to enjoy in other countries asylum from persecution' but this is not a right enforceable at the behest of the individual (Goodwin-Gill and McAdam 2007, 358) and as we have seen, wide-ranging restrictions prevent asylum seekers from obtaining access to asylum procedures within liberal democracies (Wilsher 2012, xi, 122). Liberal states generally refuse visas to individuals considered likely to make an asylum claim and place blanket visa bans on nationalities likely to require protection (Crisp 2007, 9; Goodwin-Gill and McAdam 2007, 375; UNHCR 2006, 35). They also impose carrier liability sanctions that force international carriers to police their customers for visa and passport compliance. It is common practice to post immigration officials at foreign airports and other points of international departure to vet embarking passengers and to ensure that no asylum seekers or other unauthorised immigrants obtain passage to the destination state (Goodwin-Gill and McAdam 2007, 377).

The Refugee Convention does not provide individuals with a right to enter a state in order to claim asylum, and it recognises that an asylum seeker's presence in a Convention state may be unlawful (Art. 31(2)). This, combined with the

---

countries can 'determine to what extent they ... guarantee ... economic rights ... to non-nationals'.

Convention's restrictive refugee definition, requiring that an individual has left his or her home state and is unable or unwilling to return to it because of a well-founded fear of persecution 'on grounds of race, religion, nationality, membership of a particular social group, or political opinion' (Art.1) means that it is appropriate to characterise it as an instrument of containment, used by Western states along with other border policing mechanisms to restrict access to their territories and to regulate refugee flows (Tuitt 1996; and see Dauvergne 2005, 85; 2008, 60; Gibney 2004, 3; Hathaway 1990, 144; and generally, Skran 1995, 88–94; UNHCR 2006, 1). The strongest protection afforded by the Convention is its prohibition in Article 33 on refoulement, or return 'to the frontiers of territories where [the refugee's] life or freedom would be threatened on account of [his or her] race, religion, nationality, membership of a particular social group or political opinion'. The principle of non-refoulement is not, however, considered to impose an obligation on states to facilitate access to their territory or even to accord lawful status to asylum seekers who manage to obtain access – the only obligation in the latter case is not to return a person to a place in which he or she is likely to be persecuted.

The ICCPR recognises a right to liberty of movement, but restricts this right to individuals '*lawfully* within the territory of a State' (Art. 12(1), my emphasis). The question of whether an individual is lawfully within the territory of a state is a matter for the state itself (UNHCHR 2006, 17; HRC 1999, para. 4; 1994, paras 5, 6, 9). In most liberal democracies, asylum seekers – like all other unauthorised immigrants – are treated as having arrived unlawfully, and their presence either remains unlawful, or is legally qualified after they have lodged a protection application through restrictions attached to bridging visas. While Article 31(2) of the Refugee Convention says that states should not impose penalties on refugees for unlawful entry, this is qualified to allow for the detention of asylum seekers. Furthermore, the Convention actually sets out different standards of treatment for refugees lawfully and unlawfully on a state's territory. International law generally recognises that states may deprive individuals who enter their territory without lawful authorisation from freedom of movement within the state.[15]

Detention should not, however, be 'arbitrary' (Art. 9(1), ICCPR). It should not constitute torture or 'cruel, inhuman or degrading treatment or punishment' (Arts 1 and 16, Convention Against Torture, and Other Cruel, Inhuman, or Degrading Treatment or Punishment) (CAT), and detainees should be 'treated with humanity and with respect for the inherent dignity of the human person' (Art. 10(1), ICCPR). Nevertheless, findings by treaty bodies that detention in particular instances contravenes international law have not impugned detention as such, and as I discuss below, such findings are in any event routinely ignored or disputed by the states involved.

15 In addition to Article 12 of the ICCPR, see the Declaration on the Rights of Non-Nationals, Article 5(3), and the European Convention for the Protection of Human Rights and Fundamental Freedoms, Article 5(f) and Article 2, Protocol 4.

The border regimes developed by wealthy liberal democracies are premised on preventing asylum seekers, along with other unauthorised immigrants, from accessing the territory of the state. The legality of intercepting and repelling individuals en route to Western states is considered dubious by international lawyers, who point out that it may result in refoulement. Nevertheless, Goodwin-Gill and McAdam (2007, 360) acknowledge that 'states retain considerable discretion to construct sophisticated interception and non-arrival policies within the letter, if not the spirit, of the law'. International lawyers have also expressed concerns about the legality of the non-arrival or non-migration zones that I discussed in the preceding section. Dauvergne (2008, 58) argues that it is 'nonsensical from the perspective of international law' to claim that territory excised from a country's migration zone 'is not in fact [that country's] territory for the purposes of making a refugee claim'. Goodwin-Gill and McAdam also argue that because it is 'a fundamental principle of international law that every state enjoys prima facie exclusive authority over its territory and persons within it', states cannot absolve themselves of obligations under international law within zones that form part of their territory but that they have designated as 'transit or international zones' (2007, 253). In their view, 'the state's sovereign and prima facie exclusive authority or jurisdiction over all its territory', and the 'fact of [the] control' that it exercises over the territory, means it has responsibility under international law for what occurs there (2007, 255). They admit, however, that the state is free to choose the manner in which it implements its international obligations, and that the application of 'procedures and standards' different to those applied outside the designated zones will 'not necessarily' constitute a breach of international law (2007, 255).

Weissbrodt (2008, 52) similarly argues that states must be held accountable for their actions within 'transit' or 'international' zones. He cites the 1996 decision of the European Court of Human Rights in 'Amuur v. France' that '[s]o-called "international zones" administered by states to detain non-citizens ... are a legal fiction and a state cannot thereby avoid its international human rights responsibilities by claiming that such areas have extraterritorial status' (Weissbrodt 2008, 52). As Wilsher (2012, 147–8) points out, however, the Court's decision in 'Amur' did not seriously undercut the power of governments to detain individuals in such zones and to do so in a manner sanctioned by international law. The Court accepted that detention might be appropriate in order to organise the removal of a person from the state's territory. It said that 'such holding should not be prolonged excessively' (para. 43, in Wilsher 2012, 147), but it 'endorsed the idea that migrants who seek entry may be deemed to be giving their consent to their continued detention'. (Wilsher 2012, 147) While the court said that such consent could not be inferred if an asylum seeker was in fact unlikely to be afforded protection in another country, Wilsher (2012, 148) emphasises that the decision has no application to other unauthorised immigrants unable to claim protection under the Refugee Convention. These unauthorised immigrants may be held indefinitely in 'non-arrival' zones and their incarceration will not be characterised as detention. Thus the 'legal fiction' forged by the creation of international zones continues to exert an all too real power over the individuals imprisoned within them.

The UNHCR argues that a state cannot absolve itself of legal responsibility for what happens to asylum seekers and other unauthorised immigrants whom it forcibly transports to camps funded by it in other countries. The legality of such arrangements is not, however, likely to be challenged at the international level. As Dauvergne (2008, 58) points out, individuals do not have a cause of action under the Refugee Convention, and other states do not have an interest in impugning arrangements that they may, at some point, wish to replicate. If the country in which a person is detained is a party to the Optional Protocol to the ICCPR or the Optional Protocol to the CAT, the person detained should in theory be able to argue that their detention is 'arbitrary' or 'cruel, inhuman or degrading'. In reality, however, they will be precluded from doing so by being denied access to legal assistance. Furthermore, such findings rarely have any practical impact because no enforcement mechanism exists to ensure that they are implemented (UNHCHR 2008, 31, 34, 48; Steiner, Alston and Goodman 2008, 915). While the treaty bodies argue that their views represent an authoritative interpretation of international law (see, for example, HRC 2008, para. 34), they are not binding (Kesby 2012, 96; Steiner, Alston and Goodman 2008, 892) and states commonly dispute the views or refuse to implement them (see Steiner and Alston 2000, 740–41).

It is also notable that international law actually provides warrant for many of the border policing practices that I have been discussing. UN Security Council Resolution 1373 (2001) calls on states to actively police their borders and ensure that refugee status is not 'abused' by 'perpetrators, organisers or facilitators of terrorist acts' (in Harvey 2005, 153). The UN Protocol Against the Smuggling of Migrants subsumes all forms of unauthorised migration under the rubric of transnational organised crime. While the Protocol specifies that its provisions do not affect any rights or obligations under the Refugee Convention, it makes provision for states to prevent citizens from leaving their own country 'by unauthorised or irregular measures' (Art. 19; Kneebone 2009, 25) and implicitly justifies the interception practices of destination states (Blay, Burn and Keyzer 2007, 12). The International Convention on the Protection of the Rights of all Migrant Workers and Members of their Families requires states parties to 'prevent' and 'eliminate' 'illegal and clandestine movements and employment of migrant workers' (Art. 68), and its recognition of a right to free movement within a state is limited to lawful migrants (Art. 39). While it recognises that even unauthorised migrants have a right to 'liberty and security of person' and not to be subject to 'arbitrary arrest or detention', it sanctions detention in accordance with law and with respect to immigration infringements (Arts 16 and 17). Dauvergne (2008, 27) concludes that 'sovereignty is reinforced [under the Convention] by leaving states in firm control of who can be a migrant worker and under what conditions, and by requiring states to reinforce their borders'. The Convention Relating to the Status of Stateless Persons attempts to attribute a legal personality even to stateless individuals, but allows that this identity may be severely restricted – for example, by requiring states parties to issue travel documents only to stateless persons who are '*lawfully* staying in their territory' (Art. 28, my emphasis). Finally, limitation clauses in all international rights instruments, such as those allowing rights to be curtailed in the interests of national security or public order, provide avenues for states to legitimate oppressive treatment of unauthorised immigrants, including asylum seekers, simply by characterising them as threats to national security or public order.

While official rhetoric in liberal democracies agrees that even unauthorised immigrants have *human* rights, the suggestion that these rights translate to rights that must be recognised by the state in which the unauthorised immigrant appears – in other words, that they are comparable to citizens' rights – is emphatically denied. Liberal democracies are deeply hostile to the rights claims of asylum seekers and other unauthorised immigrants because these claims are seen to threaten the political autonomy of the nation-state and its sovereign right to determine its own character and composition. Rather than stand respectfully at a distance, unauthorised immigrants arrive in the state – or attempt to scale its borders – and ask for their rights to be recognised. Increasingly, their presence is characterised as a national security problem (Wilsher 2012, xviii) and even, in some instances, 'a national emergency' (Tony Abbott in Mogelson 2013). The latter claim, made by Australia's Prime Minister in response to an increase in asylum seekers attempting to reach the country by boat, would be laughable in view of the relatively small numbers involved were the rhetoric not so politically potent.

Although the treatment of refugees as a national security issue tends to be driven by politicians, this characterisation is commonly accepted by courts, reflecting the fact that the liberal democratic government's power in respect of aliens is 'a descendent of [its] war power' (Wilsher 2012, xi). Courts typically characterise the executive's power over immigration related matters as fundamental to its capacity to determine the character and indeed the on-going viability of the political community. Wilsher (2012, xiii) suggests that courts have 'officially ceded … power over such questions … Building, shaping and protecting nations through migration policy [are seen as] political questions not within the courts' jurisdiction or competence'. In the arena of national security, judges deem parliaments and the executive better equipped than the courts to deal with sensitive policy issues.[16] It is true that some judges carefully avoid assimilating issues relating to unauthorised immigrants and those relating to national security, and there has, in some jurisdictions, been 'fierce resistance by constitutional courts' to the attempt 'to exclude judicial review of immigration decisions' (Wilsher 2012, xix fn. 13, citing Dyzenhaus 2006). Nevertheless, such resistance has ultimately failed to challenge the basic assumption that the sovereign right of the state to exercise control over its borders overrides the rights obligations that it may have towards unauthorised

16 Regarding the fact that courts have proved 'rather ineffective watchdogs' 'at times of perceived threats to national security' and 'in times of crisis', see Bingham 2006, 25.

immigrants under the international human rights system or under ordinary rule of law principles within the liberal state.

Tellingly, the attitude currently prevailing is illustrated by a war-time case. In 'O'Keefe v. Calwell', Australia's Chief Justice referred to 'the deportation of an unwanted immigrant' as 'a measure of protection of the community from undesired infiltration' (1949, 278, per Latham CJ). The Chief Justice's comments were cited with approval many years later – and no longer against the background of a country at war – by Justice McHugh in 'Al-Kateb v. Godwin' (2004, para. 45), a case in which the Australian High Court upheld the constitutionality of mandatory immigration detention even when this might foreseeably result in life-long detention. Justice McHugh concluded that

> Under the aliens power [of the Australian constitution], the Parliament is entitled to protect the nation against unwanted entrants by detaining them in custody. As long as the detention is for the purpose of deportation or preventing aliens from entering Australia or the Australian community, the justice or wisdom of the course taken by the Parliament is not examinable in this or any other domestic court. It is not for courts, exercising federal jurisdiction, to determine whether the course taken by Parliament is unjust or contrary to basic human rights. (Para.74)

Consistent with their refusal to seriously impugn immigration detention regimes, courts in liberal democracies have upheld laws that exclude unauthorised immigrants and asylum seekers from many of the other rights secured under law for citizens and residents who are lawfully present. As Wilsher (2012, xvi) points out, 'modern states have stripped away many "fundamental" rights [not only] to liberty [but also to] work, healthcare, social security, and even marriage and family life'. Even if some rights are accorded in some form, these are strictly speaking the rights of the rightless. It is impossible for those who are unlawfully present to freely enjoy their rights because any attempt to claim them – for example, by approaching social service providers or by reporting assaults and other abuses to the police, exposes them to detention or deportation on the basis of their unlawful status.[17]

The refusal by states that are parties to international human rights instruments to secure the human rights of unauthorised immigrants or to be bound by the views of the treaty bodies that oversee these instruments is ultimately justified in both legal and moral terms by reference to states' right to exercise sovereign

---

17 Amnesty International USA (2012, 12) points out that although 'US legislation makes provision for undocumented immigrants who are victims of crimes … to be given temporary legal immigration status and to pursue remedies against the perpetrator of the crime … many people [are] reluctant to come into contact with the law enforcement authorities and apply for these remedies because they fear that they will be detained and deported or lose custody of their children'. See also Kesby 2012, 110.

control over immigration and matters related to citizenship and nationality. I discuss the principle of sovereignty in greater depth in the next chapter. Now I want to discuss the impact that border policing regimes have on the rule of law within the liberal democratic state.

Erosion of the Rule of Law

Arendt argues that governments in Western democracies during the inter-war years simply devolved responsibility for refugees to the police, who were given licence to treat the refugees with impunity. Arendt focuses on the actions of the police, but it is also illuminating to consider the associated abdication of responsibility by parliaments and the courts, which in the inter-war years left the executive branch of government, and within it, particular ministries such as the French Ministry of the Interior, to set the tone for the behaviour of the police, who were then accorded great licence in the exercise of their day to day duties. Such a characterisation parallels the contemporary situation. Impunity defines the contemporary treatment of refugees, but this impunity is carefully orchestrated and managed by branches of the executive government whose powers have been repeatedly extended. As I argued in the previous section, courts have failed to arrest this general tendency, and parliaments have been similarly 'reluctant to provide *legal* entitlements for persons who are unauthorized, preferring to remove rights or leave matters to executive discretion' (Wilsher 2012, xxi, emphasis in original). This has invidious effects insofar as the integrity, impartiality and protective functions of the law are concerned. The existence of people outside the pale of the law does not leave the integrity of the legal system intact. Instead, their exclusion is upheld by the system and its functionaries, including through laws of exception that mark out those who are unlawfully present for punitive treatment. The result is an expansion in the use of arbitrary powers and a corresponding weakening of those institutions designed to constrain power and hold it to account. This is evidenced in the Australian context by a steady increase in the executive's discretionary powers, along with its increasing disdain for parliamentary processes and other accountability mechanisms.

Australia's Immigration Minister exercises powers that the Minister himself has described as 'extraordinary' (Evans 2008, 5). These powers are employed both to influence public perceptions of refugees – with the current Minister instructing his department and its contractors to refer to unauthorised boat arrivals as 'illegal maritime arrivals', and people held in immigration detention as 'detainees' rather than 'clients' (in Hall 2013); and in the management of refugees themselves. As noted already,[18] it is in the Immigration Minister's discretion whether to allow a person to lodge a protection application under

18 Page 125.

the Refugee Convention if that person arrives on Australian territory by boat – his only consideration in exercising this discretion is 'the public interest'.[19] He is also free to enter agreements with other countries to establish immigration detention centres on their territory and to arrange for the forced transfer of asylum seekers to these centres – again his only consideration is whether such an arrangement is 'in the national interest'.[20] Immigration department officers have also been accorded 'exceptional, even extraordinary' powers (Palmer 2005, ix).

At the same time as the executive branch of government wields extraordinary power, it is quick to deflect blame for its policies by implicating independent contractors who are paid to run detention centres and conduct deportations; and in the ultimate abdication of responsibility, by locating detention camps in third countries and claiming that these countries have sovereign responsibility for what happens in the camps – even though it funds the camps and exercises control over their operation (Cordell 2014, McKenna 2014). Very extensive powers have been accorded to contractors, the police and defence personnel in their dealings with refugees, and these dealings have been hidden from external scrutiny. The confidentiality of commercial contracts is relied on to deny publication of the terms of service agreements with detention and security providers, and personnel who work in detention centres are prevented under their employment contracts from discussing their work (Davies 2013a; Gordon and Whyte 2014; Gordon, Whyte and Wroe 2014). In 2001, the Australian Government sought in its Border Protection Bill to provide absolute immunity to officers of the Commonwealth for civil or criminal acts undertaken in the forced removal of asylum seekers (Poynder 2003, 1). The Bill was blocked in the Senate, but 13 years later the Chief of the Defence Force circumvented this legal constraint by using his powers under workplace health and safety laws to exempt members of the navy who are involved in border policing from the obligation to take 'reasonable care' of all individuals whom they encounter in the exercise of their duties (Wroe 2014).

In the liberal democratic tradition it is recognised that detaining people and thereby depriving them of their liberty is an extreme act that must be attended by rigorous procedural protections, yet liberal democracies now routinely detain refugees en masse without judicial consideration of the individual circumstances of their case. As Wilsher (2012, xii) argues, 'detention has … become a technique of control used in a great many different situations [in respect of] a wide variety of … foreigners, a few alleged to be individually dangerous, most not'. The Australian government itself characterises its immigration detention regime as 'an exceptional measure' (see the Human Rights Committee's decision in 'Shams et al. v. Australia', para. 4.11). Creating and maintaining such detention regimes has invidious effects on the rule of law. This is evidenced by the abusive culture within

19 Migration Act 1958 (Cth.) s.46A.
20 Migration Act 1958 (Cth) s.198AA.

immigration detention centres that I detailed above; a culture that also influences the policing of borders more broadly and the management of deportations. In the European context, Carloz-Tschapp (1997, 166–7) echoes other commentators in claiming that coercive practices associated with the detention and repulsion of refugees have corroded political processes. Contempt for the rule of law is not easily contained or restricted, and it is always a temptation to expand the use of draconian methods initially deployed only against one unpopular minority. Arguably the punitive border policing mechanisms that I have been discussing paved the way for the extraordinary anti-terrorism provisions, including provisions allowing for pre-emptive detention and, in Australia, detention of non-suspects,that were introduced by all Western democracies in the aftermath of 11 September 2001 (Galligan and Larking 2008). Wilsher (2012, 240) certainly suggests that the experience 'of holding aliens [at Guantánamo Bay] for considerable periods without legal rights such as access to lawyers, due process, judicial review or habeas corpus ... was a significant factor in the choice ... to house post-September 11 prisoners [there]'.

Conclusion

People who arrive in liberal democracies without prior authorisation, including asylum seekers, are routinely denied access to judicial review of their treatment by state authorities and, if they are imprisoned, of the circumstances in which they are detained; but they are also the objects of complex legislative regimes, not to mention the overwhelming coercive power of the state, so it may appear misleading to describe them as existing outside the pale of the law. Arendt's idiom is fitting, however, because the legislative regimes that constitute refugees as 'illegals' are extraordinary provisions falling outside the terrain of the general law.[21] Like Europe's pre-World War Two 'scum of the earth', contemporary refugees can be treated with impunity and are deprived of the legal standing that is necessary to contest their treatment. The term 'illegal' is thus an apt description for refugees, implying an illegality of status and being: the condition of the outlaw. Refugees are the West's unwanted peoples. Although occasionally objects of pity, compassion and 'humanitarian concern', they are never full subjects of justice, law and rights.

In line with the argument that I have been developing throughout this book, one cannot be a full subject of law in a democratic community without also appearing before the law as the bearer of a constituted legal personality. As I argued in Chapters 2 and 3, citizens of liberal democracies are accorded a

21 Newman and Levine (2006, 30) similarly point out that the detention of terrorism suspects by the United States at Guantánamo Bay established a space of exception that was beyond the reach of the law, but was at the same time a system within which rules and laws of exception proliferated.

legal persona and equality on the basis of their membership of 'the people' who are – problematically – assumed to be the ultimate source of law in the state. Lawful visitors and permanent residents are accorded legal status and provisional recognition of equality on the basis of the fact that 'the people', through their representatives, believe it is in their interests to welcome them. While they are not full equals in the sense of being co-legislators, their potential vulnerability is ameliorated by the fact that they have a national state capable of acting on their behalf and to which they can return. Refugees are the bearers of human rights, but without lawful authorisation to enter a state their appeal to human rights effectively marks them out as the rightless. They are objects of state power and of the laws of exception it wields, but they are not subjects of the law of equality that should – according to the argument I will make in Chapters 8 and 9 – nevertheless be extended to them if the integrity of that law is to be preserved.

Chapter 8

The International Human Rights Regime and the Sovereignty of States

Introduction

An individual's legal personality is constituted by his or her status as a national of some country. As we saw in Chapter 1, individuals' attributes as people who stand before and are recognised by the domestic law of their own and other states flow from their national membership, and their home state bears the responsibility of protecting them 'both domestically and internationally' (Weissbrodt 2008, 81). But since the UN Charter affirmed the human rights of all individuals in 1945, and the Universal Declaration of Human Rights (UDHR) spelled out these rights in 1948, individuals have also been accorded standing in international law. From this time, international law has constituted all individuals as subjects of human rights. As I have stressed throughout the course of this book, however, individual subjects of human rights are not accorded standing and the right to appear and claim rights under the domestic law of states other than their own. Even if they are excluded from rights-recognition in their own state, they are not accorded a right to claim rights elsewhere.

States are free to decide whom they will admit to their territory, and they frequently deny access to the law to those who are unlawfully present. As I demonstrated in Chapter 7, this is the case even when states exercise jurisdiction over individuals and make laws in respect of them. In such cases, although these people are subject to the power of the state – even to the point of being detained by it, they do not have standing on the basis of which to claim the rights or protections that the state affords to its own citizens and to those lawfully present in its territory. In theory, refugees can appeal to the institutions of international human rights law, but in Chapter 7 I canvassed the difficulty of accessing these institutions and of enforcing their findings. I argued as well that the sovereign autonomy of states, particularly in relation to matters relating to immigration and membership, is presupposed by international human rights law. Thus while international law recognises all people as the bearers of 'inalienable' rights, when these rights come into conflict with the sovereign rights of states over immigration and membership, they very quickly assume a mythical status. An appeal to human rights in these instances is an appeal to an imagined moral community akin to the ancient natural law community of gods and men. The appeal may have rhetorical or hortatory appeal but it binds states 'in conscience' rather than in fact. Furthermore, the appeal casts the person making it in the role of supplicant – someone who is outside the sphere of constituted equality secured by the democratic state's basic law.

Against my reading of human rights, it is increasingly common to claim that our contemporary world order is 'cosmopolitan' rather than 'international' (Benhabib 2005, 86; Habermas 2008, 335), taking individuals rather than states as the primary subjects of justice and thus ensuring that the sovereignty of states is tempered by and answerable to the sway of human rights. Human rights, meanwhile, are characterised as 'intermestic' (Nash 2009, 14–15) – influencing the development of domestic law through the creation and proliferation of international norms but also influencing international norms through their realisation and mediation in domestic and regional settings. The increasing purchase of human rights is said to have undermined the significance of citizenship, ensuring that everyone in a state's territory is treated as a subject of the rights secured by its laws, regardless of their citizenship status. There remains a huge gap, however, between the constitution of individuals as the subjects of human rights in international law and the legal constitution of individuals within particular states. This gap continues to receive normative backing through international law's recognition of state sovereignty.

Recognition of state sovereignty is the organising principle of international law and moral bedrock of the modern international order. After briefly reviewing the constitution of individuals as legal persons and subjects of human rights, I turn in this chapter to a consideration of the principle of sovereignty and the historical and moral foundations on which the sovereignty of states rests. I argue that the principle in effect protects the sovereignty of the powerful, and within liberal democratic states, of the nation – thereby echoing and endorsing the social contract tradition's implicit assumptions concerning the role of the nation. This is because sovereign recognition is accorded in international law to any government that effectively asserts control over a specified territory and its inhabitants. Nevertheless, the liberal democratic state's dual commitment to rights and to the internal sovereignty of the people provides even marginalised members of such states with a foundation on which to contest their marginalisation and to argue for equal recognition within the state. On the other hand, outsiders who are not parties to the liberal state's constitutive law of equality and who cannot demand, on the basis of an historical or social relationship to the community, that they be treated as parties to its founding law can be excluded from recognition under that law. Meanwhile, in the international arena, sovereignty trumps universalism insofar as the attribution of individual legal status and thus rights recognition is concerned. Refugees who have only their human rights to fall back on against the power of the sovereign state are not subjects of justice nor equals under the law that controls and oppresses them, yet the sovereignty of this law continues to be upheld even by the instruments and institutions of international human rights law.

The Constitution of the Individual as a Legal Person and Subject of Human Rights

As in the inter-war years, an individual's legal identity continues to depend on his or her national status. Nationality establishes a legal bond between individuals and the state of which they are members; it imposes rights and duties on both, and is often characterised as a contract between the state and the individual (Weiss 1979, 29–30). The nature of the rights and duties associated with nationality depends on the legislation of the state in question. This is because states have sovereign control over matters related to nationality, including the right to confer or deny national status (Brownlie 2003, 373 and 376). States may choose to accord non-national residents rights and recognition under their law, and this is consistent with the state's sovereign power to legislate in respect of those within its jurisdiction. Usually, nationals of other states who are lawfully resident in a host state are accorded legal recognition both on the basis of the host state's laws dealing specifically with non-nationals (including, for example, laws relating to visa requirements and qualification periods for naturalisation) and on the basis of their legal identity as established by their national states and evidenced through identity documents such as passports and birth certificates. A host state will also have obligations to non-nationals lawfully resident in its territory in accordance with bi-lateral treaties, as well as general principles of reciprocity between states and under the doctrine of state responsibility for injuries to aliens.[1]

Given that an individual's legal identity is still so closely tied to his or her national status, refugees who are not effectively represented by their national state are in an anomalous position. Nevertheless, since the establishment of the United Nations in 1945 and the signing of the UDHR in 1948, individuals everywhere have been constituted in international law as the subjects of human rights. The UN Charter tells us that the organisation was established not only to 'save succeeding generations from the scourge of war' and to promote international justice, social progress, 'and better standards of life in larger freedom', but also 'to reaffirm faith in fundamental human rights, in the dignity and worth of the human person, in the equal rights of men and women and of nations large and small' (preamble). Article 55(c) commits the UN to promoting 'universal respect for, and observance of, human rights and fundamental freedoms for all', and Article 56 says members 'pledge themselves to take joint and separate action in co-operation with the Organization for the achievement of the purposes set forth in Article 55'.[2]

In Chapter 7, I quoted Amnesty International's claim that '[a]ll immigrants, irrespective of their legal status, have human rights' (2012, 12). David Weissbrodt, UN Special Rapporteur on the rights of non-citizens similarly argues that even

1 See my discussion in Chapter 1, 17–18.

2 See also Arts 1, 62(2), 68 and 76.

asylum seekers whose protection applications have been rejected are, 'being human … entitled to the full spectrum of human rights enshrined in the Universal Declaration of Human Rights' (2008, 134). But my account of the treatment and legal status of refugees in Chapter 7 demonstrates what little comfort is offered by 'the full spectrum of human rights'. Weissbrodt's subsequent discussion in fact demonstrates the many ways in which refugees are deprived of human rights. He admits, for example, that the detention of asylum seekers is consistent with international law and practise, although it should not be indefinite (2008, 137). This is so even in the case of children, although the detention of children 'should be for the shortest necessary amount of time and … should be a last resort' (2008, 138). In a somewhat farcical conclusion to his discussion of the detention of children, Weissbrodt says, that '[r]egardless of whether child asylum seekers have been detained, they are entitled to all human rights, including those rights enshrined in the Children's Convention such as medical care, mental healthcare, and education' (2008, 138). Here there are echoes of Arendt's claim in *Origins* that the refugees detained between World Wars One and Two might have received regular meals and had more freedom of opinion than a person living 'in an ordinary despotism', but this did not in the least change 'their fundamental situation of rightlessness': 'The prolongation of their lives [was] due to charity and not to right … and their freedom of opinion [was] a fool's freedom, for nothing they [thought] matter[ed] anyhow' (1968, 296).

International rights instruments claim to recognise human rights, rather than to bring them into being. The UDHR speaks in its preamble of the 'inherent dignity' and 'the equal and inalienable rights' of all 'members of the human family', and reiterates the UN Charter's 'faith in fundamental human rights' and in 'the dignity and worth of the human person'. Article 1 says that '[a]ll human beings are born free and equal in dignity and rights. They are endowed with reason and conscience and should act towards one another in a spirit of brotherhood'. The International Covenant on Civil and Political Rights (ICCPR) and the International Covenant on Economic, Social and Cultural Rights (ICESCR) both claim that the 'equal and inalienable rights of all members of the human family' 'derive from the inherent dignity of the human person' (preamble to both Covenants). The conception of human rights endorsed by contemporary international law thus treats rights as natural and innate. While such rights may also receive explicit legal protection, and the international rights regime argues for their realisation in domestic legislation, the pronouncement of human rights does not depend upon such realisation – these are rights that individuals hold by virtue of their membership of the human species. The international human rights regime is thus based on moral foundations and posits a modern, secular version of the universal law of nature. The subjects of this law are 'born free and equal' and their status as the bearers of human rights is independent of political or legal recognition by any particular state. Despite its continued reliance on the language of law and of right, then, the international human rights regime trades on the myth of human rights and represents an ideal moral community rather than a community based on justice and law.

Habermas (2001, 108) captures the ambiguity inherent in the myth of human rights nicely when he describes human rights as 'legal norms with an exclusively moral content'.[3] He is also well known for characterising human rights as 'Janus-faced, looking simultaneously toward morality and the law', but here he emphasises that 'as legal norms [human rights] protect individual persons only insofar as the latter belong to a particular legal community – normally the citizens of a nation-state' (2001, 118). Habermas (2006; 2008) suggests that the universalisation of human rights 'as legal norms' requires a world polity that establishes, mediates, supports and enforces institutional rights protections. I argue against a global polity conceived along these lines in Chapter 9. Here my claim is that there continues to be a disjunct between the juridical and political language of the international human rights regime and the fact that its content remains 'exclusively moral' in respect of refugees. It continues to be that case that human rights are realised – if at all – through the institutional framework of states, and as I discuss in more detail in the next section, these are states that claim and are accorded sovereign autonomy. They may deny refugees legal standing and thus the capacity to appear before the law. The result is that these people are not in fact the subjects of rights. They are accorded human rights in the state's discretion, and if their human rights are taken away refugees have no basis on which to appear before the law and to challenge that deprivation.

The reliance of the international human rights regime upon states as the primary duty bearers in relation to rights, and the power accorded to states in respect of border control, fundamentally undermine Weissbrodt's argument that even failed asylum applicants are entitled to all human rights. It is true that the international human rights regime exhorts individuals and civil society to promote respect for and observance of human rights. For example, the preamble to the ICCPR (substantially replicated in the ICESCR) says that individuals as well as states are under an obligation 'to strive for the promotion and observance of the rights recognized in the present Covenant'. Nevertheless, the regime takes for granted that states are the primary addressees of rights claims. Thus, while the 1998 Declaration on the Rights and Responsibility of Individuals … to Promote and Protect Universally Recognised Human Rights … emphasises the importance of individuals and civil society in promoting human rights, it also makes clear that 'the prime responsibility and duty to promote and protect human rights and fundamental freedoms lies with the state' (preamble). Article 2(1) specifies that '[e]ach state has a prime responsibility and duty to protect, promote and implement all human rights and fundamental freedoms' and Article 3 says that '[d]omestic

3 In describing human rights as 'legal norms with an exclusively moral content' Habermas also (2001, 108) underlines the fact that the universal sphere of human rights is the sphere of morality: 'The normative model for a community that exists without any possible exclusions is the universe of moral persons – Kant's "kingdom of ends"'.

law … is the juridical framework within which human rights and fundamental freedoms should be implemented and enjoyed'. It is states that have the power to accord rights, through legal and political infrastructures that protect civil and political rights, for example, and through their monopoly on the redistribution of resources via public taxation and social welfare schemes. It is also through the coercive power of states and their functionaries that human rights abuses are committed. What is an attack on the human right to life in the case of state sanctioned violence is, among individuals, criminal violence subject to the ordinary sanctions of the criminal law.

For theorists who argue that citizenship within states can now be characterised as 'post-national', it is not necessarily a problem that states remain the primary addressees in respect of rights claims. These theorists claim that in response to international human rights norms, domestic courts have been increasingly willing to accord legal status and rights recognition to long-term residents such as guest workers who are, however, non-citizens.[4] According to Cohen (1996, 179), 'it has long been the case that under normal circumstances, non-citizens enjoy legal rights'. Cohen also points to a significant 'expansion … of the particular range of civil rights that non-citizen residents enjoy, and the explicit articulation of the principle of the right to have rights (a legal persona) for non-citizens, including even illegal aliens, in various international and national codes' (1996, 179). Meanwhile, Habermas (2008, 335) cites with approval the opinion of 'many experts' that 'the individual legal subject … is gradually acquiring the status of a subject of international law and a cosmopolitan citizen' supported by 'the emergence of a global constitutional law'. In a similar vein, Kesby (2012, 94) says that many theorists now argue that international law is strongly 'oriented towards the protection of the rights of the individual such that the individual need not be at the mercy of the protection afforded by the state'. Kesby herself, however, points to the fact that 'in terms of enforcement' 'the international human rights regime is notoriously weak' (2012, 96). More fundamentally, she acknowledges a 'counter-narrative' that 'challenges the optimism of postnational or denationalised citizenship' (2012, 101). It is this narrative that captures the reality of life for refugees. Furthermore, although it is true that citizenship is now less significant for those who are lawfully present, ultimately the lawful right to remain can be revoked, in which case those who are rendered unlawfully present will discover how little their human rights avail them. Their situation will be less precarious than that of the refugee, however, if they have a national state to which they can return or that is willing to offer them protection in the international sphere. It is also true that even citizenship may not provide robust protection in a state in which the nation has taken precedence over the rule of law: when 'right is what is good for the German (Australian/American/etc.) people', the pool of people considered 'true' nationals can shrink very rapidly. I have nevertheless argued throughout this

4 See Dauvergne's discussion of the literature arguing that citizenship is no longer an important 'determinant of life chances': 2008, 20–21 and 119–24.

book that a historical or social connection to the nation, and membership of the state that represents it, currently provides a foundation within liberal democracies on which citizens are able to demand legal recognition and to claim rights 'as of right'. Refugees who are unlawfully present in the territory of the rights recognising state, on the other hand, are immediately identifiable as strangers to its law. To the extent that they are the subjects of human rights and nothing more, their appeals are couched in the language of charity rather than justice. Given that their presence is unlawful, and thus presumed to be a threat to the state and its capacity to control its membership and national identity, their appeal to charity and their reliance on the myth of human rights is more likely to be received with hostility than with compassion.

The Principle of Sovereignty

In international law, states are conceived in the image of liberal individuals. They are independent decision-makers, entitled to act in their own interests and to regulate their affairs as they see fit, limited only by the equal rights of other states. The customary markers of statehood are summarised in the 1933 Montevideo Convention on the Rights and Duties of States.[5] Article 1 of the Convention specifies that: 'The state as a person of international law should possess the following qualifications: a) a permanent population; b) a defined territory; c) government; and d) capacity to enter into relations with … other states'. Article 2 says that '[t]he federal state shall constitute a sole person in the eyes of international law', and Article 3 stipulates that:

> … the state has the right to defend its integrity and independence, to provide for its conservation and prosperity, and consequently to organize itself as it sees fit, to legislate upon its interests, administer its services, and to define the jurisdiction and competence of its courts. The exercise of these rights has no other limitation than the exercise of the rights of other states according to international law.

Article 5 describes states as the bearers of 'fundamental rights' that 'are not susceptible of being affected in any manner whatsoever'. Article 3 also specifies that 't]he political existence of the state is independent of recognition by … other states'.[6] In practise, however, recognition within the international community – which may hinge on historical, economic, strategic or other factors – is crucial

5 Although it is an inter-American agreement, the Montevideo Convention is recognised as articulating principles of customary law and thus as an authoritative statement of the characteristics of statehood.

6 See also Article 4, which provides that: 'States are juridically equal, enjoy the same rights, and have equal capacity in their exercise. The rights of each one do not depend upon

for recognition of statehood and, despite the interplay of other factors, has turned historically on the capacity of a governing power to exercise exclusive authority over a particular territory. Once recognition of statehood has been accorded, it functions as a *fait accompli* – ensuring continued international recognition of the state regardless of who exercises power or how effectively that power is exercised within its borders, and regardless even of disputes concerning the exact location of these borders.[7] Nevertheless, the capacity to exercise exclusive territorial control remains significant. As Hubert and Weiss (2001, 6) put it, '[a]n important component of sovereignty has always been an adequate display of the authority of states to act over their territory to the exclusion of other states'.

The Montevideo Convention's characterisation of states captures in broad outlines the principle of sovereignty, which is the organising principle of modern international law. Described by the International Court of Justice (in Hubert and Weiss 2001, 6) as 'the fundamental principle on which the whole of international law rests', sovereignty accords states equal standing and authority within a global society of states and recognises every state's competence and legal jurisdiction.[8] A concomitant of the recognition of state sovereignty is the principle of non-interference, which constrains states from intervening in each other's affairs, including their political, economic, social, and cultural spheres, as well as their development of foreign policy (Hubert and Weiss 2001, 6; Montevideo Convention Art. 8). Hubert and Weis (2001, 5) point out that the concept of sovereignty 'lies at the heart of both customary international law and the United Nations ... Charter'. Article 1 of the Charter lists the purposes of the UN, which include both 'international cooperation' in the promotion of human rights and '[t]o develop friendly relations among nations based on respect for the equal rights and self-determination of peoples'. Article 2 specifies that the organization 'is based on the principle of the sovereign equality of all its Members'. The first right recognised in both the ICCPR and the ICESCR, which are otherwise dedicated to the recognition of individual rights,[9] is a right to self-determination held by

the power which it possesses to assure its exercise, but upon the simple fact of its existence as a person under international law'.

7 Article 6 of the Convention provides that recognition of statehood 'is unconditional and irrevocable'. Brownlie (1998, 37–8) points out that a state may have disputed boundaries, a shifting population, and an absence of governmental authority, and still continue to be recognised internationally as a sovereign state.

8 'Jurisdiction broadly refers to the power, authority, and competence of a state to govern persons and property within its territory. It is labelled "prescriptive" and "enforcement". Prescriptive jurisdiction relates to the power of a state to make or prescribe law within and outside its territory, and enforcement jurisdiction is about the power of the state to implement the law within its territory' (Hubert and Weiss 2001, 6–7).

9 With the exception of Article 47 of the ICCPR and Article 25 of the ICESCR, both of which specify that '[n]othing in the present Covenant shall be interpreted as impairing the inherent right of all peoples to enjoy and utilize fully and freely their natural wealth and resources'.

'all peoples'. The Covenants provide (Art. 1(1)) that the right allows peoples to 'freely determine their political status and freely pursue their economic, social and cultural development'.

All the major international rights instruments affirm the principle of sovereignty, which is generally equated – as in the ICCPR and the ICESCR – with the right of 'peoples' to self-determination. The respect paid in international law to the principle of state sovereignty, and the association between peoples, nations, and states in international human rights law, reflects the fact that modern international law developed alongside the rise of the European nation-state in the seventeenth and eighteenth centuries (Luban 1985, 207) and human rights law developed in the era of de-colonisation following World War Two.[10] As I discussed in Chapter 2, the history of European nation-states is based on the principle of national self-determination. The assimilation of nations with states in this tradition, as well as the sovereign recognition afforded to states in international law generally, means that states are presumed to constitute nations or peoples – despite the fact that multi-national and pluralist states are now common and internationally states may act as representatives of more than one people or nation. Normative justifications for the principle of sovereignty thus rely on the idea that the state represents a politically unified nation, even if this is 'a people' or a 'super-nation' that itself comprises multiple nations. The gap between the rhetoric of sovereign autonomy and the influence wielded internationally by the world's most powerful states as well as by international institutions is widely recognised (see, for example, Hubert and Weiss 2001, 5). Nevertheless, the principle of sovereignty continues to be characterised as indispensable protection for political autonomy, and in the history of anti-colonialism sovereignty has frequently been vaunted as 'the final defense' available to small or weak states 'against the rules of an unjust world' – in the words of former Algerian President Boueteflika, then President of the Organisation of African Unity (in Hubert and Weiss 2001, 7). In international law, the principle of sovereignty takes such justifications at face value and does not enquire into the representative character of the state, as evident in the account of statehood contained in the Montevideo Convention (see also Pogge 2004, 269–70). Even instruments dealing with the rights of minorities such as the UN's Declaration on the Rights of Indigenous Peoples assume that states act on behalf of a unified political community that is entitled to autonomy and self-determination. The Declaration on the Rights of Indigenous Peoples specifies that the rights of indigenous minorities cannot be used to undermine the 'territorial integrity or political unity' of the state in which they reside (Art. 46). Nevertheless, if a national minority engages in a successful secession struggle and is subsequently granted statehood, this achievement is

10 Cf. The UN's 1960 Declaration on the Granting of Independence to Colonial Countries and Peoples.

likely to be characterised, after the fact, as a realisation of the principle of self-determination.[11]

In the seventeenth and eighteenth centuries the principle of sovereignty was championed by Western European governments both in their efforts to centralise and consolidate their powers in relation to their own people and in their struggles for independence from papal and imperial authority (Beitz 1991, 236). Thus sovereignty has had what Beitz calls 'a dual reference: first, to the constitution of political and legal authority within the state, and secondly, to the state in relation to other agents in the international environment' (1991, 236). Internally, the principle of sovereignty refers to the highest source of political authority in the state – for many early theorists of sovereignty this was necessarily and appropriately undivided and absolute. The revolutions of the eighteenth century recast sovereignty as a doctrine of popular political legitimation, and I have argued that the democratic credentials of the liberal state continue to rest on the idea of the 'sovereignty of the people' where 'the people' is characterised as constituting a historically and culturally connected nation. While the language of 'popular sovereignty' is often used to invoke a people's collective right to political autonomy, however, the liberal state's rights-based foundations and the increasingly widespread assertion of human rights in international law mean that the concept of sovereignty is also increasingly used to invoke a state's obligation to protect and promote the rights of each of its individual citizens.[12] These uses of the concept of sovereignty contradict the absolutism of its original usage (Beitz 1991, 236 fn. 2). On the other hand, however, they capture the normative basis on which sovereignty continues to be defended as a principle of external autonomy: the argument is that states should be free from external interference because this respects their members' collective right to political self-determination and it is also appropriately respectful of individual rights.

As I discussed in Chapters 2 and 3, however, there is a deep tension between the recognition of individual rights and the recognition of sovereignty as a principle of political autonomy based on popular legitimation. Habermas (2001; 2001a) is famous for attempting to dissolve or at least reconceptualise this tension through his account of the co-implication of rights and popular sovereignty. He argues that within the nation-state the exercise of political autonomy and the realisation of individual rights (which he also refers to under the rubric of constitutionalism and the rule of law) should not be thought of as hierarchically ordered, with one or the other taking precedence, but instead should be recognised as interdependent, mutually supporting each other through an iterative process

11 For a discussion of the principle of self-determination (tellingly known in the past as the principle of nationalities), see Brownlie 1998, 39 and ff.

12 Hubert and Weiss (2001, 8) suggest that for many people, 'sovereignty is not becoming less relevant; it remains the ordering principle of international affairs. However, it is "the peoples" sovereignty rather than the sovereign's sovereignty' (citing Kofi Annan, 'Two concepts of sovereignty', *The Economist*, 18 September 1999).

capable of strengthening the commitment to each. Meanwhile, although his focus is not on the position of the outsider, he implies that the problem that arises when outsiders are deprived by the state of rights can be dealt with internally through citizens' activism (see 2001, 119) and externally through better relations between nation-states (see 2001, 128). Although in his later work he calls for the creation of a rights-based world polity, his earlier discussions of the co-implication of rights and popular sovereignty lead him to conclude that: 'The allegedly paradoxical relation between democracy and the rule of law resolves itself in the dimension of historical time, provided one conceives the constitution as a project that makes the founding act into an ongoing process of constitution-making that continues across generations' (2001a, 768). Thought of in this way, citizens are constantly engaged in democratic will formation that is possible only because they are also committed – and continuously recommit themselves – to the authority of a constitutive law of equality and the rights that they together agree (through their democratic will formation) express and secure that equality.

If Habermas is correct about what might be called the 'dynamic' quality of the constitutional commitment to equality, as I think he is, then the failure of the democratic community to extend democratic participation and rights to the refugee who is nevertheless subject to the community's coercive authority threatens the community's on-going constitutional project, drawing into question and undermining the law of equality that must be upheld and extended or else wither away. Habermas says, 'only those laws that lie in the equal interest of each can meet with the reasonable agreement of all' (2001a, 768) – but the 'all' in this articulation must include everyone subject on an on-going basis to the authority of the law. Laws of exception applicable only to those who are unlawfully present are at odds with the democratic state's constitutive law because even laws of exception must be made under the authority of the founding law. Laws of exception run contrary to the principles of equality and mutuality that characterise the state's constitutive law, and as a result they inevitably corrode it.

I have said that Habermas implies that the problem of refugees who are deprived of recognition and of rights can be dealt with through the activism of citizens within the democratic state. Contrary, however, to Habermas' claim in *The Postnational Constellation* (2001, 119) that the egalitarian promise of human rights has, through 'tough political struggles', eventually ensured the extension of rights *not only* to 'workers, women, Jews, Romanies, [and] gays', but also to 'political refugees', the activism of citizens, where they are in the minority, may not be enough to ensure the integrity of the law in its response to refugees given the global reach and implications of state sovereignty. Within the liberal state the rights accorded to refugees remain, where they are recognised and accorded at all, rights of exception that can be overridden at any moment. Refugees do not have standing on the basis of which they can appear before the law as equals and demand that their rights be restored. The parallels between the contemporary treatment of refugees and the treatment of Europe's inter-war refugees make this clear. The dangers for the integrity of the law where its egalitarian promise is not extended to all who come before it are again evident in the proliferation of abuses – and of legal rules and fictions that sanction and normalise these abuses – now being committed under the auspices of liberal democratic refugee regimes. The trajectory of such abuse is evident everywhere, and not least in Arendt's original 'nation-state par excellence', where not only 'political refugees' but also members of resident Roma communities have had their camps and housing bulldozed and have been rounded up and expelled (re refugees see Beardsley 2009; RTÉ News 2009; re the Roma expulsions see Davies, 2010).

In the light of such events, Habermas' account of the iterative entrenchment and extension of rights occurring in conjunction with a participatory process of democratic will formation within the liberal democratic state now appears unduly optimistic – although I argued in Chapter 3 that we must aim, through a reconceptualisation and reinvigoration of the public sphere of action, to realise the egalitarian and inclusive promise of the modern nation-state in something like these terms. As things stand, however, the rule of law that protects individual rights within liberal states often conflicts with the democratic principle of popular sovereignty. Popular sovereignty appeared first of all within the nation-state in revolutionary guise – offering the promise, although even then not the reality, of egalitarian inclusivity – but the takeover of the public sphere by partisan and commercial interests, which I charted in Chapter 2, and the consequent recourse to sentimental notions of the nation, has been conceptually supported and undergirded by liberalism's reliance on the nation as the ultimate ground of law and rights.

As I demonstrated in Part II in my discussion of Locke and Kant's accounts of political legitimacy, not only are 'the people' assumed to be the ultimate source of law and rights, but the majority stands in as decision maker for and representative of the people. While the rule of law should continue to provide some protection for individual rights, the presumed authority of the law is based on the fact that it reflects a democratic consensus that is, however, actually achieved through according power to the majority. The power of the majority within liberal democracies is a form of 'majority-rule' that can be contrasted with procedural forms of majority decision-making allowing for decisions to be made on the basis of majority support following an inclusive deliberative process. Because of the deliberative context within which it occurs, assigning decision-making power to the majority in the latter case need not have the anti-political implications associated with the power of the majority within standard liberal accounts of political legitimacy. This is a point made by Waldron (2000, 210–11), who notes that Arendt is

> not at all uncomfortable with the idea of majority decision … provided first that it is pursuant to a genuine exchange of opinions, and secondly that it does not degenerate into what she calls majority-rule – 'where the majority, after the decision has been taken, proceeds to liquidate politically, and in extreme cases, physically, the opposing minority. (2000, 211, quoting Arendt 2006, Viking Press edn, 1963, 164 [2006, 155])

Against majority-rule, Habermas counters his idea of deliberative democracy and a will formation within the bounds of reason, but the members of modern democracies have thus far failed to take up the deliberative challenge. Following Arendt, I have argued that this failure reflects an unthinking recourse to sentimental nationalism as the source of solidarity within the state, against the background of liberalism's anti-political understanding of the role of government and – related to this – its assumptions concerning the predominantly private interests and pursuits of citizens. I have also emphasised that the principle of sovereignty in international law provides normative warrant for the pursuit by states of policy solely in what are said to be their own interests, even where the effect of this is to undermine the rights of outsiders and citizens of other states. As a result, internal and external sovereignty operate along the same axis, privileging the rights and interests of the majority – which speaks for 'the nation' within states, and undermining the rights of some individuals both within the state and externally.

Despite the power of the majority within the democratic nation-state, however, because minorities' membership of the community is not obviously in question, their individual members have legal standing and thus a foundation on which to claim rights and contest their deprivation. The refugee does not have this standing and thus cannot be recognised as a subject of rights. It is true – as Habermas' reference to 'workers, women, Jews, Romanies [and] gays' reminds us – that historically many insiders have been (and in some cases continue to be) denied standing as full citizens and thus members of the community. Nevertheless, the fact of their connection to the community – whether this is a connection based on a prior relationship to the land, as in the case of indigenous peoples, or on social membership, as in the case of women – provides some foothold from which to assert participation in the social contract and membership of the people, and thus legal standing. And ever since the liberal democratic state has claimed political legitimacy on the basis of a constitutive law of equality, those members excluded from full recognition under the law have been able to appear before the law and demand that its promise of equality be extended. Refugees, by comparison, can point to the inconsistency between an impartial rule of law and the refusal to extend them recognition and equal rights, but they are self-evidently not parties to the social contract or the sovereign nation that the state represents, so they have no standing under its constitutive law. Their appeal cannot be heard according to the logic that legitimates the authority of the liberal democratic state.

The principle of sovereignty in international law, by recognising states' right to autonomy and by assimilating states with nations, serves to protect the sovereignty within states of those who claim to speak for the nation. Although nationalism and the power of the majority is qualified and constrained within liberal democracies by the countervailing universalism of rights and the institutional protections established to protect individual rights, the fostering of nationalism is supported by an international system in which nation-states are treated as autonomous actors whose interests are not constrained by global or international considerations. This is a far cry from the idea of a 'comity of nations' that Arendt applauded and that I discussed in Chapter 2 – a form of human solidarity but also of political plurality within which each nation sees itself as a member of a community of mankind and recognises obligations to that community. In my final chapter I argue for recognition of the existence of a political community of mankind – and an obligation on all states to forge a comity that qualifies, in certain respects, the sovereign rights of each. The failure to recognise and act on this obligation produces the situation that we currently confront: a world in which sovereignty has spread its net over the entire globe, forcing into a position of abject inhumanity those unfortunate individuals who fall through or must take their chances in the gaps. Hubert and Weis (2001, 6) claim that the spread of sovereignty means that we are all insiders: '[t]here [are] no longer "insiders" and "outsiders" because virtually every person on Earth live[s] within a sovereign state'. On the contrary, millions of refugees are consigned to live as outsiders and thus as inhuman within the borders of liberal democracies.

Chapter 9

The Right to Have Rights and a New Law on Earth

Introduction

Until the eighteenth century, the concept of 'humanity' or 'mankind' was no more than a 'regulative idea' (Arendt 1968, 298; 1949, 35). It was a philosophical or spiritual ideal (Arendt 1995, 82) and I have argued that within the Western tradition it was typically founded in the idea of natural law. This understanding of humanity was, however, without foundation in an existing human community. Here I follow Arendt in claiming that we now live in a global community. After discussing the nature and foundations of this world community, and its implications in terms of the need to assume political responsibility for what goes on within it, I consider the capacity of the contemporary nation-state to meet its challenges. I argue that the liberal nation-state remains a viable political form only if there is a revival of public engagement among its citizens, and only if the sovereignty of the state is constrained in the interests of all humanity. A revival of republican engagement is necessary if we are to uphold the revolutionary promise of equality within the liberal democratic state, and if we are to allow the extension of this promise to outsiders. Such an extension must be possible if the ideal of equality is to be preserved.

World Politics

Arendt claims that the status of humanity as merely an ideal changed fundamentally with the advent of atomic technology, which meant that suddenly and perversely humans found themselves in a community based on the possibility of mutual annihilation (see 1998, 6; 1995, 82–3). Ever since then, humanity has represented 'something of an urgent reality' (1995, 82). This reality was, however, pre-empted by other developments. Advances in humanity's technological capabilities since the seventeenth century have inexorably reduced the significance of geographic distance, while Western Europe's technological mastery provided the means for it to impose its laws and its political formations on much of the world (1968, 235). We have since seen the evolution of a complex web of international institutions and organisations that comprise a global 'basic structure' influencing not only individuals' life chances but the conduct of politics within and between states.[1] This structure now appears to constitute some form of political community, yet the question of how this community conceives of and governs itself continues to confound our political concepts and capacities. This is nowhere more evident than in the tension between the expressed universalism of human rights and the operation of the principle of sovereignty.

The announcement of the rights of man in the American and French Declarations posited human rights as the foundation of legitimate government and characterised securing rights as the true end of all political association, a conception that was elevated to a global consensus when the UN was formed in 1945. Yet we also confront the fact that the political sphere was restricted by the sovereignty of the nation at the same time as it was placed by the rights declarations on universal foundations, and the sovereignty of the nation was itself protected by the vigorous assertion of the sovereignty of the state. The reality of power politics may, as Arendt (1968, 269) points out, make a 'mockery' of the idea of sovereign autonomy for all but 'giant' states – even in a post-colonial era, but I have shown in the course of this book that the role played by sovereignty in international law, and its significance for the legal and political constitution of individuals and their capacity to move between states, remains very real.

When sovereignty's net tightened over the entire globe following World War One, Arendt claims that it produced in Europe's inter-war refugees a new class, unknown to the nineteenth century, of legal and political outlaws (2000, 261). Arendt argues that the problem of the stateless

> could not be repaired, because there was no longer any 'uncivilized' spot on earth, because whether we like it or not we have really started to live in One World. Only with a completely organized humanity could the loss of home and political status become identical with the expulsion from humanity altogether. (1968, 297)

As Arendt's account of the significance of the atom bomb makes clear, the political reality of 'One World' poses even more wholesale dangers than those that confront individuals severed from their own communities and often, as a result, from

1 In *A Theory of Justice*, Rawls argues that individuals' life chances are influenced in morally arbitrary ways by the basic institutional structure of society. Thus a society's political, legal, economic and social systems advantage some individuals while disadvantaging others, and do so to a significant degree irrespective of individual behaviour or dessert. Given the profound impact of society's institutional arrangements, justice requires some redistribution of the benefits and burdens that flow from these arrangements, ensuring that those members of society who may be disproportionately burdened by the arrangements are compensated. Cosmopolitan theorists such as Pogge (1989; see also 2005) and Beitz (1985) take Rawls' concept of a basic structure within particular societies and argue that such a structure also influences individuals' life chances globally (see also Wenar 2002, 55).

humanity altogether. Far from advocating global government as the solution to the 'urgent reality' posed by global politics, however, Arendt echoes Kant in claiming that a sovereign world state modelled either on the nation-state or along the lines of an empire 'would not be the climax of politics, but quite literally its end' (1995, 82). In her view, according one centralised government control over the means of violence would certainly be an invitation to tyranny and likely to totalitarianism (1995, 81; 1968, 298–9). This is not only a matter of the dangers that attend executive power backed by force, but in a much broader sense, because 'political concepts are based on plurality, diversity, and mutual limitations' (1995, 81).

I discussed in Chapter 3 the tendency of human action to 'force open all limitations and cut across all boundaries' (Arendt 1998, 190). This is because action involves the forging of relationships, which have a tendency to proliferate, and it is constantly supplemented by the entry to the public sphere of new generations and the projects that they initiate. Arendt was thus much preoccupied with the question, as Canovan (1999, 109) frames it, 'of how stable political power is possible at all in a world where mortals are continually passing on and off the human stage'. Ideally, territorial and legal boundaries act as 'mutual limitations', allowing power to flourish without being amassed in annihilating proportions and enabling the continued existence of a diversity of spaces within which new forms of power can germinate and new political actions be initiated. When they function effectively, these boundaries establish spaces that allow individuals to act collaboratively and through collective action to achieve common goals. In Chapter 2, I discussed the association that Arendt draws in *Origins* between Western European imperialism and the Central/Eastern European pan-movements, both of which exhibited 'contempt for the narrowness of the nation-state' (1968, 223). Arendt claims that politics in the imperialist era saw a 'shift from localized, limited and therefore predictable goals of national interest to the limitless pursuit of power after power that could roam and lay waste to the whole globe with no certain nationally and territorially prescribed purpose and hence with no predictable direction' (1968, xviii).

This contrast between the spirit of imperialist and subsequently totalitarian thinking, that is contemptuous of institutional limitations and claims to directly embody laws of nature or history, bypassing the intermediate constraints of positive law; and the territorially rooted and legally bounded spirit of political nationhood, serves as a potent reminder of the importance of boundaries around as well as within political communities (Arendt 1968, 461). Canovan (1999, 106) suggests that the original Western European nation-states functioned, however inadequately, 'as bulwarks against totalitarianism' because 'they were good at generating power'. They were able to 'mobili[se] people to act in concert' in defence of the state against the totalitarian threat (Canovan 1999, 106). Without, however, the additional bulwark provided by the nation-state's commitment to constitutional government, such mobilising power would constantly threaten to over-run the boundaries of the state. And in fact this is what occurred in the case of imperialism. Nevertheless, and despite the further erosion of constitutionality and the rule of law that occurred as a result of how Europe's inter-war refugees were treated, Arendt suggests that the only reason the world annihilating logic of imperial politics was ultimately thwarted lay in what remained of 'the constitutional restraint of the nation-state' (1968, xix).

Arguably, the boundaries around nation-states are crucial not only because they provide a degree of stability and moderation, but also because they protect and foster particular historical, cultural and political traditions, and in doing so, human pluralism. The vitality of these traditions within particular states relates in part to the fact that the state exists among plural others. The diversity of nations, and the states that protect the continued existence of nations, supports a plurality of perspectives in the world – perspectives that may nourish and provide alternative reference points and an inducement to an enlarged outlook for individuals everywhere. As I quoted Arendt in Chapter 2, the destruction of national traditions would result in 'a shallowness that would transform man, as we have known him in five thousand years of recorded history, beyond recognition' (1995, 87). When he accepted the Nobel prize for literature in 1970, Alexander Solzhenitsyn claimed that 'world literature is no longer an abstraction or a generalised concept invented by literary critics, but a common body and common spirit, a living, heartfelt unity reflecting the growing spiritual unity of mankind'. He was well aware, however, of the dangers of this 'growing spiritual unity', arguing not only that unity entails responsibility: '[m]ankind's salvation lies exclusively in everyone's making everything his business'; but also that political diversity must be protected. In his view, 'the disappearance of whole nations would impoverish us no less than if people were to become identical, with the same character and the same face. Nations are the wealth of humanity, its generalised personalities'.

The case against a world state is compelling, but like Solzhenitsyn, Arendt suggests that the existence of 'world politics' as 'an adjunct to politics' (2006, 44) requires the assumption of political responsibility on a new scale: 'the solidarity of mankind can be meaningful in a positive sense only if it is coupled with political responsibility' (1995, 83). As citizens 'we are held responsible' for the character of the political community within which we live, and for the decisions and projects which that community carries out (1995, 83). This is the case even in situations in which repressive regimes are in power. The assumption of political responsibility is not the same as the assumption of guilt. We must take responsibility 'regardless of personal "guilt"' (1995, 83; see also 2007, 488–9 and 492).[2] In circumstances in which the idea of mankind has become a political reality, this responsibility has 'the very serious consequence that in one form or another men must assume responsibility for all crimes committed by men, and that eventually all nations will be forced to answer for the evil committed by all others' (1969, 236). On the one hand this seems an overwhelming and impossible obligation; on the other, it

---

2 Arendt acknowledges, however, that under the absolute sway of tyranny the only option available to individuals may be withdrawal from the realm of politics altogether (1995, 3–31; 2007, 485).

is an obligation we are compelled to accept. I can think of only two alternatives. The first is to blindly embrace xenophobic nationalism, which is usually fuelled by racist ideologies and fomented by fear and insecurity, and invariably inclines towards violence and oppression. The second alternative, which may be equally destructive for humanity generally, is to retreat from politics into the worldless realm of the personal (see Arendt 1995, 83; 1949, 35). Arendt's thought represents a categorical rejection of these alternatives. Faced with humanity's obligation to assume global responsibility, Arendt called for 'a new political principle … a new law on earth, whose validity this time must comprehend the whole of humanity while its power must remain strictly limited, rooted in and controlled by newly defined territorial entities' (1968, ix).

Re-imagining the Nation-state

Over the course of her lifetime, Arendt continued to refine her account of politics as a manifestation of the human condition of plurality, but she said very little about how we might establish 'a new law on earth' while still leaving space for the flourishing of politics within particular communities. Canovan (1999, 103–4) argues that 'an Arendtian case for the nation-state' can be built on certain explicit Arendtian commitments, combined with 'the spirit' of Arendt's thinking – but she points out that Arendt herself 'believed that the nation-state was in decline and that the future lay with other types of polity'. It is certainly true that Arendt in *Origins* characterises the original nation-states as already, by the end of the nineteenth century, in fatal decline, and in *On Revolution* she describes the nation-state as a 'short-lived form of government' (2006, 44). As I argued in Chapter 2, however, she continued throughout her life to praise the virtues of constitutional states based on *political* nations, to warn of the dangers of nationalism, and to recognise the continued influence in world politics of nation-states. Canovan (103, 111 and ff.) distinguishes the nation-state form from that of a federal republic, but also points to the similarities between the two forms, and it is my argument that the positive attributes associated with political nationhood on the one hand and federal republicanism on the other are capable of being combined, producing an ideal to which contemporary liberal democracies might conform. It is true, though, that such conformity relies on significant modifications to the principle of sovereignty, as I discuss further below.

Reinvigorating the nation-state also requires unequivocal rejection of the idea that because the nation is the ultimate source of law, law must be answerable to the nation. While a *political* nation grounds the nation-state's basic law through 'the strength of mutual promises' (Arendt 1972, 87), the mutuality of these promises is derived from and evidence of the revolutionary commitment to equality. In modernity we have, at least explicitly, severed the connection between the law of the state and natural law, rejecting Plato's cautionary principle that '[n]ot man, but a god, must be the measure of all things' (Arendt 1968, 299). This is dangerous, but it is not necessarily a cause for regret given that gods are known for serving the interests of those who receive and interpret their edicts. In any case, rather than link the source of law solely to 'the people', the nation-state has taken the principle of equality as its new measure. Although the constitutional commitment to equality is not immune from the capacity of the people to change the law – thereby undoing the constitutional compact that grounds the liberal democratic state, it is most in danger not from explicit denunciation but rather from the failure to extend its promise to all who come before it. Historically, there was a gap between the commitment to equality and the constitution of all members of the state as equals, but as I have discussed in preceding chapters, through the activism of those excluded the liberal democratic state has been forced to extend its promise of equality. The realisation of political equality has been a source of strength and durability, but it will only continue to be so if it is protected and extended to all who come within the purview of the law.

Insofar as its integrity depends on the consistency with which it treats every individual who appears before it as an equal, the democratic constitution is 'no more the expression of a national will or subject to the will of a majority than a building is the expression of the will of its architect or subject to the will of its inhabitants' (Arendt 2006, 155). Thus while rights and popular sovereignty are 'co-original' in the living constitutional project, a defining virtue of the project itself is the legal recognition that it accords – not only to those who currently participate in it, but to all those who are affected by it. Arguably, however, the exercise of popular sovereignty is impossible in circumstances in which even outsiders can demand recognition under the law. Although in his later work Habermas suggests that 'the fading idea of the democratic constitution' can be severed from 'its roots in the nation-state' and revitalised 'in the postnational guise of a constitutionalised world society' (2008, 327), in his early work on the 'co-originality' of rights and popular sovereignty he claims that '[a]ny political community that wants to understand itself as a democracy must at least distinguish between members and non-members' (2001, 107). In advocating for the continued relevance and merits of the nation-state, Canovan (1999) takes for granted that this is the case. She argues that qualifying the sovereign autonomy of nation-states – at least in respect of the sovereign right to police borders – would undermine their viability *as* nation-states (1999, 114). Furthermore, she claims that, 'despite the glaring moral inconsistency in the way that liberal nation-states treat citizens as opposed to non-citizens … it would be unwise to assume that nation-states are dispensable' (1999, 115). In her view, '[b]y giving their citizens a privileged haven of rights guarded against the global torrents of modernity (including the flow of migrants), the mature nation-states do at least mitigate the misery of [global] rightlessness' (1999, 116).

Canovan is wrong to think, though, that the nation-state can provide 'a privileged haven of rights' against 'the flow of migrants'. In making laws for the militarised protection of its borders and for the inhuman treatment of the people who attempt to cross them, the nation-state undermines its constitutional commitment to equality, leading to a corrosion that will ultimately destroy its character as a 'haven of rights', even for its own citizens. It is in Arendt's account of republican politics, combined with a re-reading of her articulation of the 'right to have rights', that we may begin to chart a path out of the conundrums posed by contemporary world politics.

Reclaiming A Public Sphere of Action

In Chapter 3, I described Arendt's account of a public sphere of action within which citizens have equal shares in power and the freedom to initiate projects and to act collaboratively. If politics is reconceived in this manner, in opposition to the liberal idea that the role of government is primarily to secure equal spheres within which individuals are free to pursue their private interests, action becomes an open-ended enactment of solidarity. Its content is not prescribed, but its conduct is enabled by the constitutive law of equality that establishes the public realm as well as the equal standing of citizens within it. Action becomes the basis of the solidarity of citizens, and while some of these citizens are co-nationals, they are not inclined towards nationalism and they see themselves in solidarity with other polities committed to the principle of equality.

This is a demanding account of politics insofar as it assumes widespread public participation and the assumption by citizens of responsibility for what occurs within the public realm. Citizens are 'concerned with public affairs as the affairs of all', as opposed to members of modern mass societies, who 'judge and use all public institutions by the yardstick of [their] private interests' (Arendt 1968, 336). Arendt imagines citizens engaging together in public affairs through grass-roots organisations or councils such as those that have historically sprung up through revolutionary action, for example in Hungary in 1956 (see Canovan 1992, 235–6); but which have, she argues, been chronically ignored and undervalued by historians and political theorists (Arendt 2006, 241). In *On Revolution*, Arendt also discusses with admiration Jefferson's idea for the subdivision of America's states into 'wards' or 'small republics' within which '"every man in the state" could become "an acting member of the Common government"' (2006, 245, quoting Jefferson). Jefferson's ward system was designed to prevent the 'degeneracy of … government' that he thought would inevitably result from the concentration of governing powers not only in the hands of 'the one' or 'the few' but also 'the many':

> the ward system was not meant to strengthen the power of the many but the power of 'every one' within the limits of his competence; and only by breaking up 'the many' into assemblies where every one could count and be counted upon 'shall we be as republican as a large society can be'. (Arendt 2006, 246, quoting Jefferson).

Jefferson did not attempt to specify in any detail the role or function of his citizens' wards, claiming their tasks and concerns would be worked out in practise, as citizens themselves determined. In Arendt's view, this is evidence of the genuinely revolutionary nature of the ward proposal, and it can be contrasted with the actual outcome of the American Revolution, which failed to provide constitutional protection for the 'townships and town hall meetings' that had been 'the original springs of all political activity in the country' (2006, 23). As she puts it, '[i]f the ultimate end of the revolution was freedom and the constitution of a public space where freedom could appear, the *constitutio libertatis*, then the elementary republics of the wards, the only tangible place where everyone could be free, actually [should have constituted] the end of the great republic' (2006, 247).

The fact that these grass-roots fora did not constitute the primary aim and enterprise of 'the great republic' meant that the American Revolution never achieved its potential. Nevertheless, Arendt highlights the achievements of the Revolution which, by comparison with the French, continued to pay attention to political questions, while also successfully enshrining important protections for individual liberty by establishing a federal system and ensuring the institutional separation of government powers. Generally speaking, because only power is able to check power without thereby undermining it, investing power not only in different arms of government but in the constituent parts of a federation enables power to flourish productively but also ensures it is not co-opted for tyrannical purposes (Arendt 2006, 142–3). Thus a federated structure linking citizens' councils and providing a network of representatives to higher councils would allow, Arendt thinks, for genuinely republican engagement and provide an alternative to party political systems that encourage individuals to think of government primarily in terms of their vested interests.

It may be that Arendt's account of republicanism is overly demanding, requiring a level of public engagement beyond the commitment or capacity of the politically anaesthetised members of modern liberal democracies. But a vibrantly inclusive republican politics is possible in more mediated form, and as Waldron (2000, 210–11) points out, Arendt was not opposed to representative politics as such, but rather to 'forms of electoral politics which fail to provide people "with more opportunity to make their voices heard in public than election day"' (quoting 2006, Viking Press edn, 1963, 253 [2006, 245]). The widespread alienation and disaffection within contemporary liberal democracies is symptomatic of societies in which the only public space officially accorded citizens is 'in the ballot box' (Arendt 2006, 245). We have to a great degree lost all conception of a shared public world, along with a sense of responsibility towards that world. At the same time, however, there are many and lively civil protest movements operating within states and internationally. These include a range of conservation movements and campaigns to protect the environment; the World Social Forum (countering the World Economic Forum); and a variety of pro-refugee campaigns including the *sans pâpiers* movement in Europe and the 'No One Is Illegal' campaign in Northern America. These provide evidence of a willingness and capacity, in some sectors of liberal democratic society at least (as well as in non-liberal states), to construct public worlds committed to the principle of equality. Humanity's common future surely depends on such constructive efforts.

The Right to Have Rights

I have argued strongly that liberal democracies must extend legal recognition to all who come into contact with their laws. It is useful to engage with the implications of this through a re-reading of the 'right to have rights'. The phrase was first used by Arendt in an essay, '"The Rights of Man": What are They?' published in 1949 in response to the adoption by the United Nations of the Universal Declaration of Human Rights (UDHR). Against the Declaration's claim that all humans are the subjects of a rather extensive list of 'equal and inalienable rights', Arendt argues that there is only one human right: 'the right to have rights', or 'the right of every human being to membership in a political community' (1949, 34) and to citizenship (1949, 37).

The phrase 'a right to have rights' is puzzling. As Michelman (1996, 200) says, '[i]t's a nice expression. When you think about it, though, what possible sense can it make?' The phrase seems to be self-defeating – one can imagine a situation in which people appear to have no rights, and yet if they have the 'right to have rights' they have at least this one right – while at the same time lacking the rights that they are supposed to have 'as of right'. Similarly, if one has rights, how can one stand in need of 'a right to have' these rights, which one already holds 'as of right'? In Michelman's account, the puzzle can be resolved – although not, he thinks, in a manner consistent with Arendt's own intent – by treating the phrase as a 'a two-place expression' designating different concepts, such that the 'right to have' can be thought of as an 'acquisition right', while 'rights' can be thought of as 'object rights' (1996, 201). The coherence of the expression would then be saved, Michelman says, by understanding the acquisition right as 'an ideal matter of moral obligation or entitlement' and the object rights as 'empirical' or 'institutional' rights (1996, 201). But Michelman notes that 'this reading constructs a duality of planes or fields of rights – the moral and the empirical … and this dualistic construction, obvious and familiar as we may find it, lacks purchase in Arendt's conception of how a right comes to be and how a person comes to have it' (203–4).

Rather than reading 'the right to have rights' against the grain of Arendt's thought, Michelman suggests a reading that accepts the ambiguous and recursive nature of the phrase. In this reading, a person has rights – and does so in a sense in which the moral and empirical cannot be differentiated – only insofar as that person has 'individually participated, by "action", in the social production of moral consciousness' (1996, 204). What follows from this reading is the apparent impossibility of anyone claiming 'a right to have rights', given it presupposes that one is already engaged among others in the production of rights (1996, 206). This leads Michelman to conclude that Arendt is 'pointing to the irreparable groundlessness of rights, affirming our own precarious, existential, collective self-care when it comes to creating and maintaining in this world the conditions of civility and humanity for any or for all' (1996, 207).

My account of the right to have rights accepts Michelman's insights, but attempts to move beyond his conclusion by specifying not how we might provide a 'ground' for rights, but rather how we might generate enabling conditions for 'creating and maintaining ... conditions of civility and humanity ... for all'. In my argument, this requires recognition that the liberal democratic state's founding law of equality, which constitutes citizens as equals and grounds the authority of legitimate government, can be extended beyond the particular group of citizens who are at any one time the source of its authority. Thought of metaphorically, a constitutive law of equality is a living project that is upheld and sustained by the commitment of citizens. Through the participation of citizens, the state's law not only secures equality but reflects and gives voice to a politically distinctive culture. Given, however, that this project is dynamic and open-ended (as I argued in Chapter 8) it is capable of incorporating newcomers, who are formally recognised as equals and who then, through their democratic engagement, may have the opportunity to participate in the 'precarious, existential, collective self-care' that is required to sustain a political sphere based on the commitment to equality. As things now stand, the consistency of the law in liberal democracies is upheld in respect of outsiders who are welcome and thus whose presence is legally sanctioned because they are provided with recognition and the formal protections that the law affords to citizens. While they may not be immediately entitled to participate actively in the development of the law, most liberal democracies provide that they can become fully-fledged citizens after a certain period of residency. If this is not the case, and if the state attempts to indefinitely or permanently exclude them from citizenship, then the integrity of the law is undermined by their presence as it is undermined by the border policing regimes that are designed to exclude refugees from access to the law. Refugees who seek entry without authorisation to the liberal state come into contact with its law – even if only via the exceptional measures through which border regimes are managed, and they suffer its coercive power but they are afforded neither recognition nor protection under it. This situation is corrosive of the law and its characteristic impartiality. Even though the current authors of the law (or their representatives) would prefer to exclude them, refugees must be afforded formal recognition and protection under the law. Whether they are then entitled to participate in the law as fully constituted authors and equals depends on whether they are able to live a decent life in their home country, as I discuss further below.

Characterised as a right held by 'man as man' (Arendt 1949, 36) – or rather, 'human as human', the right to have rights appears to suffer from the same defects that Arendt critiques in the eighteenth century's announcement of human rights (defects that appear again in the twentieth century's rights declarations). It sounds like an abstract right, posited as the apolitical natural inheritance or 'birth right' of all human beings. On the contrary, although it has not yet been secured, the need for it arises from the existence of a global polity. When Arendt says that the right to have rights is the only universal human right, what she means is that it is the only right that correlates to the existence of a global community and whose realisation requires the struggle for mutual recognition within this community. Because it 'does not spring "from within the nation" [it] ... needs more than national guarantees' (Arendt 1949, 34). Its significance is fundamental: it is the only right 'without which no other can materialise' (1949, 37). Prior to the existence of a global community, however, it would indeed have been conceived in natural, and thus pre-political, terms. But in this form it could not – Arendt would argue – have been successfully defended (or understood) in the language of rights. It was simply 'a general characteristic of the human condition which no tyrant could take away' (1949, 30).

That an individual's life was rooted in the life of a particular community appeared as an incontestable fact about human life: each was born into and lived in community with others. Although the majority were excluded from the political sphere, Arendt argues that they remained members of society and participated in the fabric of social life (1969, 297).[3] Although individuals could be exiled, or choose to withdraw from a particular community, they were free to move from place to place, and were never, Arendt argues, as a result of their exile excluded from membership as such. Informal recognition of asylum as well as in medieval times of the principle '*quidquid est in territorio est de territorio*' ('whomever is in the territory is of the territory') ensured that exiles and refugees were brought within the legal jurisdiction of the country to which they fled (1968, 280).[4] It is only since the global application of the principle of sovereignty that membership of political communities has itself acquired a political cast. As something that humans can be denied altogether, it has become something that human institutions – the products of law and politics – must be created to protect.

Arguably, the right to have rights could be realised on the basis of membership of a global community in which a whole range of rights are specified and secured. This is the position at which Habermas has now arrived, suggesting that 'a politically constituted world society' must secure peaceful relations between states as well as the full range of human rights for individuals globally (2008, 316). In his view, this is possible without global society 'taking on the character of a state'

---

3 While Arendt recognises that 'the rule over slaves in antiquity' tended towards totalitarianism by depriving people 'not only of the political realm' but also of a private life (1968, 475), she suggests that even slaves 'belonged to some sort of human community; their labor was needed, used, and exploited, and this kept them within the pale of humanity' (1968, 297).

4 See also Wimmer 2004, 53: 'From the middle of the nineteenth century onwards, citizenship rights turned away from the medieval principle of *quidquid est in territorio est de territorio* and were more and more restricted to persons sharing a specific national background'. Note that Arendt's claim ignores the phenomenon of 'civil death' (see, for example, Agamben's discussion in *Homo Sacer* 1988).

(2008, 322), but to the extent that human rights are institutionalised democratically through 'the strength of mutual promises', they require the backing and support of a state-based legal system. If human rights are secured by global institutions and a coercive apparatus that is not, however, legitimated democratically, then Habermas' global rights regime will be oppressive and deprive individuals of political agency – they will be the 'beneficiaries' of rights but not authors of the law that upholds and administers these rights. In either case, political plurality will suffer. The right to have rights must be realised, insofar as this is possible, in a manner consistent with the plurality that is a precondition of politics. The right 'of every individual to belong to humanity' (Arendt 1968, 298) is a right to membership in a state among states, or 'a country among countries' (Arendt 1995, 81). Nevertheless, recognition of the right necessarily limits the sovereign autonomy of these polities.

In Arendt's account, these limits must be strictly circumscribed. In '"The Rights of Man": What Are They?' she argues against an expansive interpretation of crimes against humanity, which she says alone correspond to 'the one human right' (1949, 37).[5] Crimes against humanity are a 'specialty of totalitarian regimes' and a 'supreme ... crime' (1949, 36), involving the attempt to annihilate an entire people or group firstly by stripping them of citizenship and of all juridical and legal status and then by herding them into camps. Crimes against humanity are distinct from other forms of oppression in that they target an entire group, destroying the political agency of its members along with their private lives and ordinary human relationships (1949, 36–7).

Arendt argues that crimes against humanity alone require a law above the nations, justifying action 'that would not have to respect the rights and rules of sovereignty' (1949, 37) and involving the establishment of an international penal code and 'an international tribunal where mankind, the plaintiff, [can] bring suit against those who have offended humanity' (2007, 492). Such suit would differ fundamentally from the case brought, for example, by Israel against the Nazi Adolf Eichmann; a case that Arendt famously and controversially detailed in *Eichmann in Jerusalem*. In Arendt's view, the approach taken by the prosecution in that case was fatally flawed because it assumed that Eichmann's crimes were an attack on the Jewish people, rather than 'crimes against mankind committed on the body of the Jewish people' (1994, 7). The attempt to destroy a specific group of people is an affront to humanity as such because it destroys the human world created by plurality. Just as a plurality of individual perspectives *within* a polity may enlarge the outlook of its members, and contributes to the creation of their common world, at the level of humanity:

5 Much of what Arendt says in 'The Rights of Man' is replicated in the second half of Chapter 9 of *Origins*, although she does not discuss there the connection between the right to have rights and what she calls crimes against humanity.

> the world comes into being only if there are perspectives ... If a people or a nation, or even just some specific human group, which offers a unique view of the world arising from its particular vision of the world ... is annihilated, it is not merely that a people or a nation or a given number of individuals perishes, but rather that a portion of our common world is destroyed, an aspect of the world that has revealed itself to us until now but can never reveal itself again. (*The Promise of Politics* 2005, 175 in Owens 2007, 109)

Genocide is now recognised as a crime in international law (Convention on the Prevention and Punishment of the Crime of Genocide 1948; Rome Statute of the International Criminal Court 1998, Art.6). The concept of a 'crime against humanity' is also recognised, although it is defined in terms of a 'widespread and systematic attack' on a civilian population (Rome Statute, Art.7) and as such bears no relation to Arendt's claim that a 'crime against humanity' is an attack on human plurality. Genocide, however, is defined by reference to an attack on a 'national, ethnical, racial or religious group' 'with intent to destroy [that group] in whole or in part' and thus provides the contemporary correlate to Arendt's conception. While the attempt to hold individuals internationally accountable for involvement in genocide and other crimes against humanity is laudable, notorious difficulties have now arisen associated with using these crimes to licence armed ('humanitarian') intervention in states. Securing the 'right to have rights' in the form of a universal right to citizenship, although not an element of the right explicitly discussed by Arendt, would do more to protect individuals and minorities globally than problematic reliance on a right to intervene to prevent genocide.[6] If individuals and peoples are genuinely free to leave their own states and cross borders into other states – and particularly to leave their own regions and claim refuge in the wealthy liberal world, then genocidal attacks will be considerably less effective. Had Europe's inter-war refugees been free to leave Europe and gain entry to Britain, the Americas and other parts of the world, far fewer would have died in the gas chambers.

As well as arguing for 'a law above the nations' that allows states, acting as representatives of all humanity, to intervene to prevent genocide, Arendt implies that anyone fleeing genocide has a right to be granted citizenship in another country – although as noted already, she is not explicit about this and she does not say anything about how the right might be secured. She is clear, however, that her 'right to have rights' extends beyond the traditional right to asylum. She describes asylum as the only right ever to have 'figured as a symbol of the

6 This is so even if 'the international community' of states is acting as representative for all humanity, as Arendt argues it should. This would mean that decisions would have to be genuinely representative, on the basis of one person, one vote, and no states or groups would have veto powers – as is the case with the current UN Security Council, which is the body currently licensed to authorise intervention under Chapter VII of the UN Charter.

Rights of Man in the sphere of international relations' (1968, 280-1), but notes that historically it was offered in the discretion of the state or city of asylum to individuals persecuted in their home state for political or religious commitments that were not, however, outlawed in the place of asylum. Genocidal attacks do not focus on the religious or political convictions of individual members of groups; instead individuals are targeted simply because they are identified with a particular group. While the group itself may be defined in political or religious terms, it might also be singled out on the basis of racial, ethnic or national criteria. The right to citizenship invoked by Arendt is thus more expansive than the ancient right to asylum, and it also requires more than securing the right to asylum now contained in Article 14 of the UDHR. In my argument, a right to have rights must be secured in a global Citizenship Convention that accords legal status to victims or targets of genocide. Unlike the right to asylum in the UDHR, this would allow genocide victims to travel lawfully across borders without prior authorisation and it would accord them legal status in all countries. It would also assure them citizenship in a country other than their own. How and where citizenship would be awarded would be worked out in concert with the genocide victims themselves and states parties to the Convention, as representatives of all humanity, or by an organisation such as the UN High Commissioner for Refugees acting under the Convention on humanity's behalf. The Convention would include sanctions (such as fines) for breaches, allowing states that attempt to prevent border crossings or that do not meet their commitments under the Convention to be penalised.

A Citizenship Convention providing legal status and citizenship to victims of genocide would secure the 'right to have rights' as Arendt articulates it in 'The Rights of Man', but in this form it fails to address the issue to which she draws our attention in *Origins* – that of large scale people movements and *de facto* statelessness, not all of which could plausibly be characterised as a response to genocidal threats. While the majority of the inter-war refugees were members of minorities that were persecuted or discriminated against in their home states, the forms of discrimination they suffered were various and included economic as well as other disadvantage (see Arendt 1968, 286 and my discussion in Chapter 1). In contemporary refugee movements we see what the UN High Commissioner for Refugees refers to as 'mixed migration' streams, with a jumble of different groups fleeing a range of circumstances including group based persecution but also war, natural disaster and poverty.

If these people are deprived of legal status in the countries to which they flee and corralled into camps, as is increasingly the case throughout the industrialised as well as the developing world – even if the initial purpose of these camps is not extermination, the impact on the people detained may come precariously close to it. There is a danger that they will be rendered superfluous beings whose 'enforced abstract existence ... [and] unrelatedness to the outside world' becomes 'a constant temptation to murderers' (Arendt 1949, 33). This temptation has already proved too much in the camp run by Australia on Manus Island in Papua New Guinea.[7] It is, nevertheless, an outcome to be avoided at all costs. We who build the camps must take responsibility for what goes on within them.

As I have discussed throughout this book, the power of liberal democratic government is legitimated on the basis of universalist principles, and political equality has supplanted the idea that any individual or group is born to govern or to occupy a privileged status in society. The egalitarian and non-discriminatory principles that ground the liberal state are inconsistent with allowing the arbitrary circumstances of individuals' birth – including *where* they are born – to stunt their life chances or exclude them permanently from the possibility of a decent life. This fact provides further justification for the expansive refugee definition that I spelled out in my introductory chapter. It is for this reason – as well as to uphold laws of equality and to prevent the degeneration of our societies associated with running detention camps, that wealthy liberal democracies must agree among themselves on the terms of a multi-lateral refugee resettlement treaty, going beyond the provisions of the Citizenship Convention that I have been discussing. A core provision of a multi-lateral refugee resettlement treaty would be its recognition that all refugees are entitled to legal status within the territory of states parties, regardless of their mode of arrival. This legal status would provide the legal persona and presumptive equality that I argued in earlier chapters is a prerequisite for recognition as a subject of justice within liberal states, but which until now has been premised on national membership. The treaty would also provide for the institution of a 'worldwide migration service' (Skran 1995, 99) to facilitate global refugee movements and manage the burden-sharing of resettlement obligations among states.

Unless wealthy liberal democracies are able to forge a genuine 'comity' to support such a treaty, they will continue on their current path. States and regional groupings will compete with each other to deter refugees, with disastrous consequences not only for the refugees but also for international relations and for the rule of law within states. Fears that liberal states will be swamped by refugees if they accord them legal recognition are over-stated. Many liberal states currently have large non-humanitarian migration programs, and they could divert places currently awarded under these programs to refugees. It is certainly true, however, that if militarised border controls are dismantled and entry systems simplified, many more people will enter these countries than is currently the case.

In the event that genuine and transparent assessment processes are conducted and it is found that applicants for permanent residence are able to live a decent life – as I discussed that concept in my introduction – in their home country, liberal democracies may refuse to offer them citizenship. This refusal is consistent with the significance for all humanity of political plurality and the stability that is provided by legal and territorial boundaries. Nevertheless, liberal democracies have an obligation to accord all people, while they remain on the

---

7 See Introduction, 1 and Chapter 7, 123.

state's territory or subject to its power, equality in access to and protection under the law. Here, however, equality need not imply the equality of the subject who is author as well as object of the law. Although recognition of a global community now requires recognition of the political agency and legal status of all its members, this status need not immediately accord all membership rights within particular liberal states. Rather, it ensures that refugees are no longer treated as an anomalous category insofar as the basic protection of the law is concerned. While some differences in treatment may be justified in law – as they are in relation to ordinary visitors who are lawfully present under current immigration regimes, these differences cannot threaten fundamental rule of law principles. Among these is the principle that a person can only be detained after being convicted and sentenced in a court of law for conduct that breaches the ordinary criminal law. This is conduct of which any person may be guilty – it cannot be defined solely by reference to members of a particular class of people such as non-citizens.

Liberal states may encourage people who are *not* refugees in the expansive sense in which I have been using the term to return to their home country, but this is not the end of the story insofar as their obligations are concerned. These democracies cannot insulate their legal systems from the global basic structure in which they now participate. This multilayered web of international institutions influences the life chances of individuals everywhere. Furthermore, it disproportionately advantages the world's wealthiest states, including many liberal democracies (Pogge 2005). Its existence implicates liberal democracies in what happens in other countries around the world. This means, as I suggested earlier, that the integrity of the liberal state's constitutive law of equality may be corroded even by its involvement in international institutions or its indirect involvement in foreign countries. Given this involvement, there is a strong case to be made for recognition by liberal states of global distributive justice obligations. Such obligations might be discharged in a variety of ways, to be worked out within each state and by agreement among liberal states. Recognition of these obligations need not threaten political plurality because it will not be centrally enforced. Such recognition will in fact contribute to plurality because greater equity in global resource distribution will challenge the current concentration of power in wealthy states. If individuals' lives can be improved within their home countries to a degree that means they no longer want to leave them, then this may be a better outcome both for these individuals and for destination states. These states are currently far from being inundated by the world's refugees, but they may face considerable difficulties if they adopt border regimes guided by justice rather than by power and privilege, while at the same time failing to act on broader distributive justice obligations. All humanity has an interest in the preservation of democratic institutions and the cultural, social and economic life that supports these institutions within independent states. This is only true, however, if these institutions act as barriers to tyranny or totalitarianism and are not preserved – as I have argued they cannot be – at the cost of outsiders.

Conclusion

I have suggested that Arendt's explicit articulation of the 'right to have rights' is relatively confined – although still expansive by current standards. I have also suggested, however, that liberal democracies have obligations to refugees that extend well beyond a universal 'right to have rights'. In *Origins*, Arendt's account of the right to have rights is in fact broadly rendered (1968, 296–302), as we saw in Chapter 1. Here she describes it as a right to membership of a community within which a flourishing public sphere ensures the equality of citizens who are able to speak and to be heard, to act and to have an impact. She says that 'a right to have rights … means to live in a framework where one is judged by one's actions and opinions' (1968, 296–7).[8] Arendt also claims in *Origins* that '[o]ur political life rests on the assumption that we can produce equality through organization, because man can act in and change and build a common world, together with his equals and only with his equals' (1968, 301). As members of liberal states, we must defend the state's constitutive law of equality by extending recognition and protection to refugees, and we must act to revitalise the revolutionary promise of equality on which our common world rests. The realisation of our capacity for freedom – not merely autonomy – depends on this, as does our ability to contribute to a shared future. It is only by acting and by assuming political responsibility that we begin to build a world rather than simply subsisting in a world over which we have no control. Only by acting together with our equals do we experience genuinely emancipatory forms of solidarity free from the stain of xenophobic nationalism. Our engagement as political equals within a liberal state makes possible our engagement with a wider human community.

In *philosophical* terms, this community is sustained by dialogue and recognition of a human commonality such as that which Solzhenitsyn invoked when he accepted the Nobel Prize in 1970. Individuals and discrete political communities retain a commitment to and appreciation of their cultural and historical traditions, but they renounce 'the binding authority and universal validity which tradition and past have always claimed' (Arendt 1995, 84). The result is 'a philosophy of mankind' (Arendt 1995, 91) grounded in human plurality. While it is not politically prescriptive, it recognises the importance of politics, treating it as 'one of the great human realms of life' and a precondition for the exercise of human freedom. In *political* terms, the human community must be recognised both in the form of a comity of nations and a world polity.

8 Having an 'opinion' is not a trivial matter but relates to a person's responsibility as an equal in a collaborative sphere of action. As Waldron (2000, 209) suggests, 'it involves a serious effort to see an issue from the point of view of all those affected by it'.

Unlike the Stoic cosmopolis and the realm of natural law and innate human rights, the universal human polity is grounded in the political agency of its individual members, and a mutual commitment among them to recognise this agency. This commitment affords the right to citizenship to all people as a matter of justice. In doing so, it promises a future worthy of our human capacities and hope to those people who, because they have been severed from their own community, are now excluded from humanity and treated everywhere as the scum of the earth.

Bibliography

Newspaper Articles and Commentary, Media Reports and Media Releases

AAP/theguardian.com. 2014. 'Lifeboat reportedly used by Australia to return asylum seekers found in Java'. 1 February.

Aly, Waleed. 2014. 'The logic of PNG policy is sanctioned horror'. *The Age*. 21 February.

Andrews, Kevin. (Minister for Immigration and Citizenship). 2007. 'Media release: Status of Sri Lankan asylum seekers'. KA087/07. 12 September.

Annan, Kofi A. 1999. 'Two concepts of sovereignty'. *The Economist*. 18 September.

Australian Broadcasting Corporation. 2005. 'Removal of failed asylum seekers'. The Law Report. 10 May.

Australian Broadcasting Coroporation. 2008. 'The guards' story'. Four Corners. 15 September.

Australian Broadcasting Coroporation. 2010. 'Children remain in immigration detention'. Lateline Report. 11 October.

Australian Democrats. 2007. 'Mandatory detention action plan'. 21 November.

Bachelard, Michael. 2012. 'Asylum seekers tried to drown, says fellow fugitive'. *Sydney Morning Herald*. 20 January.

Beardsley, Eleanor. 2009. 'French police clear Calais refugee camp'. National Public Radio. 22 September.

Callinan, Rory and Whyte, Sarah. 2014. 'Suspects in death of man at Manus Island Detention Centre keep watch over his body'. *The Age*. 21 February.

Clennell, Andrew. 2000. 'Hopes fade for missing boat people'. *Sydney Morning Herald*. 13 April.

Cordell, Marni. 2014. 'Manus Camp a human "experiment": Staff'. newmatilda.com. 25 February.

Cullen, Simon and Woodley, Naomi. 2014. 'Manus Island riots: Two investigations underway as government sticks by its policies'. ABC News, 'AM program'. 19 February.

Dastyari, Azadeh. 2008. 'The detained refugees Obama will not free'. *The Age*. Melbourne, Australia, 24 November.

Davies, Julie-Anne. 2013. 'Asylum policy of deterrence threatening families'. *The Age*. Melbourne, Australia, 15 November.

Davies, Julie-Anne. 2013a. 'Abbott's new world order'. *The Age*. Melbourne, Australia, 15 November.

Davies, Lizzy. 2010. 'Back in Romania, Roma plan return to the west'. *The Guardian Weekly*. 24–30 September.

The Economist. 2013. 'Immigration reform: Getting there'. 6 April.

Flitton, Daniel. 2014. 'A conundrum at the heart of the Pacific solution'. *The Canberra Times*. 20 February.

Fraser, Malcolm. 2014. 'Manus Island: So many questions, one simple solution'. *The Age*, 'Comment'. 21 February.

Gordon, Michael and Ireland, Judith. 2014. 'Neck of asylum seeker killed on Manus Island "had been cut"'. *Canberra Times.* 22 February.

Gordon, Michael and Whyte, Sarah. 2014. 'Manus Island violence: Interpreter claims detainees attacked by locals, "there was blood everywhere"'. *Canberra Times*. 20 February.

Gordon, Michael, Whyte, Sarah and Wroe, David. 2014. 'Parliament to probe Manus Island riot'. *Sydney Morning Herald.* 5 March.

The Greens, Australia. 2013. 'Caring for refugees in our community'. Refugee Policy Statement.

Hall, Bianca. 2013. 'Human rights chief warned off islands visit'. *Sydney Morning Herald.* 5 March.

Hall, Bianca. 2014. 'Minister wants boat people called illegals'. *Sydney Morning Herald.* 20 October.

Hansen-Young, Sarah. 2010. 'Landmark High Court ruling demands changes to the Migration Act'. Greens Party Media Release. Canberra, Australia, 11 November.

Hill, Jess. 2013. 'Asylum seekers: Drowning on our watch'. Background Briefing. Australian Broadcasting Corporation, Radio National. 1 September.

Hunter, Emma (writing under a pseudonym). 2013. 'My experience as a nurse on Christmas Island changed the core of my being'. theguardian.com. 21 November.

Isaacs, Mark, et al. 2013. 'The Nauru riot: Staff condemn cruel and degrading conditions'. Statement by past and present Salvation Army staff members. 23 July. http://www.refugeecouncil.org.au/n/mr/130723-Salvos-Nauru.pdf.

Irin News. 2013. 'Tough Australian policy fails to discourage Sri Lankan asylum seekers'. 29 November.

Lagan, Bernard. 2010. 'A lean, mean America turns on its illegal migrants'. *The Age*. 14 July.

Laughland, Oliver. 2014. 'Locked up and out of Australia'. *The Guardian Weekly*. 7–13 February.

McKenna, Michael. 2014. 'Troublemakers to face "jail within a jail"'. *The Australian*. 25 February.

McQuillen, William. 2010. 'Nine States back Arizona's tough stance on migrants'. *The Age*. 16 July.

Miller, Nick. 2008. 'New mental illness hits refugees'. *The Age.* 28 May.

Mogelson, Luke. 2013. 'The dream boat'. *The New York Times Magazine*. 15 November.

Morris, Nigel. 2008. 'Britain closes door on 80,000 asylum seekers'. *The Independent*. 5 November.

Murdoch, Lindsay. 2014. 'Australia asks Cambodia to take asylum seekers amid violent crackdown'. *The Age*. 24 February.
Murphy, Katharine. 2013. 'Scott Morrison imposes information blackout on self-harm in detention'. theguardian.com. 11 October.
Narushima, Yuko. 2010. 'Self-harm rates increase fourfold'. *The Age*. 4 October.
Narushima, Yuko. 2010a. '"Security risk" refugees left in limbo'. *The Age*. 22 April.
Nicholson, Brendan. 2000. 'Hundreds die tied up to hulks'. *The Age*. 23 July.
Nyakairu, Frank. 2010. 'Xenophobia hitting asylum seekers: UNHCR'. reuters.com. 16 April.
Pearlman, Jonathan. 2009. 'UN role on refugees "has to change"'. *The Age*. 28 October.
Pilkington, Ed. 2010. 'Latinos flee Arizona's new laws'. *The Age*. 20 July.
Rhiannon, Lee. 2010. 'Government refugee policy failure: One suicide, mass hunger strike at Villawood'. Greens Party Media Release. Canberra, Australia, 20 September.
Roberts, Michelle. 2009. 'AP impact: Immigrants face detention, few rights'. foxnews.com/The Associated Press. 15 March.
RTÉ News. 2009. 'Riot police dismantle Calais refugee camp'. 22 September.
Shenker, Jack. 2013. 'Mediterranean migrant deaths: A litany of largely avoidable loss'. *The Guardian*. 4 October.
Simon, C. 2007. 'Why do they treat us like criminals?' *The Guardian Weekly*. 30 November.
Smith, Lauren. 2014. 'Ex-immigration officer: Is there asylum seeker blood on my hands?' crikey.com.au. http://www.crikey.com.au/2014/01/30/ex-immigration-officer-is-there-asylum-seeker-blood-on-my-hands/
Stevis, Matina and Ball, Deborah. 2013. 'A Cargo of Human Woe as Refugees Risk All to Reach Europe'. *The Wall Street Journal/The Australian*. 21–22 December.
Sydney Morning Herald. 2008. 'Govt denies backflip on island excision'. 21 February.
Taylor, Lenore. 2014. 'Coalition offers Indonesia extra money to help halt flow of asylum seekers'. *The Guardian*. 16 January.
Topsfield, Jewel. 2007. 'Minister condemned for "abuse of rights"'. *The Age*. 13 October.
Topsfield, Jewel. 2007a. 'We were given expired saline: Hunger strikers'. *The Age*. 14 September.
Urbina, Ian and Rentz, Catherine. 2013, 'Immigrants held in solitary cells, often for weeks'. *The New York Times*. 23 March.
Vincent, F. 2003. 'The real dangers to our rights'. *The Age*. 28 October.
Wroe, David and Callinan, Rory. 2014. 'Island MP says unrest avoidable'. *The Age*. 24 February.
Wroe, David and Swan, Jonathan. 2014. 'Abbott stands by his man'. *The Age*. 24 February.

Wroe, David, Whyte, Sarah and Wen, Philip. 2014. 'Manus Island police chief slams Tony Abbott'. brisbanetimes.com. 21 February.

Journal Articles, Books, etc.

Agamben, Georgio. 1988. *Homo Sacer: Sovereign Power and Bare Life*. Daniel Heller-Roazen (trans.). Stanford, CA: Stanford University Press.

Agamben, Giorgio. 1994. 'We Refugees'. Michael Rocke (trans.). *Symposium* 49 no. 2: 114–19.

American Civil Liberties Union. 2009. Issues Brief: Prolonged Immigration Detention of Individuals Who are Challenging Removal. USA: ACLU Immigrants' Rights Project.

Amnesty International, USA. 2012. *In Hostile Terrain: Human Rights Violations in Immigration Enforcement in the US Southwest*. New York: Amnesty International USA.

Annas, Julia. 1993. *The Morality of Happiness*. New York and Oxford: Oxford University Press.

Arendt, Hannah. 1949. '"The Rights of Man": What Are They?' *Modern Review* 3 no. 1: 24–37.

Arendt, Hannah. 1968 [1951]. *The Origins of Totalitarianism*. USA: Harcourt Inc.

Arendt, Hannah. 1972 [1969]. *Crises of the Republic*. USA: Harcourt Brace & Co.

Arendt, Hannah. 1978. 'The Jew as Pariah: A Hidden Tradition' in Hannah Arendt, *The Jewish Writings*. Jerome Kohn and Ron H. Feldman (eds). New York: Grove Press, Inc., 275–97.

Arendt, Hannah. 1992 [1982]. *Lectures on Kant's Political Philosophy*. Ronald Beiner (ed.). USA: The University of Chicago Press.

Arendt, Hannah. 1992a. *Hannah Arendt, Karl Jaspers: Correspondence, 1926–1969*. Lotte Kohler and Hans Saner (eds), Robert Kimber and Rita Kimber (trans.). New York: Harcourt Brace Jovanovich.

Arendt, Hannah. 1994 [1946]. 'The Nation' in *Essays in Understanding 1930–1954*. Jerome Kohn (ed.). USA: Harcourt Brace & Co., 206–11.

Arendt, Hannah. 1994a [1963]. *Eichmann in Jerusalem: A Report on the Banality of Evil*. USA: Penguin Books.

Arendt, Hannah. 1995 [1968]. *Men in Dark Times*. USA: Harcourt Brace & Co.

Arendt, Hannah. 1998 [1958]. *The Human Condition*. Chicago and London: The University of Chicago Press.

Arendt, Hannah. 2000 [1943]. 'We Refugees' in *Hitler's Exiles: Personal Stories of the Flight from Nazi Germany to America*. Mark M. Anderson (ed.). New York: The New Press.

Arendt, Hannah. 2003. *Responsibility and Judgment*. New York: Schocken Books.

Arendt, Hannah. 2006 [1963]. *On Revolution*. USA: Penguin Books.

Arendt, Hannah. 2007. *The Jewish Writings*. Jerome Kohn and Ron H. Feldman (eds). USA: Schocken Books.

Arendt, Hannah. 2007a [1953]. 'The Great Tradition, I. Law and Power'. *Social Research* 74 no. 3, Fall: 713–26.
Arendt, Hannah. 2007b [1953]. 'The Great Tradition, II. Ruling and Being Ruled'. *Social Research* 74 no. 4, Winter: 941–54.
Aristotle. 1976 [1955] *The Nicomachean Ethics*. J.A.K. Thomson (trans.). England: Penguin Books.
Aristotle. 1998. [1995] *Politics*. Ernest Barker (trans.). Oxford and New York: Oxford University Press.
Australian Human Rights Commission (AHRC). 2010. 'Immigration Detention on Christmas Island'.
Australian Human Rights Commission (AHRC). 2011. 'Immigration Detention at Villawood: Summary of Observations from Visit to Immigration Detention Facilities at Villawood'.
Australian Human Rights Commission (AHRC). 2012. 'Immigration Detention on Christmas Island: Observations from Visit to Immigration Detention Facilities on Christmas Island'.
Australian Human Rights Commission (AHRC). 2013. 'Asylum Seekers, Refugees, and Human Rights: Snapshot Report'.
Barry, Brian and Goodin, Robert E. 1992. *Free Movement: Ethical Issues in the Transnational Migration of People and Money.* UK: Harvester Wheatsheaff.
Bashford, Alison and Strange, Carolyn. 2002. 'Asylum-Seekers and National Histories of Detention'. *Australian Journal of Politics and History* 48 no. 4: 509–27.
Bauböck, Rainer. 1997. 'Citizenship and National Identities in the European Union'. Jean Monnet Working Paper no. 4.
Beiner, Ronald. 2000. 'Arendt and Nationalism' in *The Cambridge Companion to Hannah Arendt.* Dana Villa (ed.). UK: Cambridge University Press, 44–62.
Beiner, Ronald and Booth, William James (eds). 1993. *Kant and Political Philosophy: The Contemporary Legacy*. USA: Yale University Press.
Beitz, Charles R. 1983. 'Cosmopolitan Ideals and National Sentiment'. *The Journal of Philosophy* 80 no. 10, pt. 1: 591–600. Eightieth Annual Meeting of the American Philosophical Association, Eastern Division, October.
Beitz, Charles R. 1985. 'Justice and International Relations' in *International Ethics*. Charles R. Beitz, Marshall Cohen, Thomas Scanlon and John A. Simmons (eds). Princeton, NJ: Princeton University Press, 282–311.
Beitz, Charles R. 1991. 'Sovereignty and Morality in International Affairs' in *Political Theory Today.* David Held (ed.). Oxford: Polity Press, 236–54.
Beitz, Charles R. 1999 [1979]. *Political Theory and International Relations.* Princeton: Princeton University Press.
Beitz, Charles R. 2001. 'Human Rights as a Common Concern'. *American Political Science Review* 95, June 2001: 269–82.
Bem, Kazimierz, Field, Nina, Maclellan, Nick, Meyer, Sarah and Morris, Tony 2007. *A Price Too High: The Cost of Australia's Approach to Asylum Seekers.* Australia: A Just Australia and Oxfam Australia.

Benhabib, Seyla. 1988. 'Judgment and the Moral Foundations of Politics in Arendt's Thought'. *Political Theory* 16 no. 1: 29–51.

Benhabib, Seyla. 1996. *The Reluctant Modernism of Hannah Arendt*. USA: Sage Publications Inc.

Benhabib, Seyla. 2002. *The Claims of Culture*. Princeton and Oxford: Princeton University Press.

Benhabib, Seyla. 2002a. 'Political Geographies in a Global World: Arendtian Reflections'. *Social Research* 69 no. 2: 539.

Benhabib, Seyla. 2004. *The Rights of Others: Aliens, Residents and Citizens*. Cambridge, UK: Cambridge University Press.

Benhabib, Seyla. 2005. 'On the Alleged Conflict between Democracy and International Law'. *Ethics and International Affairs* 19 no. 1: 85–100.

Benhabib, Seyla. 2006. 'Another Cosmopolitanism' in *Another Cosmopolitanism, with Commentaries by Jeremy Waldron, Bonnie Honig, and Will Kymlicka*. Robert Post (ed.). Oxford: Oxford University Press, 13–82.

Beyani, Chaloka. 1999. 'The Legal Premises for the International Protection of Human Rights' in *The Reality of International Law – Essays in Honour of Ian Brownlie*. Guy Goodwin-Gill and Stefan Talmon (eds). New York: Oxford University Press, 21–35.

Bingham, Tom. 2006. 'The Rule of Law'. The Sixth Sir David Williams Lecture. Cambridge University: Centre for Public Law, 16 November.

Birmingham, Peg. 2006. *Hannah Arendt and Human Rights: The Predicament of Common Responsibility*. USA: Indiana University Press.

Blake, Michael. 2003. 'Immigration' in *A Companion to Applied Ethics*. R.G. Frey and Christopher Heath Wellman (eds). Malden, MA: Blackwell, 224–37.

Blay, Sam, Burn, Jennifer and Keyzer, Patrick. 2007. *Offshore Processing of Asylum Seekers: The Search for Legitimate Parameters*. Sydney: Halstead Press [No.9 UTS Law Review].

Blitz, Brad and Lynch, Maureen (eds). 2009. *Statelessness and the Benefits of Citizenship: A Comparative Study*. Geneva: Geneva Academy of International Humanitarian Law and Human Rights, and the International Observatory on Statelessness.

Bloch, Ernst. 1986 [1961]. *Natural Law and Human Dignity*. USA: The MIT Press.

Bohman, James and Lutz-Bachmann, Matthias (eds). 1997. *Perpetual Peace: Essays on Kant's Cosmopolitan Ideal*. Cambridge, MA and London, England: The MIT Press.

Bossuyt, M. 1993. 'International Human Rights Systems: Strengths and Weaknesses' in *Human Rights in the Twenty-first Century: A Global Challenge*. Kathleen E. Mahoney and Paul Mahoney (eds). The Netherlands: Martinus Nijhoff Publishers, 47–55.

Breen, Keith. 2012. 'Law beyond Command? An Evaluation of Arendt's Understanding of Law' in *Hannah Arendt and the Law*. Marco Goldoni and Christopher McCorkindale (eds). Oxford and Portland, OR: Hart Publishing, 15–34.

Brennan, Frank. 2002. 'Australia's Refugee Policy – Facts, Needs, Limits' in *Refugees, Morality and Public Policy.* Frank Brennan et al. (eds). Australia: David Lovell Publishing, 11–25.

Briskman, Linda, Latham, Susie, Goddard, Christopher. 2008. *Human Rights Overboard.* Victoria, Australia: Scribe Publications.

Brown, Adèle. (ed.). 1999. *Asylum Practice and Procedure: Country-by-Country Handbook.* Great Britain: Trenton Publishing.

Brown, Chris. 1999. 'Universal Human Rights: A Critique' in *Human Rights in Global Politics.* Tim Dunne and Nicholas J. Wheeler (eds). Cambridge, UK: Cambridge University Press, 103–27.

Brown, Chris. 2002. *Sovereignty, Rights and Justice: International Political Theory Today*. USA: Polity Press.

Brownlie, Ian. 1998. *The Rule of Law in International Affairs*. The Hague: Martinus Nijhoff Publishers.

Brownlie, Ian. 2003 [1966]. *Principles of Public International Law.* USA: Oxford University Press.

Brownlie, Ian and Goodwin-Gill, Guy. 2002 [1971]. *Basic Documents on Human Rights.* USA: Oxford University Press.

Brunkhorst, Hauke. 1996. 'Are Human Rights Self-Contradictory?: Critical Remarks on a Hypothesis by Hannah Arendt'. *Constellations* 3 no. 2: 190–99.

Brunkhorst, Hauke. 2000. 'Rights and the Sovereignty of the People in the Crisis of the Nation State'. *Ratio Juris* 13 no. 1: 49–62.

Burnside, Julian. 2007. *Watching Brief: Reflections on Human Rights, Law, and Justice*. Victoria, Australia: Scribe Publications.

Byrd, Sharon and Hruschka, Joachim. 2008. 'From the State of Nature to the Juridical State of States'. *Law and Philosophy* 27: 599–641.

Canovan, Margaret. 1992. *Hannah Arendt: A Reinterpretation of her Political Thought*. Cambridge: Cambridge University Press.

Canovan, Margaret. 1996. 'Hannah Arendt as a Conservative Thinker' in *Hannah Arendt: Twenty Years Later*. Larry May and Jerome Kohn (eds). Cambridge, MA and London, England: The MIT Press, 11–32.

Canovan, Margaret. 1996a. *Nationhood and Political Theory*. UK and USA: Edward Elgar.

Canovan, Margaret. 1998. 'Introduction' in Hannah Arendt, *The Human Condition.* Chicago and London: The University of Chicago Press, *vii–xx*.

Canovan, Margaret. 1999. 'Is There An Arendtian Case For The Nation-State?' *Contemporary Politics* 5 no. 2: 103–19.

Canovan, Margaret. 2005. *The People.* Cambridge, UK and Malden, MA: Polity Press.

Carens, Joseph H. 1987. 'Aliens and Citizens: The Case for Open Borders'. *The Review of Politics* 49 no. 2: 251–73.

Carens, Joseph H. 1992. 'Refugees and the Limits of Obligation'. *Public Affairs Quarterly* 6 no. 1: 31–44.

Carens, Joseph H. 2003. 'Who Should Get In? The Ethics of Immigration Admissions'. *Ethics and International Affairs* 17 no. 1: 95–189.
Carens, Joseph H. 2003a. 'Migration and Morality: A Liberal Egalitarian Perspective' in *Morality and Public Policy.* Steven Cahn and Tziporah Kasachkoff (eds). Prentice Hall, 257–80.
Carloz-Tschaap, Marie-Claire. 1997. 'On the Detention of Aliens: The Impact on Democratic Rights'. *Journal of Refugee Studies* 10 no. 2: 165–80.
Castillo, Manuel Angel and Hathaway, James C. 1997. 'Temporary Protection' in *Reconceiving International Refugee Law.* James C. Hathaway (ed.). The Hague and Boston: M. Nijhoff Publishers, 1–21.
Chistodoulidis, Emilios and Schaap, Andrew. 2012. 'Arendt's Constitutional Question' in *Hannah Arendt and the Law*. Marco Goldoni and Christopher McCorkindale (eds). Oxford and Portland, Oregon: Hart Publishing, 101–16.
Cohen, Jean L. 1996. 'Rights, Citizenship and the Modern Form of the Social: Dilemmas of Arendtian Republicanism'. *Constellations* 3 no. 2: 164–89.
Cole, Phillip. 2000. *Philosophies of Exclusion: Liberal Political Theory and Immigration*. Great Britain: Edinburgh University Press Ltd.
Corlett, David. 2005. *Following them Home: The Fate of the Returned Asylum Seekers*. Australia: Black Inc.
Cotter, Bridget. 2005. 'Hannah Arendt and "The Right to have Rights"' in *Hannah Arendt and International Relations: Reading Across the Lines*. Anthony F. Lang and John Williams (eds). New York: Palgrave MacMillan, 95–112.
Crisp, Jeff. 2007. 'Vital Distinction'. *Refugees* 148, issue 4: 4–14. UNHCR.
Crock, Mary. 1998. 'Apart from Us or a Part of Us? Immigrants' Rights, Public Opinion and the Rule of Law'. *The International Journal of Refugee Law* 10 no. 1/2: 49–76.
Crock, Mary. 2004. 'Judging Refugees: The Clash of Power and Institutions in the Development of Australian Refugee Law'. *Sydney Law Review* 26: 51–73.
Cronin, Ciaran and De Greiff, Pablo (eds). 2002. *Global Justice and Transnational Politics: Essays on the Moral and Political Challenges of Globalization*. Cambridge, MA: MIT Press.
Curr, Pamela. 2008. 'American Torture – Aussie Style'. Melbourne, Australia: Asylum Seeker Resource Centre.
Dastyari, Azadeh. 2006. 'Offshore Processing: An Australian Phenomenon?' Paper presented to the Castan Centre for Human Rights Law conference, *Human Rights 2006: The Year in Review*. Melbourne, Australia.
Dastyari, Azadeh and Effeney, Libbey. 2012. 'Immigration Detention in Guantánamo Bay'. *Shima: The International Journal of Research into Island Cultures* 6 no. 2: 49–65.
Dauvergne, Catherine. 1997. 'Beyond Justice: The Consequences of Liberalism for Immigration Law'. *Canadian Journal of Law and Jurisprudence* X no. 2: 323–42.
Dauvergne, Catherine. 2000. 'The Dilemma of Rights Discourses for Refugees'. *UNSW Law Journal* 23 no. 3: 56–74.

Dauvergne, Catherine. 2004. 'Making People Illegal' in *Critical Beings: Law, Nation and the Global Subject.* Peter Fitzpatrick and Patricia Tuitt (eds). Great Britain: Ashgate, 83–99.

Dauvergne, Catherine. 2005. *Humanitarianism, Identity and Nation: Migration Laws in Australia and Canada.* Toronto and Vancouver: UBC Press.

Dauvergne, Catherine. 2008. *Making People Illegal: What Globalization Means for Migration and Law.* New York: Cambridge University Press.

Davitt, Michael. 1903. *Within the Pale: The True Story of Anti-Semitic Persecutions in Russia.* London: Hurst and Blackett, Ltd.

Deák, István, Gross, Jan Tomasz and Judt, Tony. 2000. *The Politics of Retribution in Europe: World War II and Its Aftermath.* Princeton, USA: Princeton University Press.

Dembour, Marie-Benedicte. 2003. 'Human Rights Law and National Sovereignty in Collusion: The Plight of Quasi-Nationals at Strasbourg'. *Netherlands Quarterly of Human Rights* 21 no. 1: 63–98.

Derrida, Jacques. 2000. *Of Hospitality.* Stanford, CA: Stanford University Press.

Derrida, Jacques. 2001. *On Cosmopolitanism and Forgiveness.* London and New York: Routledge.

Derrida, Jacques. 2002. 'Declarations of Independence' in *Negotiations: Intervention and Interviews, 1971–2001.* Elizabeth Rottenberg (ed.). Stanford, CA: Stanford University Press, 46–54.

Derrida, Jacques. 2002a. 'Derelictions of the Right to Justice (But What are the "Sans-Papiers" Lacking?)' in *Negotiations: Intervention and Interviews, 1971–2001.* Elizabeth Rottenberg (ed.). Stanford, CA: Stanford University Press, 1330144.

Donnelly, Jack. 1999. 'The Social Construction of International Human Rights' in *Human Rights in Global Politics.* Tim Dunne and Nicholas J. Wheeler (eds). Cambridge, UK: Cambridge University Press, 71–102.

Donnelly, Jack. 2003 [1989]. *Universal Human Rights in Theory and Practice.* USA: Cornell University Press.

Douzinas, Costas. 2000. *The End of Human Rights: Critical Legal Thought at the Turn of the Century.* Oxford: Hart.

Dummett, Ann and Nicol, Andrew G.L. 1990. *Subjects, Citizens, Aliens and Others: Nationality and Immigration Law.* London: Weidenfeld and Nicolson.

Dummett, Michael. 2001. *On Immigration and Refugees.* USA and Canada: Routledge.

Dunn, J.M. 1989. '"Bright Enough for All Our Purposes": John Locke's Conception of a Civilized Society'. *Notes and Records of the Royal Society of London* 43 no. 2: 133–53.

Dunne, Tim and Wheeler, Nicholas J. 1999. *Human Rights in Global Politics.* Cambridge, UK: Cambridge University Press.

Dyzenhaus, David and Thwaites, Rayner. 2007. 'Legality and Emergency – The Judiciary in a Time of Terror' in *Law and Liberty in the War on Terror.* Andrew

Lynch, Edwina MacDonald and George Williams (eds). Leichhardt, NSW: Federation Press, 9–27.
Erskine, Andrew. 1990. *The Hellenistic Stoa: Political Thought and Action.* New York: Cornell University Press.
Evans, Senator Chris. 2008. 'New Directions in Detention, Restoring Integrity to Australia's Immigration System'. Seminar presented at the Centre for International and Public Law, Australian National University, Tuesday 29 July.
Fitzpatrick, Peter and Tuitt, Patricia. (eds). 2004. *Critical Beings: Law, Nation and the Global Subject.* Great Britain: Ashgate.
Flikschuh, Katrin. 2000. *Kant and Modern Political Philosophy.* UK: Cambridge University Press.
Flikschuh, Katrin. 2010. 'Kant's Sovereignty Dilemma: A Contemporary Analysis'. *The Journal of Political Philosophy* 18 no. 4: 469–93.
Galligan, Brian and Larking, Emma. 2008. 'The Separation of Judicial and Executive Powers in Australia: Detention Decisions and the Haneef case'. Australasian Political Science Association Conference, University of Queensland, 6–9 July, Refereed Proceedings.
Galligan, Brian and Larking, Emma. 2009. 'Rights Protection: Comparative Perspectives'. *Australian Journal of Political Science* 44 no. 1: 1–11.
Gearty, Conor. 2007. 'Terrorism and Human Rights'. *Government and Opposition* 42 no. 3: 340–62.
Gibney, Mark (ed.). 1988. *Open Borders? Closed Societies? The Ethical and Political Issues.* Connecticut, USA: Greenwood Press.
Gibney, Mark J. 2004. *The Ethics and Politics of Asylum: Liberal Democracy and the Response to Refugees.* United Kingdom: Cambridge University Press.
Gibney, Mark and Stohl, Michael. 1988. 'Human Rights and US Refugee Policy' in *Open Borders? Closed Societies? The Ethical and Political Issues.* Mark Gibney (ed.). Connecticut, USA: Greenwood Press, 151–83.
Gierke, Otto. 1958 [1934]. *Natural Law and the Theory of Society: 1500 to 1800.* Cambridge: Cambridge University Press.
Glendenning, Phil et al. 2004. *Deported to Danger: A Study of Australia's Treatment of 40 Rejected Asylum Seekers.* Sydney, Australia: Edmund Rice Centre.
Global Detention Project. 2009. 'France: Detention Profile'. http://www.globaldetentionproject.org/countries/europe/france/introduction.html.
Goldoni, Marco and McCorkindale, Christopher. 2012. 'Introduction' in *Hannah Arendt and the Law.* Marco Goldoni and Christopher McCorkindale (eds). Oxford and Portland, Oregon: Hart Publishing, 1–11.
Goldoni, Marco and McCorkindale, Christopher (eds). 2012a. *Hannah Arendt and the Law.* Oxford and Portland, Oregon: Hart Publishing.
Goldston, James A. 2006. 'Holes in the Rights Framework: Racial Discrimination, Citizenship and the Rights of Noncitizens'. *Ethics and International Affairs* 20 no. 3: 321–47.
Goodin, Robert E. 1988. 'What Is So Special about Our Fellow Countrymen?' *Ethics* 98 (July): 663–86.

Goodwin-Gill, Guy S. 2011. 'The Right to Seek Asylum: Interception at Sea and the Principle of Non-Refoulement'. *International Journal of Refugee Law* 23 no. 3: 443–57.

Goodwin-Gill, Guy S. and McAdam, Jane. 2007. *The Refugee in International Law*. USA: Oxford University Press.

Gorman, Robert Francis. 1992. 'Citizenship, Obligation, and Exile in the Greek and Roman Experience'. *Public Affairs Quarterly* 6 no. 1 (July): 5–22.

Grayling, Anthony Clifford. 2008 [2007]. *Towards the Light: The Story of the Struggles for Liberty and Rights that Made the Modern West*. Great Britain: Bloomsbury Publishing.

Gregor, Mary. 1993. 'Kant on "Natural Rights"' in *Kant and Political Philosophy: The Contemporary Legacy*. Ronald Beiner and William James Booth (eds). USA: Yale University Press, 50–75.

Greig, D.W. 1976. *International Law.* London: Butterworths.

Grewcock, Michael. 2006. *Border Crimes: Australia's War on Illicit Migrants*. NSW: Institute of Criminology Press/The Federation Press.

Gross, Leo. 1984. 'The Peace of Westphalia, 1648–1948' in Leo Gross, *Essays on International Law and Organization* Vol. 1. New York: Transnational Publishers Inc., and The Hague: Martinus Nijhoff Publishers.

Habermas, Jürgen. 1997. 'Kant's Idea of Perpetual Peace, with the Benefit of Two Hundred Years' Hindsight' in *Perpetual Peace: Essays on Kant's Cosmopolitan Ideal*. James Bohman and Matthias Lutz-Bachmann (eds). Cambridge, MA and London, England: The MIT Press, 113–53.

Habermas, Jürgen. 2001. *The Postnational Constellation*: *Political Essays*. Max Pensky (ed. and trans.). UK: Polity Press.

Habermas, Jürgen. 2001a. 'Constitutional Democracy: A Paradoxical Union of Contradictory Principles?' *Political Theory* 29 no. 6: 766–81.

Habermas, Jürgen. 2006. 'Does the Constitutionalization of International Law Still Have a Chance?' in *The Divided West*. Ciaran Cronin (ed. and trans.). USA: Polity Press, 115–93.

Habermas, Jürgen. 2008. 'A Political Constitution for the Pluralist World Society?' in *Between Naturalism and Religion*. Ciaran Cronin (ed. and trans.). Cambridge, UK: Polity Press, 312–52.

Habermas, Jürgen. 2008a. 'Prepolitical Foundations of the Constitutional State?' in *Between Naturalism and Religion*. Ciaran Cronin (ed. and trans.). Cambridge, UK: Polity Press, 101–13.

Harvey, Colin. 2005. 'And Fairness For All? Asylum, National Security, and The Rule of Law' in *Global Anti-Terrorism Law and Policy.* Victor V. Ramraj, Michael Hor and Kent Roach (eds). Cambridge and New York: Cambridge University Press, 152–78.

Hathaway, James C. 1984. 'The Evolution of Refugee Status in International Law: 1920–1950'. *The International and Comparative Law Quarterly* 33 no. 2 (April): 348–80.

Hathaway, James C. 1990. 'A Reconsideration of the Underlying Premise of Refugee Law'. *Harvard International Law Journal* 31 no. 1 (Winter): 129–83.

Hathaway, James C. 1991. 'Reconceiving Refugee Law as Human Rights Protection'. *Journal of Refugee Studies* 4 no. 2: 113–131.

Hathaway, James C. 2005. *The Rights of Refugees Under International Law*. Cambridge and New York: Cambridge University Press.

Hathaway, James C. 2006. 'The False Panacea of Offshore Deterrence'. *Forced Migration Review* 26 (August): 56–7.

Hayden, Patrick. 2008. 'From Exclusion to Containment: Arendt, Sovereign Power, and Statelessness'. *Societies Without Borders* 3: 248–69.

Held, David. 1991. 'Democracy, the Nation-State and the Global System' in *Political Theory Today*. David Held (ed.). Oxford: Polity Press, 197–235.

Heller, Agnes. 1991. 'The Concept of the Political Revisited' in *Political Theory Today*. David Held (ed.). Oxford: Polity Press, 330–343.

Holborn, Louise W. 1938. 'The Legal Status of Political Refugees, 1920–1938'. *American Journal of International Law* 32: 680–703.

Hruschka, Joachim. 2004. 'The Permissive Law of Practical Reason in Kant's "Metaphysics of Morals"'. *Law and Philosophy* 23: 45–72.

Hubert, Don and Weiss, Thomas G. (primary authors). 2001. *The Responsibility to Protect: Supplementary Volume to the Report of the International Commission on Intervention and State Sovereignty*. Ottawa, Canada: International Development Research Centre.

Human Rights and Equal Opportunity Commission (HREOC). 1998. 'Those Who've Come Across the Seas: Detention of Unauthorised Arrivals'. Canberra, Australia. www.humanrights.gov.au/human_rights/immigration/seas.html, accessed 10 November 2010.

Human Rights and Equal Opportunity Commission (HREOC). 2001. 'A Report on Visits to Immigration Detention Facilities by the Human Rights Commission'. Canberra, Australia.

Human Rights and Equal Opportunity Commission (HREOC). 2004. 'A Last Resort? National Inquiry into Children in Detention'. Canberra, Australia. www.humanrights.gov.au/human_rights/children_detention_report/index.html.

Human Rights Law Resource Centre (HRLRC). 2008. 'Submission in Relation to Draft General Comment 33 of the Human Rights Committee on States Parties' Obligations Under the First Optional Protocol to the International Covenant on Civil and Political Rights'. Melbourne, Australia.

Human Rights Law Resource Centre (HRLRC). 2008a. 'Submission to the Joint Standing Committee on Migration Review of Immigration Detention'. Melbourne, Australia.

Human Rights Law Resource Centre (HRLRC). 2008b. *Bulletin* 26 (June). Melbourne, Australia.

Human Rights Watch. 2013. 'Barely Surviving: Detention, Abuse, and Neglect of Migrant Children in Indonesia'. USA. http://www.hrw.org/sites/default/files/reports/indonesia0613webwcover.pdf.

Hutchings, Kimberly. 1999. 'Political Theory and Cosmopolitan Citizenship' in *Cosmopolitan Citizenship*. Kimberly Hutchings and Roland Dannreuther (eds). Houndmills, Basingstoke, Hampshire: Macmillan Press and NewYork: St. Martin's Press, 3–32.

Isaac, Jeffrey C. 1996. 'A New Guarantee on Earth: Hannah Arendt on Human Dignity and the Politics of Human Rights'. *The American Political Science Review* 90 no. 1: 61–73.

Jenkins, Philip. 1988. 'Policing the Cold War: The Emergence of New Police Structures in Europe 1946–1953'. *The Historical Journal* 31 no. 1 (March):141–57.

Jennings, Robert Ywedall. 1939. 'Some International Law Aspects of the Refugee Question'. *British Yearbook of International Law* 20: 98–114.

Jones, Peter. 1994. *Rights*. London, England: Macmillan.

Jones, Peter. 1996. 'International Human Rights: Philosophical or Political?' in *National Rights, International Obligations*. Simon Caney, David George and Peter Jones (eds). Boulder, CO: Westview, 183-284.

Kant, Immanuel. 1948 [1785]. *The Moral Law: Groundwork of the Metaphysics of Morals*. Herbert James Paton (trans.). USA: University of Chicago Press.

Kant, Immanuel. 1963 [1795/6]. 'Perpetual Peace' in *On History*. Lewis White Beck (ed.). USA: The Bobbs-Merrill Company Inc., 85–135.

Kant, Immanuel. 1963a [1784]. 'Idea for a Universal History from a Cosmopolitan Point of View' in *On History*. Lewis White Beck (ed.). USA: The Bobbs-Merrill Company Inc., 11–26.

Kant, Immanuel. 1970 [1798]. 'The Contest of Faculties' in *Kant's Political Writings*. Hans Reiss (ed.). Cambridge, NY: Cambridge University Press, 176–90.

Kant, Immanuel. 1970a [1792]. 'On the Common Saying: "This May be True in Theory, But it Does Not Apply in Practice"' in *Kant's Political Writings*. Hans Reiss (ed.). Cambridge, NY: Cambridge University Press, 61–92.

Kant, Immanuel. 1996 [1797]. *The Metaphysics of Morals*. Mary Gregor (ed.). Great Britain: Cambridge University Press.

Kelsen, Hans. 1969. 'Sovereignty and International Law' in *In Defence of Sovereignty*. Wladyslaw J. Stankiewicz (ed.). New York: Oxford University Press, 115–31.

Kerber, Linda K. 2007. 'The Stateless as the Citizen's Other: A View from the United States'. Presidential address delivered at the annual meeting of the American Historical Association, Atlanta, Georgia.

Kesby, Alison. 2012. *The Right to Have Rights: Citizenship, Humanity and International Law*. New York: Oxford University Press.

Kjaerum, Morten. 2002. 'Refugee Protection Between State Interests and Human Rights: Where is Europe Heading?' *Human Rights Quarterly* 24: 513–36.

Kleingeld, Pauline. 2012. *Kant and Cosmopolitanism*. New York, USA: Cambridge University Press.

Kneebone, Susan. 2002. 'Natural Justice and Non-Citizens: A Matter of Integrity?' *Melbourne University Law Review* 26 no. 2 (August): 355.

Kneebone, Susan. 2006. 'The Legal and Ethical Implications of Extra-Territorial Processing of Asylum Seekers: Europe follows Australia' in *Seeking Asylum in Australia: 1995–2005 Experiences and Policies*. Susan Aykut and Jessie Taylor (eds). Monash University, Melbourne, Australia: Institute for Public History and the Australian Centre for the Study of Jewish Civilisation, 53–60.

Kneebone, Susan. (ed.). 2009. *Refugees, Asylum Seekers and the Rule of Law: Comparative Perspectives*. New York, USA: Cambridge University Press.

Koestler, Arthur. 1991 [1941]. *Scum of the Earth*. London: Eland Publishing Ltd.

Kohn, Jerome. 1996. 'Evil and Plurality: Hannah Arendt's Way to "The Life of the Mind", I' in *Hannah Arendt: Twenty Years Later*. Larry May and Jerome Kohn (eds). Cambridge, MA and London, England: The MIT Press, 147–78.

Kohn, Jerome. 2000. 'Freedom: The Priority of the Political' in *The Cambridge Companion to Hannah Arendt*. Dana Villa (ed.). UK: Cambridge University Press, 113–29.

Kohn, Jerome. 2002. 'Arendt's Concept and Description of Totalitarianism'. *Social Research* 69 no. 2 (Summer): 621–56.

Kohn, Jerome. 2007. 'Guest Editor's Introduction to "The Great Tradition I"' and 'Guest Editor's Introduction to "The Great Tradition II"'. *Social Research* 74 no. 3 (Fall): xiii–xxi and *Social Research* 74 no. 4 (Winter): xvii–xxxii.

Krause, Monika. 2008. 'Undocumented Migrants: An Arendtian Perspective'. *European Journal of Political Theory* 7 no. 3: 331–48.

Kumin, Judith. 2007. 'Control vs. Protection: Refugees, Migrants and the EU'. *Refugees* 148 no. 4. UNHCR.

La Caze, Marguerite. 2004. 'Not Just Visitors: Cosmopolitanism, Hospitality, and Refugees'. *Philosophy Today* 48 no. 3 (Fall): 313–24.

Lafitte, Francois. 1940. *The Internment of Aliens*. Great Britain: Penguin Books (Allen Lane).

Lamb, Robert and Thompson, Benjamin. 2009. 'The Meaning of Charity in Locke's Political Thought'. *European Journal of Political Theory* 8 no. 2: 229–52.

Larkin, LaRae. 1996. *The Legitimacy in International Law of the Detention and Internment of Aliens and Minorities in the Interest of National Security*. Symposium Series Vol. 40. USA: The Edwin Mellen Press.

Leclerc, Philippe and Colville, Rupert. 2007. 'In the Shadows'. *Refugees* 147 no. 3: 4–17. UNHCR.

Lee, H.P., Hanks, Peter J. and Morabito, Vincenzo. 1995. *In the Name of National Security: The Legal Dimensions*. Sydney, Australia: LBC Information Services.

Lefort, Claude. 1986. *The Political Forms of Modern Society: Bureaucracy, Democracy, Totalitarianism*. John B. Thompson (ed.). UK: Polity Press.

Lindhal, Hans. 2009. 'In Between: Immigration, Distributive Justice and Political Dialogue'. *Contemporary Political Theory* 8 no. 4: 415–34.

Locke, John. 1952 [1690]. *The Second Treatise of Government*. Thomas Peardon (ed.). NJ: Prentice-Hall, Inc.

Locke, John. 2003 [1690]. *Two Treatises of Government*. Ian Shapiro (ed.). New Haven and London: Yale University Press.

Loughlin, Martin. 2003. 'Ten Tenets of Sovereignty' in *Sovereignty in Transition*. Neil Walker (ed.). Oxford and Portland, Oregon: Hart Publishing, 55–86.

Lowe, Vaughan. 2006. 'Jurisdiction' in *International Law*. Malcolm D. Evans (ed.). USA: Oxford University Press, 335–60.

Luban, David. 1985. 'Just War and Human Rights' in *International Ethics*. Charles R. Beitz, Marshall Cohen, Thomas Scanlon and A. John Simmons (eds). Princeton, NJ: Princeton University Press, 195–216.

McClure, Kirstie M. 1996. *Judging Rights: Lockean Politics and the Limits of Consent*. Ithaca and London: Cornell University Press.

McCorquodale, Robert. 2006 [2003]. 'The Individual and the International Legal System' in *International Law*. Malcolm D. Evans (ed.). USA: Oxford University Press, 307–31.

McHugh, Michael. 2002. 'Tensions Between the Executive and the Judiciary'. Australian Bar Association Conference, Paris, 10 July.

Macken, Claire. 2005. 'Preventive Detention and the Right of Personal Liberty and Security Under the International Covenant on Civil and Political Rights, 1966'. *Adelaide Law Review* 26: 1–28.

McBeth, Adam, Nolan, Justine and Rice, Simon. 2011. *The International Law of Human Rights*. Australia: Oxford University Press.

McKim, Robert and McMahan, Jeff (eds). 1997. *The Morality of Nationalism*. New York: Oxford University Press.

McMaster, Don. 2001. *Asylum Seekers: Australia's Response to Refugees*. Australia: Melbourne University Press.

Madison, James, Hamilton, Alexander and Jay, John. 1987. *The Federalist Papers*. Isaac Kramnick (ed.). Harmondsworth: Penguin.

Mares, Peter. 2002. *Borderline: Australia's Response to Refugees and Asylum Seekers in the Wake of the Tampa*. Sydney: UNSW Press.

Marr, David and Wilkinson, Marian. 2003. *Dark Victory*. NSW, Australia: Allen & Unwin.

Marrus, Michael R. 1982. '"A Body, a Soul, a Passport …": Refugees in the '30s'. *Encounter* 339 (January): 82–6.

Marrus, Michael R. and Paxton, Robert O. 1982. 'The Nazis and the Jews in Occupied Western Europe, 1940–1944'. *The Journal of Modern History* 54 no. 4 (December): 687–714.

May, Larry and Kohn, Jerome (eds). 1996. *Hannah Arendt: Twenty Years Later*. Cambridge, MA and London, England: The MIT Press.

Mendus, Susan. 1995. 'Human Rights in Political Theory'. *Political Studies* XLIII: 10–24.

Menke, Christoph. 2007. 'The "Aporias of Human Rights" and the "One Human Right": Regarding the Coherence of Hannah Arendt's Argument'. *Social Research* 74 no. 3 (Fall): 739.

Michelman, Frank I. 1996. 'Parsing "A Right to Have Rights"'. *Constellations* 3 no. 2: 200–208.

Mickalsen, Kjartan Koch. 2011. 'In Defense of Kant's League of States'. *Law and Philosophy* 30: 291–317.

Miller, David. 1988. 'The Ethical Significance of Nationality'. *Ethics* 98 (July): 647–62.

Miller, David. 1995. *On Nationality*. Oxford: Clarendon Press.

Miller, David. 2011. 'Property and Territory: Locke, Kant, and Steiner'. *The Journal of Political Philosophy* 19 no. 1: 90–109.

Mills, Jennifer. 2008. 'The Long Graveyard'. *newmatilda.com*. 15 August.

Moyn, Samuel. 2010. *The Last Utopia: Human Rights in History*. Cambridge, MA: Belknap Press of Harvard University Press.

Murphy, Kerry. 2013. 'Protection Visa Sequel Worse than the Original'. *Eureka Street*. 21 October.

Muthu, Sankar. 2000. 'Justice and Foreigners: Kant's Cosmopolitan Right'. *Constellations* 7 no. 1: 23–45.

Nardin, Terry. 1983. *Law, Morality, and the Relations of States*. Princeton, NJ: Princeton University Press.

Nardin, Terry, and Mapel, David R. 1993. *Traditions of International Ethics*. Cambridge and Melbourne: Cambridge University Press.

Nash, Kate. 2009. *The Cultural Politics of Human Rights*. UK: Cambridge University Press.

Ngo, May. 2010. 'On the Edge of an Ambivalent Europe'. *Inside Story*. 22 October. http://inside.org.au/on-the-edge-of-an-ambivalent-europe.

NGO Submission to the Human Rights Committee. 2008. 'Freedom, Respect, Equality, Dignity: Action'. Australia: National Association of Community Legal Centres, Human Rights Law Resource Centre, and Kingsford Legal Centre.

Nicholls, Glenn. 2007. *Deported: A History of Forced Departures from Australia*. NSW, Australia: University of New South Wales Press.

Noll, Gregor. 2003. 'Visions of the Exceptional: Legal and Theoretical Issues Raised by Transit Processing Centres and Protection Zones'. *European Journal of Migration and Law* 5: 303–41.

Noll, Gregor. 2010. 'Why Human Rights Fail to Protect Undocumented Migrants'. *European Journal of Migration and Law* 12 no. 2: 241–72.

Nussbaum, Martha C. 1997. 'Kant and Cosmopolitanism' in *Perpetual Peace: Essays on Kant's Cosmopolitan Ideal*. James Bohman and Matthias Lutz-Bachmann (eds). Cambridge, MA and London, England: The MIT Press, 25–57.

Owens, Patricia. 2007. *Between War and Politics: International Relations and the Thought of Hannah Arendt*. Great Britain: Oxford University Press.

Oxfam. 2007. *A Price Too High: The Cost of Australia's Approach to Asylum Seekers*. Melbourne, Australia: Oxfam.

Pagden, Anthony. 2000. 'Stoicism, Cosmopolitanism, and the Legacy of European Imperialism'. *Constellations* 7 no. 1: 3–22.

Pagden, Anthony (ed.). 2002. *The Idea of Europe*. UK: Cambridge University Press.

Pangle, Thomas L. 1998. 'Socratic Cosmopolitanism: Cicero's Critique and Transformation of the Stoic Ideal'. *Canadian Journal of Political Science* 31 no. 2 (June): 235–62.

Peardon, Thomas P. 1952. 'Introduction' in John Locke, *The Second Treatise of Government*. NJ: Prentice-Hall, Inc.

Pocock, John Grenville. 1993. 'A Discourse of Sovereignty: Observations on the Work in Progress' in *Political Discourse in Early Modern Britain.* Nicholas Phillipson and Quentin Skinner (eds). Great Britain: Cambridge University Press, 377–428.

Pogge, Thomas W. 1989. *Realising Rawls*. Ithaca: Cornell University Press.

Pogge, Thomas W. 2004. '"Assisting" the Global Poor' in *The Ethics of Assistance: Morality and the Distant Needy*. Deen K. Chaterjee (ed.). Cambridge: Cambridge University Press, 260–88.

Pogge, Thomas W. 2005. 'Severe Poverty as a Violation of Negative Duties'. *Ethics and International Affairs* 19 no. 1: 55–83.

Popkin, Jeremy D. 1994. *A History of Modern France*. USA: Prentice-Hall.

Pouilly, Cécile. 2007. 'Stateless Achievers'. *Refugees* 147 no. 3: 18–19. UNHCR.

Poynder, Nicholas. 2003. 'When All Else Fails: The Practicalities of Seeking Protection of Human Rights under International Treaties'. Lecture presented by the Castan Centre and Australian Lawyers for Human Rights, Melbourne, 28 April.

Rancière, Jacques. 2004. 'Who Is the Subject of the Rights of Man?' *South Atlantic Quaterly* 103 no. 2/3: 297–310.

Rawls, John. 1971. *A Theory of Justice*. Cambridge: Harvard University Press.

Rawls, John. 1999. *The Law of Peoples, with 'The Idea of Public Reason Revisited'*. Cambridge: Harvard University Press.

Rosas, Allan. 1995. 'State Sovereignty and Human Rights: Towards a Global Constitutional Project'. *Political Studies* XLIII: 61–78.

Ruddock, Philip. 2000. 'Refugee Claims and Australian Migration Law: A Ministerial Perspective'. *UNSW Law Journal* 23: 1–12.

Rummery, Ariane. 2007. 'Diverted to Nauru'. *Refugees* 148 no. 4: 29–30. UNHCR.

Sabates-Wheeler, Rachel. 2009. 'The Impact of Irregular Status on Human Development Outcomes for Migrants'. *Human Development Research Paper Series* 26 no. 2009.

Schofield, Malcolm. 1991. *The Stoic Idea of the City*. Great Britain: Cambridge University Press.

Shapiro, Ian. 2003. 'Introduction' in John Locke, *Two Treatises of Government.* New Haven and London: Yale University Press.

Sicilianos, Linos-Alexander. 2012. 'The Human Face of International Law – Interactions Between General International Law and Human Rights: An Overview'. *Human Rights Law Journal* 32 nos 1–6: 1–11.

Silverman, Stephanie and Hajela, Ruchi. 2013. 'Immigration Detention in the UK'. Oxford: The Migration Observatory. 29 November. http://migrationobservatory.ox.ac.uk/briefings/immigration-detention-uk.

Simmons, John A. 1979. *Moral Principles and Political Obligations*. Princeton, NJ: Princeton University Press.

Simmons, John A. 1992. *The Lockean Theory of Rights*. Princeton, NJ: Princeton University Press.

Simmons, John A. 1993. *On the Edge of Anarchy: Locke, Consent, and the Limits of Society*. Princeton, NJ: Princeton University Press.

Simmons, John A. 2001. 'Human Rights and World Citizenship: The Universality of Human Rights in Kant and Locke' in John A. Simmons, *Justification and Legitimacy: Essays on Rights and Obligations*. USA: Cambridge University Press, 179–96.

Simmons, John A. 2001a. '"Denisons" and "Aliens": Locke's Problem of Political Consent' in *Justification and Legitimacy: Essays on Rights and Obligations*. USA: Cambridge University Press, 158–78.

Sinha, S. Prakash. 1971. *Asylum and International Law*. Netherlands: Martinus Nijhoff Publishers.

Skinner, Quentin. 1978. *The Foundations of Modern Political Thought*. USA: Cambridge University Press.

Skran, Claudena M. 1995. *Refugees in Inter-War Europe: The Emergence of a Regime*. Oxford: Clarendon Press.

Slaugher, Joseph. 2007. *Human Rights Inc.* New York: Fordham.

Smith, Anthony D. 2004. 'Ethnic Cores and Dominant Ethnies' in *Rethinking Ethnicity: Majority Groups and Dominant Minorities*. Eric P. Kaufmann (ed.). London and New York: Routledge, 17–30.

Solzhenitsyn, Alexander. 1970. 'Nobel Lecture'. Franklin D'Olier, Reeve (trans.). http://www.columbia.edu/cu/augustine/arch/solzhenitsyn/nobel-lit1970.htm.

Spinks, Harriet. 2013. 'Destination Anywhere? Factors Affecting Asylum Seekers' Choice of Destination Country'. Research Paper No. 1, 2012–13. Parliament of Australia, Parliamentary Library.

Stalley, Richard F. 1995. 'Introduction' in Aristotle, *Politics*. Ernest Barker (ed.). Great Britain: Oxford University Press, vii–xxxviii.

Stankiewicz, Wladyslaw J. (ed.). 1969. *In Defense of Sovereignty*. New York: Oxford University Press.

Staples, Kelly. 2012. *Retheorising Statelessness: A Background Theory of Membership in World Politics*. Edinburgh: Edinburgh University Press.

Steiner, Hillel. 1992. 'Libertarianism and the Transnational Migration of People' in *Free Movement: Ethical Issues in the Transnational Migration of People and Money*. Brian Barry and Robert E. Goodin (eds). Great Britain: Harvester Wheatsheaf, 87–94.

Steiner, Henry J. and Alston, Philip. 2000. *International Human Rights in Context*. Oxford: Oxford University Press.

Steiner, Henry J., Alston, Philip and Goodman, Ryan. 2008. *International Human Rights in Context*. Oxford: Oxford University Press.

Sullivan, Roger J. 1996. 'Introduction' in *The Metaphysics of Morals*. Cambridge: Cambridge University Press, vii–xxvi.

Tan, Kok-Chor. 2004. *Justice Without Borders: Cosmopolitanism, Nationalism and Patriotism.* USA: Cambridge University Press.

Taylor, Jessica. 2009. *Behind Australian Doors: Examining the Conditions of Detention of Asylum Seekers in Indonesia.* Wordpress. http://www.law.monash.edu.au/castancentre/news/behind-australian-doors-report.pdf.

Tiburcio, Carmen. 2001. *The Human Rights of Aliens under International and Comparative Law.* The Hague: Martinus Nijhoff Publishers.

Torpey, John. 2000. *The Invention of the Passport: Surveillance, Citizenship and the State.* UK: Cambridge University Press.

Tuck, Richard. 1979. *Natural Rights Theories: Their Origin and Development.* Great Britain: Cambridge University Press.

Tuitt, Patricia. 1996. *False Images: Law's Construction of the Refugee.* East Haven, CT: Pluto Press.

Tully, James, 1980. *A Discourse on Property: John Locke and His Adversaries.* Great Britain: Cambridge University Press.

Tully, James. 1993. *An Approach to Political Philosophy: Locke In Contexts.* Great Britain: Cambridge University Press.

Tully, James. 1993a. 'Placing the "Two Treatises"' in *Political Discourse in Early Modern Britain.* Nicholas Phillipson and Quentin Skinner (eds). Great Britain: Cambridge University Press, 253–80.

Tully, James. 2002. 'The Kantian Idea Of Europe: Critical And Cosmopolitan Perspectives' in *The Idea of Europe.* Anthony Pagden (ed.). UK: Cambridge University Press, 331–58.

Villa, Dana R. 1999. *Politics, Philosophy, Terror: Essays on the Thought of Hannah Arendt.* Princeton, New Jersey: Princeton University Press.

Vincent, Raymond John (R.J.). 1986. *Human Rights and International Relations.* UK: Cambridge University Press.

Vincent, Raymond John (R.J.). 1993. 'The Idea of Rights in International Ethics' in *Traditions of International Ethics.* Terry Nardin and David R. Mapel (eds). Cambridge and Melbourne: Cambridge University Press, 250–69.

von Sternberg, Mark R. 2002. *The Grounds of Refugee Protection in the Context of International Human Rights and Humanitarian Law: Canadian and United States Case Law Compared.* Netherlands: Martinus Nijhoff Publishers.

Waldron, Jeremy. 1984. 'Locke, Tully, and the Regulation of Property'. *Political Studies* XXXII: 98–106.

Waldron, Jeremy. 2000. 'Arendt's Constitutional Politics' in *The Cambridge Companion to Hannah Arendt.* Dana Villa (ed.). UK: Cambridge University Press, 201–19.

Walzer, Michael. 1990. 'The Communitarian Critique of Liberalism'. *Political Theory* 1 (February): 6–23.

Ward, Lee. 2006. 'Locke on the Moral Basis of International Relations'. *American Journal of Political Science* 50 no. 3 (July): 691–705.

Weber, Leanne. 2010. 'Knowing-and-yet-not-knowing about European Border Deaths'. *Australian Journal of Human Rights* 15 no. 2: 35–57.

Weis, Paul. 1979 [1956]. *Nationality and Statelessness in International Law*. The Netherlands: Sijthoff and Noordhoff.
Weissbrodt, David. 2008. *The Human Rights of Non-Citizens*. Great Britain: Oxford University Press.
Wellman, Christopher Heath and Cole, Phillip. 2011. *Debating the Ethics of Immigration*. New York: Oxford University Press.
Wenar, Leif. 2002. 'The Legitimacy of Peoples' in *Global Justice and Transnational Politics: Essays on the Moral and Political Challenges of Globalization*. Ciaran P. Cronin and Pablo De Grieff (eds). Cambridge, MA: The MIT Press, 53-76.
White Beck, Lewis. 1993. 'Kant's Two Conceptions of the Will in Their Political Context' in *Kant and Political Philosophy: The Contemporary Legacy*. Ronald Beiner and William James Booth (eds). USA: Yale University Press, 38–49.
Whyte, Jessica. 2009. 'Particular Rights and Absolute Wrongs: Giorgio Agamben on Life and Politics'. *Law Critique* 20: 147–61.
Wilsher, Daniel. 2012. *Immigration Detention: Law, History, Politics*. USA: Cambridge University Press.
Wimmer, Andreas. 2004. 'Dominant Ethnicity and Dominant Nationhood' in *Rethinking Ethnicity: Majority Groups and Dominant Minorities*. Eric P. Kaufmann (ed.). London and New York: Routledge, 40–58.
Young-Bruehl, Elisabeth. 2004 [1982]. *For Love of the World*. USA: Yale University Press.
Zifcak, Spencer. 2006. 'No Way Out: The High Court, Asylum Seekers and Human Rights' in *Seeking Asylum in Australia: 1995–2005 Experiences and Policies*. Susan Aykut and Jessie Taylor (eds). Monash University, Melbourne, Australia: Institute for Public History and the Australian Centre for the Study of Jewish Civilisation, 97–108.
Žižek, Slavoj. 1999. 'Human Rights and Its Discontents'. Olin Auditorium, Bard College. 15 November. http://www.lacan.com/zizek-human.htm.
Zucotti, Susan. 1993. *The Holocaust, The French and The Jews*. New York: Basic Books.

Cases, Legislation, International Instruments, Official Government Documents and Publications Produced by International Organisations

Australia

'Al-Kateb v. Godwin'. [2004] HCA 37.
'Chu Kheng Lim v. Minister for Immigration'. (1992) 176 CLR 1.
Commonwealth Ombudsman. 2005. 'Inquiry into the Circumstances of the Vivian Alvarez Matter'. Report No. 03/2005. Canberra: Commonwealth of Australia.
Joint Committee of Public Accounts and Audit (JCPAA). 2001. 'Answers to Questions Taken on Notice by DIMA from Committee Hearing on 30 January'. *Inquiry into Coastwatch*. March.

Migration Act 1958 (Cth).
'Minister for Immigration and Multicultural and Indigenous Affairs v. Al Khafaji'. [2004] HCA 38.
Palmer, Mick. 2005. 'Inquiry into the Circumstances of the Immigration Detention of Cornelia Rau: Report'. Canberra: Commonwealth of Australia, July.
Phillips, Janet and Millbank, Adrienne. 2005. 'The Detention and Removal of Asylum Seekers'. Australian Parliamentary Library E-Brief, 5 July. aph.gov.au/library/intguide/SP/asylum_seekers.html.
'Victorian Council of Civil Liberties Inc. v. Minister for Immigration & Multicultural Affairs'. [2001] FCA 1297.

Europe

Council of Europe. 1950. (European) Convention for the Protection of Human Rights and Fundamental Freedoms. Rome.
Council of Europe. 1997. European Convention on Nationality. Strasbourg.
Council of the European Union. 2003. 'Council Directive 2003/9/EC of 27 January 2003 Laying Down Minimum Standards for the Reception of Asylum Seekers'.
Drzemczewski, Andrew. 1985. 'The Position of Aliens in Relation to the European Convention on Human Rights'. Strasbourg: Council of Europe, Directorate of Human Rights.
European Commission. 2007. 'Achieving Common EU Standards on Reception of Asylum Seekers: Report on Transposition and Implementation of the Reception Conditions Directive'. Brussels: press release of 27 November, IP/07/1759.
European Commission. 2008. 'Questions and Answers on the Commission Proposal to Amend the Reception Conditions Directive'. Brussels: press release of 3 December, MEMO/08/760.

United Kingdom

United Kingdom Home Office. 2008. 'Control of Immigration: Quarterly Statistical Summary, July 2008–September 2008'. http://rds.homeoffice.gov.uk/rds/pdfs08/immiq308.pdf.

United States

United States Congress. 1989. 'The French Declaration of the Rights of Man and of the Citizen and the American Bill of Rights: A Bicentennial Commemoration Issued Pursuant to S.J.Res. 317, 100th Congress'. Public Law 100–482.
United States Government Accountability Office (US GAO). 2006. 'Illegal Immigration: Report to the Honorable Bill Frist, Majority Leader, U.S. Senate'. GAO-06–770. August.

United States Supreme Court. 2002. 'Hoffman Plastics Compounds Inc. v. NLRB'. 535 US 137.

International

'A v. Australia'. Communication No. 560/1993, UN Doc CCPR/C/59/D/560/1993 (1997).
Bhagwati, P.N. (Justice, Regional Advisor for Asia and the Pacific of the United Nations High Commissioner for Human Rights). 2002. 'Human Rights and Immigration Detention in Australia'. Report of Mission to Australia, 24 May–2 June.
'C v. Australia'. Communication No. 900/1999, UN Doc CCPR/C/76/D/900/1999 (2002).
Cartagena Colloquium. 1984. Cartagena Declaration on Refugees.
'Elles, Diana. 1980. International Provisions Protecting the Human Rights of Non-Citizens. E/CN.4/Sub.2/391/Rev.1. New York: United Nations.
F.K.A.G. et al. v. Australia'. UN Doc CCPR/C/108/D/2094/2011 and 'M.M.M. et al. v. Australia'. UN Doc CCPR/C/108/D/2136/2012 (2013).
Goodwin-Gill, Guy S. 2001. 'Article 31 of the 1951 Convention Relating to the Status of Refugees: Non-penalization, Detention and Protection'. Paper prepared at the request of the Department of International Protection for the UNHCR Global Consultations.
Guterres, António. 2005. 'Remarks by Mr António Guterres, UN High Commissioner for Refugees, on the Occasion of the European Union Council of Ministers of Justice and Home Affairs'. Luxembourg, 12 October. www.unhcr.org/cgi-bin/texis/vtx/admin/opendoc.htm?tbl=ADMIN&id=435612ec4.
International Commission on Intervention and State Sovereignty (ICISS). 2001. 'The Responsibility to Protect – Report of the International Commission on Intervention and State Sovereignty'. Ottawa, Canada: International Development Research Centre.
Montevideo Convention on Rights and Duties of States (Inter-American). 26 December, 1933.
Organisation of American States. 1954. Caracas Convention on Territorial Asylum. OAS Treaty Series No. 19, UN Registration 03/20/89 No. 24378.
Organization of African Unity. 1969. Convention Governing the Specific Aspects of Refugee Problems in Africa.
'Shams et al. v. Australia'. Communication Nos 1255, 1256, 1259, 1260, 1266, 1268, 1270, 1288/2004, UN Doc CCPR/C/90/D/1255, 1256, 1259, 1260, 1266, 1268, 1270 and 1288/2004 (2007).
United Nations. 1948. Universal Declaration of Human Rights. GA Res. 217A (III).
United Nations. 1948. Convention on the Prevention and Punishment of the Crime of Genocide. GA Res. 260 (III) A.

United Nations. 1951. Convention relating to the Status of Refugees. GA Res. 429(V). As amended by the 1966 Protocol relating to the Status of Refugees. GA Res. 2198(XXI).

United Nations. 1954. Convention relating to the Status of Stateless Persons. UN Treaty Series vol. 360, p. 117.

United Nations. 1965. International Convention on the Elimination of All Forms of Racial Discrimination. GA Res. 2106(XX).

United Nations. 1966. International Covenant on Civil and Political Rights. GA Res. 2200A(XXI).

United Nations. 1966. International Covenant on Economic, Social and Cultural Rights. GA Res. 2200A(XXI).

United Nations. 1967. Declaration on Territorial Asylum. GA Res. 2312(XXII).

United Nations. 1969. Vienna Convention on the Law of Treaties. Treaty Series vol. 1155, p. 331.

United Nations. 1984. Convention Against Torture, and Other Cruel, Inhuman, or Degrading Treatment or Punishment. GA Res. 39/46.

United Nations. 1985. Declaration on the Human Rights of Individuals Who are Not Nationals of the Country in Which They Live. GA Res. 40/144 ('Declaration on the Rights of Non-Nationals').

United Nations. 1990. International Convention on the Protection of the Rights of all Migrant Workers and Members of their Families. GA Res. 45/158, UN GAOR, 45th Sess., Supp. No. 49A, UN Doc. A/45/49 (1990) 261 (entered into force 1 July, 2003).

United Nations. 1998. Declaration on the Right and Responsibility of Individuals, Groups and Organs of Society to Promote and Protect Universally Recognized Human Rights and Fundamental Freedoms. GA Res. 53/144.

United Nations. 2000. Convention against Transnational Organised Crime. UN Doc. A/55/383. Supplemented by the 'Protocol to Prevent, Suppress and Punish Trafficking in Persons, Especially Women and Children', UN Doc. A/55/383, Annex II; and the 'Protocol against the Smuggling of Migrants by Land, Sea, and Air', UN Doc. A/55/383, Annex III.

United Nations. 2002. *Human Rights: A Compilation of International Instruments*. New York and Geneva.

United Nations Ad Hoc Committee on Refugees and Stateless Persons. 1949. 'A Study of Statelessness'. Lake Success, New York, E/1112;E/1112/Add.1. http://www.unhcr.org/refworld/docid/3ae68c2d0.html, accessed 15 September 2008.

United Nations Committee Against Torture. 2008. 'Concluding Observations on Australia – Australia's Compliance with the Convention Against Torture and Other Cruel, Inhumane or Degrading Treatment'. 40th Session, Geneva.

United Nations Committee on Economic, Social and Cultural Rights. 1998. 'General Comment 9: The Domestic Application of the Covenant'. E/C.12/1998/24.

United Nations Committee on Economic, Social and Cultural Rights. 2009. 'General Comment 20: Non-discrimination in Economic, Social and Cultural Rights'. E/C.12/GC/20.

United Nations Committee on the Elimination of Racial Discrimination. 2004. 'General Recommendation XXX on Discrimination against Non-Citizens'. CERD/C/64/Misc.11/rev.3.
United Nations High Commissioner for Human Rights, Office of the (UNHCHR). 2006. *The Rights of Non-Citizens*. New York and Geneva. HR/PUB/06/11.
United Nations High Commissioner for Human Rights, Office of the (UNHCHR). 2008. 'The United Nations Human Rights Treaty System: An Introduction to the Core Human Rights Treaties and the Treaty Bodies'. *Fact Sheet No. 30*. http.//www.ohchr.org, accessed 8 October 2008.
United Nations High Commissioner for Human Rights, Office of the (UNHCHR). 2008a. 'International Human Rights Law; Commission on Human Rights; The Human Rights Council; Human Rights Treaty Bodies'. http.//www.ohchr.org/EN/ProfessionalInterest/Pages/InternationalLaw.aspx; http.//www2.ohchr.org/english/bodies/chr/index.htm; http.//www2.ohchr.org/english/bodies/hrcouncil/; http.//www2.ohchr.org/english/bodies/treaty/index.htm.
United Nations High Commissioner for Refugees, (UNHCR). 1979. *Handbook on Procedures and Criteria for Determining Refugee Status under the 1951 Convention and the 1967 Protocol relating to the Status of Refugees*. HCR/IP/4/Eng/REV.1 Reedited, Geneva. January 1992.
United Nations High Commissioner for Refugees (UNHCR). 2002. 'The International Legal Framework Concerning Statelessness and Access for Stateless Persons'. Contribution by Carol A. Batchelor to the European Union Seminar on the Content and Scope of International Protection organised by the Ministry of Internal Affairs, Spain (Madrid, 8–9 January). http://www.unhcr.org/refworld/docid/415c3be44.html.
United Nations High Commissioner for Refugees (UNHCR). 2006. *The State of the World's Refugees: Human Displacement in the New Millennium*. Great Britain: Oxford University Press.
United Nations High Commissioner for Refugees (UNHCR). 2008. 'Note on International Protection'. EC/59/SC/CRP.10. 11 June. Reprinted in *Refugee Survey Quarterly* 27 no. 3: 129–48.
United Nations High Commissioner for Refugees (UNHCR). 2009. 'The Year in Review: Global Report 2009'. Geneva: UNHCR.
United Nations High Commissioner for Refugees (UNHCR). 2010. *Asylum Levels and Trends in Industrialized Countries, 2009*. Geneva: UNHCR Division of Programme Support and Management. 23 March.
United Nations High Commissioner for Refugees (UNHCR), Executive Committee. 2011. *A Thematic Compilation of Executive Committee Conclusions* 6th edition. UNHCR: Division of International Protection. June. http://www.unhcr.org/3d4ab3ff2.html.
United Nations High Commissioner for Refugees (UNHCR). 2012. 'Guidelines on the Applicable Criteria and Standards relating to the Detention of

Asylum-Seekers and Alternatives to Detention'. http://www.refworld.org/docid/503489533b8.html.

United Nations High Commissioner for Refugees (UNHCR). 2012a. 'UNHCR Concerned at Detention of Asylum-Seekers, Releases New Guidelines'. *Making a Difference*. UNHCR. 21 September. http://www.unhcr.org/505c33199.html.

United Nations High Commissioner for Refugees (UNHCR). 2012b. 'UNHCR Asylum Trends 2012: Levels and Trends in Industrialized Countries'. http://unhcr.org.au/unhcr/files/2012_Asylum_Trends.pdf.

United Nations High Commissioner for Refugees (UNHCR). 2013. 'Mid-Year Trends 2013'. 19 December. http://www.unhcr.org/52af08d26.html.

United Nations High Commissioner for Refugees (UNHCR). 2013a. 'UNHCR Monitoring Visit to the Republic of Nauru 7 to 9 October 2013'. http://unhcr.org.au/unhcr/images/2013–11–26%20Report%20of%20UNHCR%20Visit%20to%20Nauru%20of%207–9%20October%202013.pdf.

United Nations High Commissioner for Refugees (UNHCR). 2013b. 'UNHCR Monitoring Visit to Manus Island, Papua New Guinea 23 to 25 October 2013'. http://unhcr.org.au/unhcr/images/2013–11–26%20Report%20of%20UNHCR%20Visit%20to%20Manus%20Island%20PNG%2023–25%20October%202013.pdf.

United Nations Human Rights Committee (HRC). 1989. 'CCPR General Comment 18: Non-discrimination'. UN Doc. HRI/GEN/1/Rev.1 at 26.

United Nations Human Rights Committee (HRC). 1994. 'General Comment 15: The Position of Aliens under the Covenant'. UN Doc. HRI/GEN/1/Rev.1 at 18 (adopted 1986, published 1994).

United Nations Human Rights Committee (HRC). 1999. 'General Comment 27: Freedom of Movement (Art.12)'. UN Doc. CCPR/C/21/Rev.1/Add.9.

United Nations Human Rights Committee (HRC). 2001. 'General Comment 29: States of Emergency (Art.4)'. UN Doc. CCPR/C/21/Rev.1/Add.11.

United Nations Human Rights Committee (HRC). 2008. 'Draft General Comment 33: The Obligations of States Parties under the Optional Protocol to the International Covenant on Civil and Political Rights'. CCPR/C/GC/33/CRP.3. 2nd revised version. 18 August 2008 (Distr. RESTRICTED).

United Nations Working Group on Arbitrary Detention ('UN Working Group'). 2002. 'Civil and Political Rights, Including the Question of Torture and Detention: Report of the Working Group on Arbitrary Detention; Addendum – Visit to Australia'. E/CN.4/2003/8/Add.2. 24 October.

World Conference on Human Rights. 1993. Vienna Declaration and Programme of Action. GA Res. 421(v) pt. 1, UN Doc. A/CONF.157/23.

Index

For Product Safety Concerns and Information please contact our EU representative GPSR@taylorandfrancis.com Taylor & Francis Verlag GmbH, Kaufingerstraße 24, 80331 München, Germany

Batch number: 10725973

Printed by Printforce, the Netherlands